The Courts and the Development of Commercial Law

Comparative Studies
in Continental and Anglo-American Legal History

Vergleichende Untersuchungen zur kontinentaleuropäischen und anglo-amerikanischen Rechtsgeschichte

Herausgegeben von

Prof. Dr. Dr. h. c. mult. Helmut Coing

und

Prof. Dr. Knut Wolfgang Nörr

Band 2

The Courts and the Development of Commercial Law

Edited by

Prof. Dr. Vito Piergiovanni

DUNCKER & HUMBLOT / BERLIN

Gedruckt mit Unterstützung der Gerda-Henkel-Stiftung, Düsseldorf

CIP-Kurztitelaufnahme der Deutschen Bibliothek

The **courts and the development of commercial law** /
ed. by Vito Piergiovanni. – Berlin: Duncker und
Humblot, 1987.
(Comparative studies in continental and
Anglo-American legal history; Bd. 2)
ISBN 3-428-06176-4

NE: Piergiovanni, Vito [Hrsg.]; GT

Satz: Klaus-Dieter Voigt, Berlin 61
Druck: Berliner Buchdruckerei Union GmbH, Berlin 61
Printed in Germany

ISBN 3-428-06176-4

Foreword

The first contribution given by the working Group "The Courts and the Development of Commercial Law" (which is a part in the wider research program "Anglo-American and Continental Legal History") evidences the difficulties connected to the historical-comparative researches between the Continental European and the Anglo-American law.

The prior problem, common to both experiences, is certainly the knowledge of sources (being these the evidence of the work of Courts or lawyers) and has the consequence of making difficult any effort to generalize.

For Continental Europe, the existence of a wide range of printed or handwritten material, produced by the Courts, emerges from the contributions collected in this volume, which deal with cases coming from Italy, Netherlands and Germany. Such material is still waiting for being considered and studied.

Also for the reconstruction of the British juridical scenario, Coquilette (whose studies are published in the third volume of the series) goes back, in addition to the printed works, also "to the Court records and the professional diaries and papers of prominent judges and practitioners", still handwritten.

The need for a more complete and deeper knowledge, offering the means for the elaboration of well based opinions, applies also to the doctrine: in fact even if the most famous works are printed, it is possible to find important contributions still in their handwritten form, and unknown, as evidenced by the study of Savelli.

For a more concrete perception of the scarcity of studies on the commercial doctrine, it should be sufficient to compare our knowledges to the list of the juridical books which are part in the library of Lord Mansfield, published by Rodgers as an addendum to his paper.

Rodgers went better in details, on single themes, about the importance of the European literary tradition on Lord Mansfield, and has identified four cathegories of works: "the continental codes and other models of commercial law, the technical treatises on the law merchant, the theoretical works of the natural lawyers, and the leading works of the continental civilians". Lord Mansfield, in his activity as judge, employs with great competence these sources aiming to create the basis of the British commercial law.

The theme of the connection between the Courts (both as institutions and as producers of judgements) and the commercial doctrine, can be certainly considered as the leading theme which connects the contributions of the volume; they differ in the subject but are all equally emblematic in perspecting, in different milieu, the different typology of the connection between the writers in commercial law and the judicial praxis. The studies by Coquilette offer a wide outline of conflicts, inside the Anglo-Saxon world, between lawyers and Courts of "civil law" and those of "common law", each one bound to manage, in a more or less monopolistic way, the professional and trial spaces opened by the development of the commercial relationships.

A less conflictual correspondence between doctrine and Courts emerges from the reconstruction of the Dutch experience on the theme of the "bill of exchange", made by Asser, and we find a more constructive and original dialectic in the judgements issued by the Admiralty Court in Hamburg, studied by Eva-Christine Frentz, or in the decisions of the Rota of Genoa, by Piergiovanni.

These are, as it is obvious, the reconstructive elements coming from different experiences which, in order to be compared, need some further element, but I guess that they do already contain very interesting suggestions.

I think, for instance, of the reconsideration or, we may even say, of the reevaluation of the British "civilians" made by Coquillette, with results which are rather different with respect to the historiographical British tradition: a continuous dialectic with the Romanistic tradition is evidenced from this study; and, inside this more general process, the rising of a special attention by the civilians to the development of the merchant-law doctrine, evidences very good chances of comparing with continental Europe in this branch of law.

An example of the results which may derive from such comparison and a significant methodological guideline for future studies are contained in the work by Nörr, who, in a previous study, had noticed how in a first stage of evolution of the English commercial law, the Admiralty Court in charge for "relation to foreign trade", "was manned by civilians who applied the continental doctrines"[1].

The comparison of the specific elements of a juridical experience with supernational negotiable and judicial practice, typical of the evolution of the commercial law, is fundamental for trespassing the obstacles and bindings produced by the political, regional or national conditions.

---

[1] *K. W. Nörr*, The European side of the English Law: a Few Comments from a Continental Historian, in Englische und kontinentale Rechtsgeschichte: ein Forschungsprojekt (vol. 1 of Comparative Studies in Continental and Anglo-American Legal History), Berlin 1985, p. 22.

It is significant, in this respect, the correspondence set by the same Nörr in the English middle age world, between the first development of the commercial law and the canonical beneficial law.

In the modern age the fight between the students of civil law and those of common law is, by itself, a significant aspect of the conflicts existing in the English society: the almost natural result, after the differences have become less marked, is found, in the XVIII century, in Lord Mansfield. He, in elaborating some principles of the English commercial law, adopts widely the continental European experience, filtered from the "civilians" and makes it effective in a period of great economic expansion and increasing political importance of Great Britain, as demonstrated by Coquilette and Rodgers.

The same evaluation on the functional aspect of the commercial law to the still expanding political reality is documented by the work by Asser on the XVIII Century Netherland and, even in different dimensions, corresponds to the XVI Century Genoa, that was going to become, through the refinement of the credit instruments, one of the most important financial centres in Europe.

The judgements of the Admiralty Court of Hamburg, for which the motto "non urbi sed orbi" corresponds to the real action of the judging organ, are even more explicit in looking for improvements to their jurisprudence even out from close juridical boundaries.

The research for new sources and the reconsideration of those already known, the connection Court - Doctrine and the functionality of the development of commercial law to the economic-political processes taking place during the Modern Age, are the themes common to all researches of this first volume of the working Group "The Courts and the Development of the Commercial Law". In a close future the study of the bank and the credit will take the Group to compare the specific experiences on the same theme.

The wish which is being expressed by the Coordinator is that this first experience of team work, important also from the human viewpoint due to the spirit of cooperation and friendship established among the components of the Group, can continue to give sound and serious scientific results.

Vito Piergiovanni

University of Genoa, Italy

Inhaltsverzeichnis

VITO PIERGIOVANNI

Courts and Commercial Law at the Beginning of the Modern Age

The medieval origin of commercial law is now a generally accepted fact and a starting point for studying commercial law. Similarly, at the other extreme, the French commercial code of 1807 comes at the end of a process which, even though it shows lesser internal development, nonetheless remains fundamentally coherent.

It may be useful, for this purpose, to refer to the most recent suggestions for classifications proposed by two German researchers, Pohlmann and Scherner, to schematize the history of commercial law and its study in the Middle Ages and in the Modern Age[1].

In the Middle Ages one can observe two movements of diverse origin, but which are basically convergent. On the one hand, common commercial practice was established along geographical lines extended to commercially homogenous areas (the Mediterranean, the Atlantic, Northern Europe), and essentially consisted of the relevant contracts connected to maritime trade (these practices are also compiled in widely-spread collections, such as the Book of the Consulate of Barcelona and the Rules of Visby and of Oleron). On the other hand, commercial law, which became dependent upon the requirements of a more and more powerful merchant-class, was progressively being compiled in volumes of *Statuti* within each individual State[2].

Medieval law scholars obviously could not ignore this phenomenon, which, like the feudal one[3], had considerable professional and economic potential.

The work of law scholars consisted in relating the regulation of the new mercantile practices to the long-standing categories of Roman law, but, the new emphasis on the professional rather than scientific value of the

---

1 *H. Pohlmann*, Die Quellen des Handelsrechts, in Handbuch der Quellen und Literatur der neuren europäischen Privatrechtsgeschichte, I, Mittelalter (1100 - 1500), Die gelehrten Rechte und die Gesetzgebung, ed. *H. Coing*, München 1973, pp. 801 - 802; *K. O. Scherner*, die Wissenschaft des Handelsrechts, ibidem, II/1, Neuere Zeit (1500 - 1800), Das Zeitalter des gemeinen Rechts, Wissenschaft, ed. *H. Coing*, München 1977, pp. 799 ss.

2 *H. Pohlmann*, Die Quellen, 802.

3 *M. Bellomo*, Società e istituzioni in Italia dal Medioevo agli inizi dell'età moderna, Catania 1982, 438 - 440.

phenomenon, is best illustrated by the *consilia*. The influences of everyday commercial activity and of maritime activity in particular, were the dynamic force which, tending to link legal theory with practice, gave rise to the attempts at incorporating the new legal practices within the wider scope of the Roman law tradition.

In this practice itself, in its dynamism, in its requirements for legal precision, requiring a quick settlement of controversial situations, and in its peculiarities, connected with a thorough evaluation of behaviour inspired by honesty and good faith, we must look for the persistence, however limited, of the presence of learned lawyers and of their contribution to its development. Justice, in the field of trade, was entrusted to Courts composed of merchants, who were familiar with customs and were mostly inclined, by an accurate and close examination of the case in point, to both search for the quickest solution, by simplifying and shortening time-limits and requirements in legal proceedings, and by using their criteria of common sense and good faith[4].

In some cases, though, a correct legal definition may have substantial effects regarding the fair conclusion of a law suit: so, there was now room for learned lawyers and we can explain the presence of some of the most important names, such as Baldo and Paolo di Castro, who were called by the judges or by the parties involved, to settle disputes or to support the claims of their respective clients. Such interventions, which made use of concepts and references taken from the Roman tradition, were the first, somewhat limited, contribution to what would in the future become the independent science of commercial law[5].

Another contribution derived from moral and theological speculations[6], which is more difficult to evaluate in its tangible effects and raises problems concerning the real influence it had on the lawyers' work: probably the greatest importance lies in the creation of an economic and commercial lexicon and in the specific reference to more and more complex cases, often with the aim of offering a means of overcoming ecclesiastical prohibition of usury.

The XVIth century brought considerable modifications to the medieval picture outlined above: a renewed interest in the theological and moral field regarding economic subjects, which grew out of the Second Scholastica, was counterbalanced by the development of the first treaties of lay commercial law.

---

[4] *H. Pohlmann*, Die Quellen, 802. See *M. Ascheri*, La decisione nelle Corti giudiziarie italiane del Tre-Quattrocento e il caso della Mercanzia di Siena, in print in the Group "Law Reporting and Records" (Comparative Studies in Continental and Anglo-American Legal History).

[5] *K. O. Scherner*, Die Wissenschaft, 799.

[6] Ibid.

Some scholars, like Scherner, when discussing this topic talk about a classical period in the science of commercial law[7]: This science tends to vary along national grounds only from the second half of the XVIIth century onwards. In Italy, in particular, the scientific treatment of commercial law took place, to a considerable extent, by means of the routine procedure of Court decisions, and mostly through the famous *Rotae* of Rome, Florence, Genoa and others[8], from the XVIIth century onwards. The basic concept of this process is a kind of unity, present in commercial science at the beginning of the Modern Age, which was afterwards replaced by a disunifying process due to the rise of national peculiarities.

As for Italy, I think that this picture can be enriched by some specific elements: firstly, Italian commercial law between the XVIth and the XVIIth centuries (which is actually restricted to the works of Stracca and Scaccia) was connected with the historical and political context and was largely conditioned in its development by the environment. The second element concerns the Courts and the importance of their law-making: in my opinion, they played a basic role from the XVIth century onwards in the process of making commercial law autonomous and lay. From the outset it is necessary to examine the lawyers and the Courts more closely, pointing out that my analysis will consider three subjects; the personalities and works of both Stracca and Scaccia and the setting up of the Genoese civil Rota with its law-making. In my opinion, the reasons for a different and more detailed evaluation of the evolution of commercial science in Italy will be evident from this analysis.

The beginnings of commercial law as an independent science are traditionally connected with the names of three jurists: Benvenuto Stracca, from Ancona, who lived between 1509 and 1578, whose main work *De mercatura seu mercatore tractatus* was first published in 1553[9]; the Portuguese Pedro de Santarem (Petrus de Santerna), author of a *Tractatus de assecurationibus et sponsionibus mercatorum*, whose activity, carried out in Italy, has recently been re-examined from the chronological point of view by Domenico Maffei[10]; and, finally, the Roman lawyer Sigismondo Scaccia, who practised law between the second half of the XVIth century and the beginning of the XVIIth and who wrote a *Tractatus de commerciis et cambio*, published in Rome in 1619[11].

---

[7] Ibid., 799 - 800.

[8] Ibid., 800.

[9] Infra, 14.

[10] *D. Maffei*, Il giureconsulto portoghese Pedro de Santarém, autore del primo trattato sulle assicurazioni (1488), Coimbra 1983 (Separata do número especial do Boletin da Faculdade de Direito de Coimbra – Estudes em Homenagen aos Profs. Manuel Paulo Merêa e Guilherme Braga da Cruz, 1983), 703 - 728.

[11] Infra, 16.

On the basis of the above-mentioned research by Maffei, the earlier dating by several decades of Santerna's work, and also the greater importance of it with respect to Stracca's work will probably cause historians to attach an earlier date to this new scientific period of commercial law.

It will be necessary, to make more detailed assessment of the range and influence of the work by Pedro de Santarem, by examining the sources and the content and to attribute to him the probable role of preparing the way for the more complex work by Stracca.

Stracca's scientific personality is certainly the best known, mostly thanks to Franchi, a scholar of commercial law, who shows reliable historical accuracy, and afterwards through Lattes. The figure of Stracca certainly deserves all this attention, even though his work was not constantly appreciated by subsequent authors and historians.

The detailed and accurate biography by Franchi, published in 1888, underlined the lawyer's cultural development and vocational education, Stracca's detailed knowledge of the humanities and his *cursus honorum*. His political and administrative career began in 1538, when the papal dominion over Ancona became definitive and Stracca's profession was practised in full accordance with the new political situation[12].

In 1889, just one year after Franchi's work was published, Giuseppe Tamassia, in a review, positive on the whole but permeated with Risorgimento-feeling and anticlerical harshness, underlined the dedication of this character "to the Roman court and to the most outstanding members of it"; the fact that in the council of Ancona Stracca's opinion "turned out nearly always to be the most moderate and that he never shared the attitude of opposition against papal outrages"; and, finally, that our lawyer joined the group of those who praised the Jesuits who were tolerated by the Council of Ancona in 1565[13].

The points of criticism, aroused by the brilliant polemic spirit of Tamassia, were re-examined in a different and more thorough way in 1909 in an article by Alessandro Lattes.

The historian of commercial law was given the task by Sraffa and Vivante of commemorating the four hundredth anniversary of the birth of Stracca, in the "Rivista di Diritto Commerciale"[14].

---

[12] *L. Franchi*, Benvenuto Stracca giureconsulto anconitano del secolo XVI, Note bio-bibliografiche, Roma 1888, 18 - 35.

[13] *G. Tamassia*, rev. *L. Franchi*, Benvenuto Stracca giureconsulto anconitano del secolo XVI: Note bio-bibliografiche, Archivio giuridico diretto da Filippo Serafini, XLII (1889), 368.

[14] *A. Lattes*, Lo Stracca giureconsulto, Rivista di Diritto commerciale, VII/1 (1909), 624 - 649.

From the scientific point of view, Stracca is highly praised: Lattes states that "the subject of modern commercial law itself had never been gathered together in a single volume before Stracca wrote his work. The individual issues could be read in books, here and there in a disorderly way, in commentaries on civil and Curch law, in counsels and opinions expressed on individual specific cases; controversies were settled exclusively according to Roman law and its principles, whenever there were no precise binding regulations of the *Statuti* to be applied".

Lattes continues, declaring that "Stracca was the first to draw up a treaty dealing exclusively with mercantile subjects, where texts of sources and by learned lawyers referring to trade and merchants were collected, leaving aside all the issues of mere civil law, either without mentioning them at all or simply making a short reference to them[15].

Having acknowledged the importance of this work of identification of the subject and sources, I think the problem that Lattes raises is negligible: that is whether Stracca is an expert in commercial law and is aware of this, or whether he is a civil lawyer who admits the importance of the new elements.

As far as I am concerned, the remarks connecting the Author and the events of his life to certain doctrinal choices, which are evident in his work, are much more noteworthy.

Lattes, in fact, moderates Tamassia's negative view, on the basis of his personal comments, according to which: "papal dominion in Ancona was a limitation of freedom enjoyed till then, rather than the actual suppression of municipal liberties and a subjection to a new lord". Therefore, in Lattes's opinion, Stracca's agreement with the new régime does not mean he betrayed the ideal of former independence[16].

The dispute and the more or less positive political evaluation of the attitude of Stracca is quite significant, if we connect it with the concrete results that the new situation in Ancona brought about also in the Author's scientific activities.

In fact, the work is not complete and it can be supposed that for some subjects, such as companies, exchange or insurance (insurance being dealt with an individual treaty) – I am quoting from Lattes – "the gaps have been left on purpose, probably because such subjects in particular implied to the utmost the question of usury, and fictitious contracts were very frequently used in order to get out of it". Furthermore, "Stracca wavered amid the open conflict between merchants and canonists ... and he was neither able nor willing to take a precise stand", and, finally, he left "aside the most

[15] Ibid., 642.
[16] Ibid., 626.

embarassing topics, on the pretext of the intensive studies made of them by scholars, but with the real intention of maintaining a more ambiguous position"[17].

But, in my opinion, Lattes does not draw the right conclusions from these statements for a wider evaluation of the Author and of his work.

I believe that the reason for the lack of consideration and limited resonance of Stracca's work in the subsequent development of commercial science actually lies in this reticence and ambiguity, deriving from political conditioning, and also in the fact that he too often takes the merchant background of Ancona as a reference point, while it certainly was not among the most advanced in either Italian or European economic life.

Stracca's political choice of prudence, which consists, on a scientific level, of avoiding or getting around the basic theoretical problems of the new discipline, has the effect, generally speaking, of restricting his contribution to the process of making commercial law more lay in its nature.

On the contrary, external influences though present and not less impending and potentially dangerous, seem to have a lesser influence on the work of another great scholar of commercial law, Sigismondo Scaccia, who was active between the end of the XVIth and the beginning of the XVIIth century[18].

Unlike Stracca, who spent almost all his life in Ancona, Scaccia, besides practising the legal profession in Rome, performed the duty of Judge of the Rota in Genoa in 1614 and possibly in Florence in 1620[19].

Actually, this lawyer still lacks a serious biographer to investigate the importance of his role, not only regarding commercial law, but also trials.

Although Scaccia too practised in the papal states, he succeeded in using his deep knowledge of moral and theological culture as an instrument for continuing the process of decanonising commercial law.

The general topics are developed in the first part of his work, whereas in the second part he takes advantage of his practical experience as a lawyer and a judge to examine closely the problems connected with the contract of exchange[20].

---

17 Ibid., 638, 641.

18 *P. Mandosio*, Bibliotheca romana, Roma 1682, 305; *C. Schwarzenberg*, Scaccia Sigismondo, Novissimo Digesto Italiano, XVI, Torino 1969, 670.

19 Leges novae Reipublicae Genuensis, Genuae 1617, p. 129: De Sp. Sigismondo Scaccia. 1614. Die 4 Februarij. Sp. Sigismondo Scaccia existens in Rota civili, extractus fuit pro Rota criminali, et declaratus impeditus, et in urnam reponendus, a minori Concilio ...; *G. Gorla*, Sulla via dei „motivi“ delle „sentenze“: lacune e trappole, Il Foro Italiano, 1980, col. 204, „Lo Scaccia ... fu membro della Rota fiorentina intorno al 1620“; *R. Savelli*, Between law and morals: interest in the dispute on exchanges during the 16th century, in this volume.

The *quaestio prima* from the *Tractatus de commercio et cambio*, published in 1619, is fundamental in assessing the contribution made by Scaccia to the independence process of commercial law.

Through a rich confrontation of arguments of theologians and lawyers, Scaccia wishes to show that decisions concerning usury and illicit trade are mainly taken by learned lawyers, whose opinion prevails over the theologists'.

Since abstention from all trade would be too detrimental to all countries, the Author maintains that it is necessary to make a distinction between trade which endangers the salvation of the soul and that which does not, and that in any case it is necessary to verify the presence of the correct legal and moral requirements every time for each form of trade[21].

This contrivance allows Scaccia to attenuate the settlement of these issues in an exaggerated and circumstantial number of cases, thus eventually reassessing the function of theology and underlining the difference between moral and legal judgments.

The traditional survey restricting the first period of commercial law studies to the works of Santerna, Stracca and Scaccia must, in my opinion, be enlarged by other sources, such as the judgments of some Courts, which exerted their legal power between the XVIth and XVIIth centuries as an integral part of the new discipline[22].

These Courts too are the fruit of a specific historical and political context, which, to a certain extent, should not be excluded from the general events of the modernization of the European States in the Modern Age.

Concerning the discourse on commercial law, I believe that the events of the Genoese civil *Rota* and of its mercantile law-making are particularly significant, but first it is necessary to make some short general remarks about Italian Courts in the Modern Age.

Not many years ago, Mario Ascheri evaluated the publications of "Decisiones" by famous Italian Courts in the Modern Age, in an integral text published under the patronage of the Max Planck Institute of Frankfurt. This operation has enabled scholars by means of the bibliographical structure, to understand the condition of the relevant historical writings, and has

---

20 *S. Scaccia*, Tractatus de commerciis et cambio, Romae 1618. Further editions Coloniae 1619, 1620, 1738, Francofurti 1648, Venetiae 1650, Genevae 1664, Coloniae 1738 (*K. O. Scherner*, Die Wissenschaft, 864), and also Venetiis 1669.

21 *S. Scaccia*, Tractatus de commerciis et cambio, Venetiis 1669, 1 - 92.

22 *G. Gorla*, I Tribunali Supremi degli stati italiani preunitari quali fattori della unificazione del diritto nello Stato e della sua uniformazione fra Stati, Atti del terzo congresso Internazionale della Società Italiana di Storia del Diritto, Firenze 1977, 447 - 532.

confirmed the idea that these Courts still retain the fascination of mysterious spheres.

These Courts are scarcely talked about, with great caution and nobody dares put forward hypotheses or conclusions which may lead to generalizations[23].

Caution seems justified if we consider that some research into this subject shows a highly varied situation, keeping to the individual institutional contexts whereby the Courts establish and exercise jurisdiction rather than to general notions which rationalize the legal system.

Some magistratures are recent, that is starting approximately from the beginning of the XVIth century, such as the Florentine and the Genoese *Rotae*; others are ancient, such as the Roman *Rota*, but all of them aim to gain legal supremacy within the individual States and some of them even to expand this beyond the borders of their States.

Within the States, obviously it is not a question of precedents, as in the case of Anglo-Saxon law, but, more simply, of a necessary and due regard to the conclusions of predecessors.

Outside the States, on the contrary, we realize the progressive presence of the decisions made by these Courts in common law.

Printing collections of legal documents is an extremely valid tool for the wider knowledge and circulation of this material, which, more often than one might think and not only in the case of the Roman *Rota*, is remarkable for its technical and legal content which is of a generally high standard.

On the basis of the considerations expressed so far, I think it is necessary to distinguish between the two aspects they present: firstly, the institutional and operative life of these magistratures, which, in their origin and evolution are functional within the settings in which they are established; secondly, the course of their decisions, which, collected and printed, have an independent life connected to common law-making and are raised above the subjective and particular circumstances which produced them.

The scheme of this concept shows two lines, which come close at times, but remain largely independent: one representing the events taking place within the individual Courts, and the other the adoption outside the Courts of the material produced.

By inserting also the history of the Genoese *Rota* and of its published *decisiones* within this framework, we get a more precise and, from certain

---

[23] *M. Ascheri*, Rechtsprechungs- und Konsiliensammlungen, Italien, Handbuch der Quellen und Literatur der neurer europäischen Privatrechtsgeschichte, II/2, Neure Zeit (1500 - 1800), Das Zeitalter des gemeinen Rechts, Gesetzgebung und Rechtsprechung, ed. *H. Coing*, München 1976, 1113, 1221.

points of view, a more emblematic view of the situation of the famous Italian Courts in the Modern Age.

Included in the complex institutional reform, which in 1528 renewed the structure of the Genoese Republic, the Civil *Rota* was needed in order to eliminate a series of magistratures composed of non-technical judges and to replace them with learned lawyers[24]. Besides the guarantee of impartiality, deriving from the fact that they were outsiders these judges were obliged to offer further guarantees of a professional nature, such as University law studies and, at least, a five-year period of training as judges or lawyers.

Among others, almost all merchants controversies were brought before them and submitted to their judgement whereas these controversies had formerly been settled by the *Uffici di Mercanzia, Gazaria, Banchi and Rotti.*

Nevertheless, the new Court could not completely eliminate the features of the abolished magistratures, as it was ordered to solve cases taking into account, besides its own *regulae*, the *inveterata consuetudo* firmly established in the Ligurian commercial world[25].

The technical ability of learned lawyers was soon adapted to the lively and demanding Genoese mercantile setting, and offered extremely interesting results.

Tradition, or even the influence of the mercantile Courts' law-making which the *Rota* replaced and the new *regulae* of the judicial body led learned judges to examine closely the theoretical notions put forward by merchants and to endavour to transfer them into the rigorous framework of *ius commune.*

The fundamental contribution to the rising science of commercial law actually came by passing through this process, using the tool of the *Rota*'s justified *decisiones*[26].

In 1582, a collection of the *Rota*'s *decisiones de mercatura* was published in Genoa, and an identical volume appeared one year later in Venice, due to personal and political disagreement between the printers[27].

---

[24] *V. Piergiovanni*, The rise of the Genoese civil Rota in the XVIth century: The "decisiones de mercatura" concerning insurance, in this volume.

[25] Ibid.

[26] Ibid.

[27] *N. Calvini*, Una strana cinquecentina genovese: Decisiones Rotae Genuae de Mercatura, La Berio, 1968/1, 24 - 29; *A. Cioni*, Bellone Antonio, Dizionario Biografico degli Italiani, VII, Roma 1965, 759 - 760; *M. Chiaudano*, Rotae Genuae (Decisiones de Mercatura), Novissimo Digesto Italiano, XVI, Torino 1969, 273 - 274; *M. Ascheri*, Rechtsprechungs- und Konsiliensammlungen, 1153 - 1154, 1181 (where the editions are enumerated in which the Decisiones are published alone: Genova 1582, Venezia 1582, 1599, 1601, 1606).

The importance of this collection was definitely confirmed by inserting it in the Lyons edition of the *De mercatura Decisiones et Tractatus varii*, and in subsequent editions in Frankfurt and in Amsterdam[28].

I cannot express my opinion on the commercial aspects of law-making of other Italian *Rotae* in the early part of the Modern Age, other than by referring to a few elements which are scarcely verified by specialised researchers: undoubtedly, above all the Roman and the Florentine *Rotae*, besides the Genoese Rota, have a position of great prestige and authority in this matter too.

I recently started research in collaboration with some colleagues, aiming at assessing the judges of some famous *Rotae*, such as those of Genoa, Florence, Siena and Lucca and I hope that it will be a positive step towards a better understanding of these Courts.

Even though we have little knowledge of other judicial sources, in the end, it is a question of estimating to what extent the experience of the Genoese Court may be generalized and considered valid for an overall understanding of the history of commercial law between the XVIth and the XVIIth centuries.

I think I can state that the necessary keeping with Roman practice, the loss of interest in theological and moral aspects, the consideration for local law and mercantile customs, make their judgements a basic tool in the process of decanonisation of commercial law.

I do not agree with those scholars who, within the scope of common law, give different values to systematic and case literature: I think it is an error deriving from an intellectual outlook which does not belong to the period we are studying.

Some years ago, as far as Casaregi was concerned, my opinion was that the underestimation of his work shown by Goldschmidt and Lattes were not acceptable: their views were based on systematical incompleteness and implied a negative consideration of the relevant literature dealing with legal practice.

It was my impression that, besides the consideration for the intrinsic qualities of Casaregi's work, his fame among both his contemporaries and later scholars raised doubts about the credibility of such an evaluation[29].

---

[28] *M. Chiaudano*, Rotae Genuae, 274, e *M. Ascheri*, Rechtsprechungs- und Konsiliensammlungen, 1181, report the editions Lyons 1582, 1590, 1592, 1593, 1608, 1610, 1621 and Frankfurt 1612, 1652, Cologne 1622, Amsterdam 1669; *L. Franchi*, Benvenuto Stracca, 144 - 146 affirms that the first Lyons edition of De Mercatura decisiones et tractatus variis was published in 1592.

[29] *V. Piergiovanni*, Dottrina, divulgazione e pratica alle origini della scienza commercialistica: Giuseppe Lorenzo Maria Casaregi, Appunti per una biografia, Materiali per la storia della cultura giuridica, IX (1979), 325 - 326.

I wish to repeat the same notion regarding the law-making of the Genoese civil *Rota*, its application and frequent appreciation in law-making and legal practice following its publication.

This work, like those by Stracca and Scaccia, must however be considered as the fruit of particular historical conditions which existed in Italy in the XVIth century, linked to the process of political and institutional modifications, which, however tentatively, aimed at extending State control to fundamental activities, such as commerce and justice.

The outlook of these works is not scientifically neutral and if they only underline the differences observed during the second half of the XVIIth century, this means once again that one has to choose an interpretative scheme, taking the French legislative model as a reference point.

This view degrades and schematizes, perhaps too arbitrarily, the wealth of the historical implications of this complex phenomenon, which is only appreciated as far as it can be compared to some models of codification which in any case are considered as being of a higher standard.

On the contrary, as I stated above, it is necessary to re-appraise and bring our historical implications, if we do not want to believe that the commercial science of the XVIth century started from nothing, by the intuition of some isolated minds.

On the contrary, the works by Santarem, Stracca and Scaccia and the law-making of the Genoese *Rota* grew out of a particular environmental and political context, which produced and influenced them: they are the fruit of a society and an economy endeavouring to rationalize bureaucratic structures and to provide a legal system adapted to the changing political situation.

This situation, if not new, is certainly different from that of the Middle Ages.

I certainly do not intend to assert that we are talking about modern States, such as France, but I think it is neither historically correct to ignore the ferment and the changes which stirred these societies at the beginning of the Modern Age.

The institutional results are interesting and the reasons why they had no further evolution are many and complex and there is no point in talking about them here.

Within this picture and with such connections, the Authors and texts that I have examined and, more generally, Italian commercial science of the XVIth century, may justify its present features and the reasons which allowed it to create innovations of content, interpretation and systemization all of which guaranteed its spread and fame throughout Europe.

VITO PIERGIOVANNI

The Rise of the Genoese Civil Rota in the XVIth Century: The "Decisiones de Mercatura" Concerning Insurance

Summary: I. The rise of the civil Rota; II. Events concerning the rules of the Genoese civil Rota between the XVIth and the XVIIth centuries; III. *Decisiones* concerning insurance.

I. The rise of the civil Rota

The origins and rise of Central Courts in the Modern Age are connected with the process of the centralization of public bodies and met the demand for the better operation and uniformity of justice for those who were subject to one power within the State.

The judgements made by these Courts reflect the realization of such legal policies, but are also a reliable indication of the problems and tension which the economic and social life of the State was prone to.

Within this jurisprudence the quantity and quality of the judgements related to trade, which were expressed in monetary terms, and the range of relevant geographical extent, can best show the extent and complexity of economic relations, and the means and skill used by the merchant classes.

Favourable environmental conditions were a stimulus to the process of specialization and the technical and legal improvement of the individual mercantile institutions and explain the greater fame and diffusion of the *decisiones* of some central Courts as opposed to those of others.

These historical and environmental considerations give a clearer insight into the events surrounding the Genoese civil Rota, which can be graphically represented, in the space of a century, from 1530 to 1630, by a rise and then decline in close connection with the economic and social life of the *Repubblica di S. Giorgio.*

The most interesting documents showing the activity and the results achieved by this Court is the collection of judgements entitled *Decisiones Rotae Genuae de mercatura et pertinentibus ad eam,* which was printed for the first time in Genoa in 1582. This collection consists of 215 *decisiones* gathered by a private citizen, offering to dealers and to practical and theoretical lawyers the best cases from one of the most important authorities in the Mediterranean area.

The law-court had been constituted fairly recently, having started its activity in 1530, when a rationalization process in Genoese legal life led to the abandoning of the previous system of magistrates. The tribunal of the Rota, in fact, fell within the reform plan wich in 1528, mostly through Admiral Andrea Doria, aimed at achieving both the political goal of rendering the local ruling class homogeneous and the institutional goal of simplifying and qualifying the bureaucratic and law giving structure of the State[1].

The choices adopted for such modernization were quite common: in the field of jurisdiction some special non-technical magistratures were replaced by a single Bench, formed of foreign learned lawyers with a 2-year term of office, who were not immediately re-eligible and were subject to control *finito munere*.

The refom laws[2] simply gave quick lines which a committee of four greatly respected citizens stove to implement: they were assigned the task of "... revidendi, commemorandi et refferendi quae ad rem ipsam pertinerent et iustitiae et veritatis, considerata natura ipsarum causarum, et pro litibus minuendis, ac quanto citius fieri potest, cum minori iactura litigantium expediendis ..."[3].

The members of the committe were required, in short, to both determine more precisely the main features of the activity (the *natura causarum*), assigned to the new Court, and to establish codes of procedure in order to

[1] Le Leggi et Riforme della ... Repubblica di Genova, fatte ... l'anno MDXXVIII, Pavia 1575, p. 30 v., 12 marzo 1529: "I predetti Mag. Signori Dodici Reformatori della Eccelsa Repubblica di Genova, ragunati in sufficiente e legittimo numero, mossi per degni rispetti, in ogni miglior modo, et c. hanno deliberato, che fra'l primo giorno di Gennaio prossimo sia istituita una Rota di cinque Dottori forastieri dall'Illustrissimo Duce e Magnifici Governatori, con quel salario, emolumento, autorità, e balia; con appellatione e senza, come loro parrà; togliendo via e rimovendo e tenendo per tolta e rimossa, finito il presente anno, tutta quella autorità e balia, che hanno nelle cose civili i magistrati de cittadini, ò altri qualsivoglia nella presente Città; cioè l'ufficio della mercatantia, della Gazaria, de banchi e tutt'altri uffici de cittadini. Intendendo però che la predetta Rota sia obligata guidicare secondo le regole, ordini e decreti, e secondo la natura dei suddetti ufficii respettivamente; eccettuando nondimeno dal predetto rimover di balia, della quale si è detto, l'ufficio de consoli della ragione. Il quale ufficio resti fermo in sua possanza ...". For a general historical setting *C. Costantini,* La Repubblica di Genova nell'età moderna, Torino 1978 (Storia d'Italia diretta da *G. Galasso,* IX).

[2] As the text of the laws establishing the civil Rota, three copies bearing no significant defferences have been taken into account. Two copies are kept at Archivio Storico del Comune di Genova (A.S.C.G.), ms. N. 89, Constitutiones Rotae Civilis Genuae 1529, fo. 2r. - 10 v., fo. 18r. - 26r. (we shall make reference to the latter later on, as it also includes the subsequent laws concerning the Rota); while the third can be found at the Archivio di Stato di Genova (A.S.G.), ms. N. 128, fo. 69v. - 77r.

[3] A.S.C.G., ms. N. 89, Constitutiones Rotae, fo. 18r. The appointed jurisconsults are Giovan Battista Cattaneo Lazagna, Giovan Battista de Nigro fu Oberto, Jacopo Cattaneo, Giovanni Imperiale Baliano.

shorten the times of judicial proceedings and to reduce Court costs borne by the parties.

At the same time, the amount of salary to be paid to the new judges was fixed, and it was decided to forward this deliberation *per litteras ad diversas Italiae civitates,* in order to urge any candidate to apply for these posts[4].

On January 8th, the definitive text of the *Constitutiones Rotae* was published and it came into force at the same time as the effective start of the new Court[5].

The problem of the activity of the new Court, which underwent subsequent stages of adjustment from the decree of institution of 1530 up to the *Statuta* of 1589, must be linked to the above-mentioned first element of the judges' professional qualities which were estimated according to the normal requirements of a university *curriculum* concluded by a degree and a subsequent *cursus honorum* in the law-courts and in the forum.

In fact, the first decree states literally:

„Et in primis statuunt, imponunt, et ordinant Magistratum unum Rotae quinque Iurisperitorum, et Doctorum in Civitate Genuae, sub modis et formis inferius declarandis elligendorum, cuius Magistratus iurisdictio incipiat in KL. Januarii proximi anni Millesimi quingentesimi trigesimi, qui Magistratus Rotae intelligatur habere et habeat iurisdictionem, authoritatem et bailiam, ac competens sit, et esse intelligatur super omnibus et singulis causis, quaestionibus, et differentiis, et in dependentibus ab eis de quibus sunt et esse consueverunt tam ex regulis ordinamentorum Januae, quam etiam ex inveterata consuetudine sp. Officiales mercantiae, Bancorum, et Gazariae tam officii Gazariae simpliciter, quam officii Gazariae Commissarii, et Delegati etc., ac etiam officiales Ruptorum, ac etiam de causis, quae ex forma Capituli Januae positi sub Rubr. de causis civilibus et pecuniariis bonis viris committendis, possunt committi duobus bonis viris de tabula, ita et tali modo, quod omnes et singulae causae, et jurisdictiones praedictae, et quaelibet earum devolvant, et intelligantur devolutae, et spectare, et spectent iudicio, iurisdictioni, ac determinationi dicti Magistratus Rotae praedictae, de quibus omnibus et singulis causis praedictis dictus Magistratus Rotae sit competens, et de praedictis causis nullus alius Magistratus possit nec debeat se intromittere. Declarato semper ad cautelam quod dictus magistratus Rotae non sit competens, nec possit se intromittere de causis quae ex forma capituli Januae positi sub rubr. De causis non commissibilibus bonis viris, non possint nec debeant bonis viris committi, nec etiam de causis de quibus officiales Monetarum sunt competentes, nec etiam de causis spectantibus DD. Consulibus rationis, nec etiam de causis Ruptorum seu Rupendorum possit se intromittere dictus Magistratus Rotae, nisi prius per DD. Antianos Januae, seu alium superiorem fuerit declaratum aliquem Bancherium sive alium ruptum esse, seu rumpendum, facta transmissione Praefato Magistratui Rotae"[6].

The activity of the new Court did not extend to all civil controversies, but it rather tended to reunify all such controversies under the authority of a

---

[4] Ibid., De salario Rotae.

[5] The precise date can be drawn from the copy A. S. G., Constitutiones Rotae, ms. N. 128, fo. 69v.

[6] A. S. C. G., ms. N. 89, Constitutiones Rotae, fo. 18v. - 19r.

body composed of qualified public magistrates, while controversies had formerly been settled by *boni viri* and by non-technical judges.

Indeed, people had previously had recourse to the *boni viri* for all issues which were not within the competence of the *Praetor* or of his *Vicarius*[7], as they concerned neither the public interest nor the prerogatives of State sovereignty.

In matters of great economic importance, for instance problems of succession, the *boni viri* would often have to turn to a jurisconsult for advice, in order to clear up and settle the most controversial legal problems.

Since the establishment of the Rota, legal aspects concerning these controversies were also better examined and more thoroughly assessed than they had been by non-technical judges.

Undoubtedly, the field in which this change in judicial development was most fruitful was the mercantile field.

The Rota, as the charter of institution claims, assumed the functions and the competence of some old special Courts: firstly of the *Officium Mercantiae,* the members of which, according to the ancient *Statuta,* of 1414: "... Qui officiales et officium mercantiae sint et esse intelligantur et debeant magistratus super omnibus et singulis differentiis, quaestionibus et controversiis quae coram eis movebuntur mercandi causa, scilicet occasione mercantiae, vel alicuius mercati de quibus non sit instrumentum publicum. Quas quidem differentias, quaestiones et controversias dictum officium teneatur et debeat declarare terminare et diffinire summarie et de plano, sine strepitu et figura iudicii ac etiam pignore bandi, quam cicius fieri poterit bona fide, vinculo iuramenti servato iuris ordine et modo (rectius, *non*) servato, oretenus et in scriptis, habendo cum per (rectius, *semper*) intuitum ad dictum (rectius, *deum*) et veritatem negotii ... sine consilio iurisperiti nisi ad utriusque partis istantiam ..."[8].

The authority of the 'Ufficio di Gazaria' (which had been replaced by the Rota) was instead more specific, responsible *super facto navigandi,* while the *Officium Banchorum* governed the *compere, paghe* and *luoghi* of the *Commune.*

The Rota's authority in the matter of bankruptcy was peculiar: in fact, it could only act when a political body, such as the *Magistratus Antianorum* considered it opportune, not only by legal criteria, to start proceedings[9].

---

[7] Statuta et decreta Communis Genuae, *A. M. Visdomini* ed., Bononiae 1498, L. I, cap. 8, c. 6r. "De causis civilibus et pecuniariis bonis viris committendis"; cap. 9, c, 9r., "De causis non commissibilibus bonis viris".

[8] Ibid., L. IV, cap. 96, c. 81r., "De potestate et bailia Officii Mercantiae".

[9] *V. Piergiovanni,* Banchieri e falliti nelle "Decisiones de mercatura" della Rota civile di Genova, Diritto comune, diritto commerciale, diritto veneziano, a cura di K.

Unlike other central Tribunals, which, in the same period, tended to organize their activities in an exclusive way for all civil and criminal matters, the Genoese civil Rota tended to act mainly as a specialized Court in mercantile and maritime matters.

The decree of institution was very clear in this matter when, taking up the notion expressed by the reformers in 1528, it insisted on respect for the rules, orders, decrees and also the features of the previous mercantile Courts, which had now been replaced by the Rota, and reminded lawyers that *Uditori* had the faculty of judging *tam ex regulis quam ex inveterata consuetudine*[10].

Formally, the rules of procedure that can be found in the decree of institution are rather similar to the rules of other tribunals, and take up the texts quoted above regarding the *Officium Mercantiae* almost literally[11]: in two contexts specific reference is made to the peculiarity of the mercantile Court. Indeed a passage claims: "... Insuper pro maiori deliberatione, attentis regulis et ordinamentis Ianuae, ac inveterata consuetudine declarant et statuunt, quod in causis cambiorum et recambiorum, exationis securitatis et exationis naulorum, et in aliis causis executionis, videlicet illae quae iurisdictioni Praefati Magistratus spectant, debeat procedi et terminari executive et sub illis modis et formis prout continetur in Decretis, ordinamentis, et regulis antea conditis et prout antea servari consuevit, quantum ad modum et formam procedendi, praedictis non obstantibus, in quibus causis executionis de quibus supra non possit nec debeat dari, nec concedi dilatio de foris informatoria, nec etiam probatoria ..."[12].

Later on we read: "... Praeterea pro tollendis difficultatibus, declarant et statuunt quod Cartulariis Bancheriorum Ianuae scriptis per Notarium publicum de Collegio Notariorum Genuae adhibeatur plena fides tam pro Bancheris, quam contra Bancherium, ac etiam inter alias extraneas Personas ..."[13].

The founding decree of the Rota, after establishing the distinctive principles of the Court and the references to the rules and customs of the mercantile tradition and regular practice that it must follow, goes back to the traditional hierarchy of sources, including Roman law: "... Magistratus Rotae,

---

Nehlsen-von Stryk e D. Nörr, (Centro Tedesco di Studi Veneziani, Quaderni, 31) 17 - 38.

[10] Constitutiones Rotae, fo. 18r.

[11] The *Constitutiones Rotae* deal exhaustively with specific procedural aspects concerning evidence, testimonies, time limits in judicial proceedings, delays of information and probation appeals, which have many points of contact with the previous Genoese regulations of the *Statuti,* dating back to 1414. These regulations were supplemented and modified by reforms many times, see below paragraph 2.

[12] Constitutiones Rotae, fo. 19v. - 20r.

[13] Fo. 23r - 23v.

salvis semper et servatis contentis in praesentibus constitutionibus, quae observari debeant, quod observent et observare teneantur capitula, et ordinamenta Ianuae tam condita quam condenda coram eis exhibenda et ipsis defficientibus iura romana ..."[14].

In this particular circumstance, that is at the moment of the constitution of the new tribunal, this reference to Roman law is more significant than it normally is in legal systems which were intended to cover a wider and wider range of dealings with one particular form of legislation, and thus tended to anticipate all foreseeable cases and to be based on rules of necessity which increasingly aimed at excluding possible outside influences. It is necessary to add to these general considerations that, in the specific case of Genoa, the new Court had to judge mercantile relations which often developed separately from local tradition and which were, instead, connected with customary forms and procedures which at the wish of the law-makers, the new judges hat to obey.

It would appear to be a very difficult situation for Roman law, but the innovation of the Genoese Rota lies in the personalities of the new judges, who, thanks to their ability to reconcile mercantile regular practice with school tradition, were to give success to the jurisprudence of the Courts.

The *Officium Mercantiae, Gazariae, Banchorum,* which the civil Rota replaced, were not composed of legal experts but of citizens, especially merchants who, thanks to their experience, wisdom and honesty were called to sit on the Benches. The composition of the Rota was, instead, governed by other criteria, as the requirements were: "DD. Iudices Rotae eligendi ad ipsam rotam sint Doctores utriusque iuris et canonici et civilis, et seu saltem civilis tantum, ac bonis moribus ornati, et iusti habeantur, et tractentur ..."[15].

In addition to this, they were requested to have been born and to dwell within at least 50-miles of the town of Genoa, to be older than 35 and that: "... postquam fuerint doctorati, quod se exercuerint in dicto exercitio Doctoratus advocando, et seu iudicando, et consulendo, seu practicando saltem per annos quinque ..."[16].

Therefore, merchant-judges were replaced by graduate-judges with experience in practice and in the Courts, who were shifted to an environment with its own rules and customs to which they had to adapt and which, above all, they had to enforce.

A study of the origin and previous experience of these judges would be interesting and appreciated; anyway, we think that they carried out two very important technical operations with very profitable consequences.

14 Fo. 24r.

15 Fo. 24r.

16 Fo. 24r.

Firstly, through the incorporation of the most valid parts of mercantile regular practice and their fusion with the new rules of the Court procedures (both those issued by law-makers and those arising from the everyday activity and previous experience of the new judges), a *stilus* gradually developed, which, from time to time, was justified and theorized and eventually contributed to introducing the most significant example of mercantile law (not only regarding Genoa, but, at least, the Mediterranean area). The previously quoted examples of *causae cambiorum et recambiorum* or of *cartularii bancheriorum* are peculiarities of the Genoese *stilus*.

Secondly, the judges' effort to use the traditional notions of the jurists of Roman formation and the *auctoritates* which supported them, leads to corresponding research into the subject emerging from a mercantile Court.

These two experiences, one practical and one theoretical, were combined in the same group of persons and helped to give a valid contribution to the rising science of commercial law. We shall give some examples of this with regard to insurance, later on.

The possibility of circulating the material worked out by the Genoese civil Rota was made concrete from the time when it was decided that the *Auditores* would be obliged to justify the judgements of the Court.

The procedure of appeal against the decisions of the Rota, which was provided for by the decree of 1530, already quoted several times, established the practice of giving grounds for decisions. The decree states: "... Item statuunt, declarant et decernunt, quod a sententiis ferendis per D. de Rota quando fuerint quinque, vel quator ex eis vere concordes in iudicando, a sententiis eorum non possit, nec debeat appellari, revocari, reclamari, nec de nullitate dici, sed ipso iure et facto transeant in rem iudicatam, et exequantur, et exequi debeant; si vero non essent concordes in iudicando ut supra, tunc et eo casu possit reclamari a sententiis eorum ad DD. Procuratores Praefatae Reipublicae. Qui causas dictae appellationis ut supra interpositae committant tribus prout eis melius videbitur, et quam commissionem faciant tribus Doctoribus extraneis ecclesiasticis, si adessent in civitate Ianuae, si eis videbitur sine suspicione eisdem possit committi, et quod ab eis administrari debeat iudicio eorum, consideratis considerandis, alioquin possit eam committere Iurisperitis ex Collegio Iurisperitorum Ianuae, quam etiam aliis non Iurisperitis et tam coniunctim quam in societate, quam aliter, et prout melius videbitur Dominis Procuratoribus Praefatae Reipublicae ..."[17].

In 1534 the obligation of giving grounds was introduced in order to increase the chance of appeal in those cases where the judges of the Rota disagreed: "Si enim inter ipsos D. Auditores in proferendis eorum sententiis in

[17] Fo. 21v. - 22r.

illis scilicet causis, quibus ex forma institutionis Rotae appellatio data est discordes fuerint teneantur et debeant in utraque eorum sententia inserere substantialiter eorum motiva, quibus moti fuerint ad sic iudicandum ..."[18].

The definitive institution and generalization of the obligation of ground can be found in the *Reformationes Rotae Genuae aeditae anno MDLVII,* according to which: "... Rationes et causas, quibus moti fuerint ad iudicandum, in omnibus et singulis sententiis per eos ferendis, sive fuerint concordes, sive discordes, teneantur Domini Auditores intra octo dies dare notario causae, allegando iura, rationes, et decisiones, quibus moti fuerint ad sic iudicandum, et non per relationem ad acta vel processus, exceptis causis minoris summae librarum ducentarum, et exceptis iis causis executivis, in quibus iura partium sunt reservata in iudicio ordinario, quae motiva subscribi debeant per unumquemque ex ipsis Dominis Auditoribus et remanere debeant penes acta causae, et de eis fiat copia parti, quae illam petierit. Declarato, quod omissio motivorum non viciet sententiam nec etiam expressio ipsorum, quamvis esset iniusta et erronea, ex eo tantum, quod in ipsis sententiis apposita fuerint, non noceat aut nocere possit sententiis, adeo quod ex eo quod fuerint expressa motiva, vel non expressa, vel iniusta, vel erronea, nullo modo possit dici de nullitate, vel excessu nec aliquid opponi contra ipsas sententias, respectu ipsorum motivorum, perinde ac si ipsa motiva, et rationes in sententiis vel actis redditae non fuissent. Dicti tamen auditores debeant syndicari de praedictis, arbitrio syndacatorum ..."[19].

In 1559 the system seems to have been consolidated and the *Auditores* asked for a pay increase "respectu maioris laboris in extendendis motivis in sententiis, quae deinceps extendere debebunt"[20].

A portfolio of these decisions based on grounds had been published in two editions, a Genoese and a Venetian one, some years earlier, in 1582, while the definitive sanction, leading to circulation and renown in Europe was to be obtained by the insertion of these judgements in the Lyons volume *De mercatura decisiones et Tractatus varii et de rebus ad eam pertinentibus* (1582), also reprinted in the XVIIth century in Cologne, Frankfurt and in Amsterdam. The press was a primary sounding board for the Genoese *decisiones* and established them as one of the cornerstones in the rising science of European commercial law[21].

---

[18] Fo. 28r.

[19] Reformationes Rotae Genuae aeditae anno MDLVII, Genuae 1557, 10 - 11.

[20] Constitutiones Rotae, fo. 29, De salario Dominorum Auditorum Rotae (1559, feb., 22).

[21] *V. Piergiovanni,* Courts and Commercial Law at the beginning of the Modern Age, in this volume.

II. Events concerning the rules of the Genoese civil Rota between the XVIth and XVIIth centuries

While the publication of the *Decisiones de mercatura* marks the height of glory of the Genoese Court, the supplements and adjustments of legislation, following the *Constitutiones Rotae* of 1530, and which continued up to the first decade of the XVIIth century, show the initial eagerness and the progressive decline of the Court[22].

The first important integration into the *Constitutiones Rotae* of 1530 took place after a few years, in 1534: in addition to the obligation of stating grounds we have already discussed, some internal regulations of the Court were established such as the distribution of lawsuits among the *Uditori*, relations with parties and lawyers, documents relating to preliminary investigations and, finally, the decision[23].

In 1538, the first printed text of the *regulae* was issued at the initiative of the Genoese Government, as the laws concerning the Rota were incomplete and vague and needed to be *reformatae, locupletatae, distinctae*.

It consists of a rather peculiar text, which, by concise directive statements, besides summarizing the *Constitutiones* of 1530, explains some aspects the *Constitutiones* merely touched on, such as execution proceedings, delays and terms, interventions in cases of *cambia et recambia*, insurance and sea freight[24].

In spite of this legislative clarification, the way of operating of the fledgling Court turned out to be defective; in fact, only two years later, in 1540, the Genoese Government realized the need to consult some jurists, and to ask them to draft the reform bills of the Rota's regulation.

Some of these reports, which have been preserved, are still in our hands and point out the problems and expectations of the lawyers and citizens concerning the Court.

The judges' behaviour is debated, mostly because of the tendency to avoid the rule of giving the *relatio processus* in the presence of the parties and of the lawyers for the defence; lawyers are accused of the tendency to lodge *cavillationes et exceptiones inutiles*, and it is advised that they be obliged to sign all their deeds in order to contest the habit as a pretext of many Court records. In the mercantile branch, it is suggested that the rules concerning insurance and exchanges should be cleared up, but, perhaps, the most inter-

---

[22] Supra, 25.

[23] Constitutiones Rotae, fo. 27r. - 28r.; another copy, Ordo et regula servanda per Auditores Rotae, in A.S.G., Bibl., Legum n. 6, fo. 66v. - 68r.

[24] Leges Rotae Genuensis nuper reformatae, Genuae 1538 (the copies are extremely rare and the one I refer to can be found in the British Museum of London).

esting aspect is the request, regarding the appeals of the *causae mercantiles,* to set up a body in which a merchant joins with two learned lawyers[25]. This is proof that the mercantile environment did not accept the total replacement of its own members with learned lawyers and it is a prelude to the partial return to special magistratures we shall talk of later on.

The instance concerning the trial report by the *Uditori* was granted by a short reform law enforced one year later, in 1541[26], while the presence of merchants in the appeal of mercantile suits was accepted by a subsequent reform of the Rota regulations issued in 1557[27].

The above-mentioned edition of 1557 is a complete text which takes up, with little innovation, all previous legislation.

Some aspects of execution proceedings are better determined, above all, as far as insurance payment and compensation in case of average are concerned[28].

Moreover, in 1572, an appendix to these reforms was issued to settle certain procedural aspects again[29].

Then, a very difficult economic and political period troubled the Genoese Republic, harassed by internal conflicts and by the ruinous consequences of Spanish bankruptcy[30], and the Rota seemed by that time to have ended its most creative period.

Owing to spanish bankruptcy, it was decided, in order to cope better with the wave of insolvencies, to deprive the Court of its activity in this field, by establishing an *Ufficio dei Rotti* not composed of lawyers but of trade experts[31].

The civil *Statuti* of 1589 definitely seemed to confirm the reappraisal of the Rota[32]: the *Uditori* entrusted with ordinary lawsuits were reduced from

---

[25] A.S.G., Senato 1540 - 41, Sala Bartolomeo Senarega, filza 1231, Commemorationes sp. d. io. Baptistae Cattanei Lazanie et Nicolai de Senarega et soci. super regulis rotte reformandis.

[26] Constitutiones Rotae, fo. 28r. - 29r.

[27] Reformationes Rotae aeditae anno MDLVII, 12 - 13, "... Qui Magnifici D. Procuratores teneantur dictas appellationes committere tribus iudicibus, tam Doctoribus, et iuris peritis de collegio iudicum Civitatis Genuae vel extraneis aut ecclesiasticis, quam aliis civibus et mercatoribus, habentibus tamen domicilium Genuae, vel etiam mistim mercatoribus, et Doctoribus prout eis videbitur, ea tamen habita consideratione, quod ubi causa fuerit mercantilis, plures sint iudices mercatores, quam Doctores, et ubi fuerit de apicibus iuris, plures sint iurisperiti et hoc arbitratu, et coscientia ipsorum Magnificorum D. Procuratorum ...".

[28] Ibid., 16 - 18.

[29] Ad Reformationes Rotae, et Statuta Genuae, appendix aedita, anno MDLXXII, Genuae 1572.

[30] *R. Savelli,* La Repubblica oligarchica. Legislazione, istituzioni e ceti a Genova nel Cinquecento, Milano 1981.

[31] *V. Piergiovanni,* Banchieri e falliti nelle "Decisiones de mercatura" della Rota civile di Genova, 24.

five to three and a Rota competent for *causae executivae et breviores*, also composed of three *Uditori* was added[33].

The criminal Rota, which arose in 1576[34], grew much more politically important within the Republic, to the extent that, in 1629, the civil *Uditori* addressed a sorrowful petition to the Government of the Republic asking to be made equal to criminal judges, considering the high-level services they performed for the Republic[35].

In the space of a century, that is, since the time when the civil Rota had first been established in 1529, the Genoese Court followed the destiny of the Republic, which from protagonist declined into a spectator of the great European political and economic events.

From the golden age, that is about halfway through the XVIth century, these remain the collection of the *Decisiones de mercatura* which, with its subsequent reprints and its circulation in Europe, stood as one of the first pillars of the rising science of commercial law.

III. Decisiones concerning insurance

In order to esemplify the role of the Genoese civil Rota in the mercantile field, let us examine the *decisiones* concerning insurance contracts.

Insurance controversies are present in the law-making collection of the Genoese Rota to a more limited extent than might be expected (and we would point out that, in this period, the almost exclusive form in which this contract appears is connected with navigation). Although the matter is an inexhaustible source of dispute, mainly concerning the determination of the elements that were the real cause of accidents and compensantion, perhaps, lawsuits used as a pretext were curbed by the Court's attitude, which was very firm and resolute in rejecting legal corruption to the advantage of good faith and informality, which were typical of the merchants' activity and of the mercantile Courts.

So, in *decisio III,* in reply to the demand of the invalidity of some testimonies, the Rota recalls both its one *regulae* and the mercantile regular practice: "... secuta quoque est ordinatio rotae, ut testes hinc inde examinati publicarentur salvis iuribus, et exceptionibus partium; verum nos, qui a regulis admonemur, ut Deum et veritatem prae oculis habeamus, et quos non

[32] Statutorum civilium Republicae Genuensis nuper reformatorum libri sex, Genuae 1589.

[33] Ibid., L. I, cap. 7, 11 - 14, "De Rota civili et eius iurisdictione".

[34] *R. Savelli,* Potere e giustizia. Documenti per la storia della Rota criminale a Genova alla fine del '500, Idee e atteggiamenti sulla repressione penale, Materiali per una storia della cultura giuridica, V (Bologna 1975), 29 - 172.

[35] Constitutiones Rotae, cit., fo. 41 r. - 41 v., Memoriale M. Auditorum Rotae civilis.

latet in curia mercatorum, ubi negotia veritate terminantur reiectis iuris apicibus, qui subtilitatem magis aspiciunt, quam facti veritatem ut per Bart. ... multa de stricto, et summo iure solere remitti, ut per Strac. in tract. de mercatura ... non pluris fecissimus hanc nullitatis oppositionem, quam par fuisset, et forte ad veritatem facti tantum libenter respexissemus ..."[36].

Another indication of the open-minded discretion used by the Court in insurance lawsuit and in the evaluation of subjective elements can be found in the same *decisio:* "Qua ex re forte factum fuit, ut ipse suis probationibus non admodum invigilaverit, et eo magis concedenda fuit dicta reservatio, quod de notabili quantitate agitur, ex qua non leve damnum sensurus est dictus reus, contra vero assecuratores si quandoque succumbuerint, non aequalem iacturam sunt facturi, quippe qui in totali summa assecurationis habeant particulas ..."[37].

Therefore, the refusal of legal corruption is absolute: "... in causis securitatum, quae fiunt inter mercatores, non sunt curandi apices iuris ..."[38]; "... veritati inhaerendo prout moris nostri est, contrariam sententiam de iure veriorem, et magis foro mercatorum et aequitati consonam esse duximus ..."[39]; "... cum maxime coram Rota procedatur habito intuitu ad Deum, et veritatem negotii, vel saltem quia allegatum oretenus, et in scriptis videbatur sufficere ..."[40].

On this basis of greater understanding of the merchants' needs and of mercantile regular practice, the Rota judges tried to identify the characteristic elements of the contract and, above all, to bring them back to the tradition of common law.

With regard to the dogmatic qualification of the contract, the references found in the decision are few, but sufficient to confirm the line of Genoese jurisprudence and tradition, that, after a short time in which the insurance contract had been considered as a false loan, then it came to treat it as a false sale, too.

So, *decisio III:* "... Dictum vero reum dignum existimavimus, qui recuperaret consteum securitatum, vel illud retineret respective, ex quo non fuit locus assecurationi, et sic emptioni periculi: est enim contractus iste

---

[36] Decisiones Rotae Genuae de mercatura et pertinentibus ad eam, *in* De mercatura decisiones et tractatus varii et de rebus ad eam pertinentibus, Lugduni 1610 (repr. Torino 1971), decisio III, 26. For a general setting and bibliography, *G. Giacchero,* Storia delle assicurazioni marittime. L'esperienza genovese dal Medioevo all' età contemporanea, Genova 1984, e *M. J. Pelaez,* Cambios y seguros maritimos en derecho catalan y belear, Bolonia 1984 (Studia Albornotiana XLII).

[37] Decisiones, dec. III, 29.

[38] Dec. V, 38.

[39] Dec. XL, 162.

[40] Dec. LV, 176.

emptionis, et venditionis, seu emptioni assimilatur cum sit innominatus, facio, ut des, vel do, ut facias, ratione pretii quod datur: quia qui assecurationem facit, propter pretium dicitur emere eventum periculi ..."[41].

And again *decisio XXXVI:* "... Consideravimus quoque, quod contractus assecurationis dicitur contractus innominatus ... unde debet regulari iuxta naturam contractuum nominatorum, quibus assimilatur, et cum assimiletur emptioni, et venditioni propter pretium, quod datur ratione periculi ..."[42].

In two other decisions, however the relation between the validity of the contract and the condition occurred is obvious: "... tunc non aderat subiectum, super quo assecuratio fieri posset, ad quid enim assecurare, quod iam amissum est? Est enim contractus assecurationis contractus conditionis ut dicit Lusitanus ... et natura conditionis est respicere futurum casum, et cum iam casus sit praeteritus, non potest verificari conditio ..."[43].

As far as the subjects are concerned, the figure, the professional integrity and the presumed prudence of the merchant play an important role in judges' evaluations and there are several examples of this. *Decisio LV,* concerning insurance made when the ship is already lost, states: "... Ex parte etiam assecuritatis absurdum oriebatur, si diceretur eum voluisse assecurare super periculo secuto, cum non sit hoc credendum de mercatore, qui habetur pro viro provido, ut not. Lusit. ..."[44]; *Decisio LXIII* arguing the question of whether the captain's change of course frees the insurance company, reminds us that: "... considerata intentione contrahentium quae in omnibus inspicienda est ... et maxime quia hoc dictat aequitas inter mercatores observanda ..."[45].

Again, the characteristics of the mercantile profession are decisive in *decisio CLXVI:* "... assecuratos eius nomine fuisse, et esse mercatores, qui solent negotiari, et non tenere suas pecunias otiosas, sed solitos lucrari in negotiis mercium, et aliis ... merito condemnavimus reum conventum ad solvendum dicto Antonio interesse lucri cessantis a die morae ..."[46].

Two decisions regarding the joint and several liability of partners, which was ratified, as the Rota claims, because "emptum fuisse ... periculum et iam insolidum, cum non sit dubium, quin ex facto unius socii alii insolidum teneantur ..."[47].

---

[41] Dec. III, 29.
[42] Dec. XXXVI, 154.
[43] Dec. CII, 238 e dec. LXIII, 187.
[44] Dec. LV, 174.
[45] Dec. LXIII, 187.
[46] Dec. CLXVI, 302.
[47] Dec. CLXVI, 301 e dec. XXIX, 134.

It was decided, however, that the insured parties' heirs may take action against the insurance company, even if they had not been expressly mentioned in the *apoca assecurationis*[48].

In fact, the greatest importance is given to the content and expressions of the insurance document, as is stated again in *decisio CII:* "... verba etiam assecurationis ponderanda sunt ... quia certissimi iuris est, quod ii contractus recipiunt legem a pactis et conventionibus ..."[49]; and again, concerning the authority of Santerna and other authors *decisio XXV* reads: "... verba assecurationis potissime ponderanda sint ...; ... clarum est, quod dicti assecuratores de alio casu, et de alio viagio non tenentur, nisi de promisso, et comprehenso in assecuratione ..."[50].

Therefore, the text of the insurance policy was fundamental in determining the extent of the risk, from which the *baratteria del capitano* was excluded by custom in Genoa, as we shall see later on, but other cases, such as *iactus et avaria* may be excluded as well, as we can read in *decisio CXXIX*[51].

Another element for determining risk is the sea voyage for which the contract of insurance has been drawn up, and, according to the Genoese Rota too, *viagium* means the first voyage (unless otherwise specified): *decisio XXV* declares, in fact, that when the ship begins its second voyage the insurance company covering the first is freed[52]. In the same way, the insurance company is freed in case of change of course and the Rota decides this according to *decisio LXIII*[53].

In another case, when the counterpart does not succeed in proving that there has actually been a *mutatio viagii,* the decision is, instead, judged in favour of insured parties[54]. The judges oppose all contestations put foraward by the insurance companies and accept Santerna's opinions, who "... quaerit an assecurator possit opponere assecurato quaestionem, quod res non erant suae, et per consequens quamvis illas sint deperditae, quod non debet habere earum aestimationem, et respondet ibi allegando iura, et decisiones, quod quando aliquis convenitur ex contractu, non potest opponere contra agentem, quaestionem dominii, quod dicit esse notandun, quia assecuratores, quando venit tempus solvendi, securitates multas perquirunt, ut excusentur, et ut solutionem aufugiant"[55]. Again, a voyage not cairred out

---

[48] Dec. CII, 238.
[49] Ibid.
[50] Dec. XXV, 118.
[51] Dec. CXXIX, 264.
[52] Dec. XXV, 118.
[53] Dec. LXIII, 187.
[54] Dec. V, 35.
[55] Ibid., 38.

leads the Rota to consider insurance policy on non-loaded goods null and void, against the insurance company's advice.

The text shows the Court's will to follow mercantile customs rather than the rules of strict law: ... satis est quod ex mutatione viagii destinati resolutus sit contractus, vel illi locus non fuerit ..."[56].

It is known that in Genoa the risks that insurance companies took upon themselves were the same as in other markets, with the exception of the *baratteria del capitano.*

Among the Rota's decisions only one set of examples can be found in *decisio CI* and this is not an exhaustive list. In case a ship is captured and kept for three days, even if it is afterwards salvaged, the Rota considers that an accident has taken place, with the consequent liability of the insurance company: "... quoniam in processu constat navem assecuratem fuisse ab infidelibus captam, et per eos in eorum dominio, ac fortiis per tres dies detentam, et merito censuimus casum sinistrum evenisse, et propterea assecuratores iuxta promissa teneri: casus enim latronum, hostium incursus, piratorum insidiae, naufragium, et incendium aequiparantur ..."[57].

This was regular Genoese practice and, therefore, the Rota took a particular stand in the case of *baratteria del capitano,* in opposition to Santerna's opinion and the notions of common law. *Decisio III* (and in the same terms decisio CLXVI) reads: "... et licet Santerna lusitanus in suo tract. de spons. mercat. videatur tenere quod culpa commissa per gubernatores navis non excuset assecuratorem, et propterea quod assecurator, qui damnum periculi patitur, ipse agere debeat contra eum, cuius occasione periculum contigit, nihilominus in casu proposito aliud concludendum esset, in quo perinde habetur, ac si conventum expresse fuisset in apodisia securitatis, quod excepta esset fraus navarchi, ex quo reus praesuposuit in processu, quod iste casus in securitate exceptus fuisset: hic est quod ipse notificari fecit praesentem litem dicto Lambruschino, ut in processu constat: praeterea vulgo observari in hanc civitatem accepimus, ut assecuratores non teneantur de dolo, et barattaria patroni, quicquid a iure in contrariorum disponatur ..."[58].

The last, most interesting subject concerns compensantion and its procedure, and is linked on the one hand to the evidence that the accident has taken place and, on their other hand, to the possibility of taking action with executory judgement sooner than with ordinary judgement.

Decisio XXXVI is perhaps the one which best clarifies the characteristics of regular Genoese Insurance practice. Discussing the validity of an insur-

[56] Dec. XL, 162.

[57] Dec. CI, 236.

[58] Dec. III, 25 e dec. CLXVI, 301.

ance contract made for a ship, which, at the time when the contract is drafted has already been captured, the Rota recalls that a decree was in force in Genoa which considered even one testimony alone as being sufficient to substantiate the news, the loss of the ship. In order not to alter the well-established traditions of common law too much, which required at least two testimonies, the single witness must be at least above all suspicion[59].

The effort to justify infringements of common law was not justified by upholding the indisputable application of customary law, but rather by seeking support within common law itself: in this case, the judges claimed that there were *auctoritates* that gave the judge the power to assess evidence and that in difficult matters, such as the loss of a ship or of an accident, the law was satisfied with lesser evidence.

The relation between an executory judgement, instituted in order to obtain more rapid compensation and an ordinary judgement brought by the insurance company to recover what they believed they unduly paid, are dealt with in other *Decisiones*.

Decisio III, in the basis of the *regulae Rotae* and of common law considers that evidence in executory judgement does not count in ordinary judgement[60]; *decisio V* obliges insurance companies to ask to be refunded for what they paid in the executory judgement to prove a change of course[61]; *decisio C* permits a foreigner to ask for payment, in an executory way, of compensantion as *modus executionis attenditur locus contractus*[62].

It should be mentioned, even though the topic deserves to be dealt with in more detail that the *auctoritates,* to which the Rota judges referred when forming their judgements, gave particular attention to Bartolo's and Baldo's quotations regarding jurisprudence and the Roman school traditions. As far as modern lawyers are concerned, the work concerning insurance by Santerna has found great support, while Stracca seems to be used to a much more limited extent.

We have given examples of insurance matters contained in the collection of the Genoese Rota decisions *de mercatura,* considering the various aspects, which, put together, contribute to making a complete reconstruction of the institution. Apart from some local peculiarities, such as the different consideration of Captain's corruption, the solutions seem on the whole to conform to regular Italian legal practice in the XVIth century.

---

59 Dec. XXXVI, 153 e dec. XLII, 164.

60 Dec. III, 23.

61 Dec. V, 35.

62 Dec. C, 235.

RODOLFO SAVELLI

Between Law and Morals: Interest in the Dispute on Exchanges during the 16th Century

"Qui facit usuras vadit ad infernum,
et qui non facit vergit ad inopiam"

Benvenuto Rambaldi da Imola

to my brother Daniele

I. Sigismondo Scaccia and the problem of exchanges in Genoa

1. "Sinuosissimus labyrinthus" was the definition adopted by Sigismondo Scaccia to characterize in a suggestively significant way the complexity of the problem of exchanges.

Since then the juridical-theological literature and the historiographical research (a first example of this is effectively represented by the *De commerciis et cambio* by Scaccia) has not failed to add pages to pages. The opinion by Raymond de Roover is also well known: according to it "sur la controverse de changes on pourrait facilment réunir toute une bibliothèque"[1]. It

Abbreviations:

ACG	Archivio Storico del Comune di Genova
ARSI	Archivum Romanum Societatis Jesu
ASF	Archivio di Stato Firenze
ASG	Archivio di Stato Genova
ASLSP	Atti della Società Ligure di Storia Patria
ASV	Archivio Segreto Vaticano
BAM	Biblioteca Ambrosiana Milano
BAV	Biblioteca Apostolica Vaticana
BCB	Biblioteca Civica Berio Genova
BNF	Biblioteca Nazionale Firenze
BNN	Biblioteca Nazionale Napoli
BUG	Biblioteca Universitaria Genova
DBI	Dizionario Biografico degli Italiani

1 *R. De Roover,* La structure des banques au moyen âge, in Troisième conférence internationale d'Histoire économique, Munich 1965, vol. V, Paris - La Haye 1974, p. 162.

may, thus, be advisable to avoid further contributions to this ever increasing bibliography. However interest on this subject leads one to trespass the limits of prudence: the fascination of the labyrinth, in fact, attracts both the prudent and incautious.

To these reasons we have also to add that the figure of Scaccia himself is practically so unknown that research into his cultural background seemed to be of great interest. The first, and fragmentary, results of this study are contained in this work[2].

A book written by Antonio Merenda, professor at the University of Pavia, during the first half of the 17th Century, contains a controversial evaluation of *De commerciis et cambio* which is useful to recall:

> Supervenit deinde tractatus de cambjis Sigismundi Scacciae, qui anxie in tutandis abusibus campsorum adeo versatus fuit, ut rarissime ab ipsis discedat: noluit quippe ingratus videri suis magistris, campsoribus videlicet Genuensibus, a quibus, dum ibi Auditor esset Rotae Civilis, universam cambiendi formam didicit[3].

The unkind judgement by Antonio Meranda, who certainly is not the last one to remain steadfast to rigorist attitudes, contains important elements of truth and interest. Persons who studied the pages written by Scaccia know the clear evidence of the Genoese "example". But Merenda recalls that these are not simply examples. The charge is precise: the Genoese bankers were the teachers of Scaccia.

It would be misleading now to think that the short period in which Scaccia held the position of judge in the Civil Rota in Genoa, from July 1612 to July 1615[4], might have been the only source for a work of the importance and complexity of the *De commerciis et cambio;* and this is proved by the fact that the first ecclesiastical authorization was issued in December 1616[5]. But it is certain, and Merenda clearly realizes it, that the Genoese period,

---

[2] Still in the Novissimo Digesto Italiano XVI (1969) p. 670, the error of considering Scaccia Genoese is repeated. Evidently not even the frontispiece of his works is read, wherein the indication "civis romanus" is always present.

[3] A. Merenda, De cambio nundinali, Papiae, apud Ioannem Andream Magnum, 1645, p. 89.

[4] In 1609 - 1610 the first indications of his person as possible candidate for both the civil and the criminal Rota are found. The accompanying judgement is always highly gratifying: "passa 50 anni, di molta virtù e valore nella sua professione . . . ha scritto in legge e scrive tuttavia con molta lode universale, è stato podestà in Lucca, e soprattutto è huomo da bene e di molta isperienza e integrità" (ASG, Rota criminale 366). Being drawn by lot on 9th January 1612 he took his office on 11th July (ASG, Archivio Segreto 860). On 6th August 1615 he obtained the positive final judgement from the Sindacatori (ASG, Senato, Sala Gallo, 1066). In 1613 he was also chosen for the criminal Rota and "attese le buone qualità", he was proposed for the immediate approval and transfer to the criminal Rota, which was in great need of good judges; this proposal was not approved (ASG, Archivio Segreto 861 and 1031). During the last months of his stay in Genoa he received threats and was physically attacked by some noble men (ASG, Archivio Segreto 1031 and 1563, Rota Criminale 366).

[5] S. Scaccia, De commerciis et cambio, Romae, sumptibus Andreae Brugiotti, ex typographia Iacobi Mascardi, 1619, c. [3] r.

together with his role as judge at the Rota, was for Scaccia an absolutely fundamental experience.

Among the few decisions, still extant, issued by Scaccia, there is one in which we find some concepts which will be systemized in the work in question[6]. This suit is intriguing, "difficilis et periculosa" (to use Scaccia's words to define the subject of exchanges), a case "mutui ad negotiandum pro determinato lucro": at the level of an ecclesiastic court, the contract is clearly illicit, but Scaccia comes to the conclusion that the secular judge may acknowledge an interest when this is owed for other obligations.

At present, however, it is important to stress two further concepts. They are:

> In civitate Genuae est expeditum quod debetur interesse alterius interesse, etiam si excedat sortem, probata solita negotiatione cambiorum ... Omnis enim Genuensis est mercator, forus est semper paratus volentibus dare et accipere cambio, et cambia responderunt tot.

The importance of the conclusions arrived at by Scaccia is evident in itself, and does not need much comment: it is however worth underlining some of the arguments used. The habits of the place justify what would be difficult to justify (interests on interests, higher than the capital). In his quality of judge at the Civil Rota he cannot but conform to the local uses. The Genoese market, however, is not only peculiar for its uses, but presents some general peculiarities which involve the merchants and the whole of the subjects and their qualities. It has to be considered how the *topos* "omnis genuensis est mercator" is reconsidered in the *De commerciis:*

> Genuae ... omnes fere cives, sive nobiles, sive plebei, sive divites, sive pauperes, sive magistratum gerentes, sive privatam vitam agentes, sive in dignitate constituti, ut Doctores, sive alius quisque adeo negotijs cambiorum et mercium incumbunt, ut res etiam ad mulieres pervenerit, et nemo ex his momento temporis suas pecunias otiosas tenet[7].

It should be noted, moreover, that the above passage has been literally copied from another judgement of the Genoese civil Rota, one of those judgements which had the honour of being printed in 1581 - 1582[8]. Scaccia thus reconsiders the habits of the merchants, the rotal tradition, and expands on them through a systematic consideration.

The other aspect of the problem, i.e. that of the interests and of the ratio between those and the exchanges, has also to be considered. In the treatise, dealing with the problem of the determination of the quantity and of the settlement of interests, he reminds us, once more, of the Genoese use:

---

[6] ASG, Rota Civile, 4 (judgement dated 30th October 1614).

[7] Scaccia, pp. 217 - 218; see also p. 236: "omnes genuenses sunt mercatores in tantum ut valeat consequentia est genuensis ergo mercator".

[8] Decisiones Rotae Genuae de mercatura, Genuae, s. t., 1582, nº CXXXVII (c. 200 v). On the Decisiones and their edition see ultra § IV.

> Genuenses ut se eximant ab hac difficili quantitatis liquidatione ... negotiantur in cambijs, quorum interesse facillime liquidant, faciunt enim listam cambiorum et recambiorum de foro in forum, cum reditibus cuiusque fori, eamque listam faciunt ostendi testibus examinandis ... vel exhibent listam confectam a Cancellario gabella cambiorum[9].

This is a typical procedure, several examples of which have been found among the papers of the Genoese notaries. Through the courses of exchanges and "re-exchanges", from fair to fair, the current rate of interest on money is determined[10]. This procedure to define the interest connected to the problem of the interest on interests had already been widely accepted by the Genoese Rota. A predecessor of Scaccia, Luca Albrizzi, was thus able to write in a judgement dated 1587:

> Non obstat quod dicebatur ultimo loco de interesse interessuum ad rationem cambiorum et recambiorum, quod de iure non debetur cum fructus fructus parere nefas est; nam istud procedit in mercatore et solito negotiari cui, ut predixi, omne interesse cambiorum et recambiorum in quibus quotidie versatur et lucrari solet, absque scrupolo debetur[11].

But the combination of these principles with the one that each Genoese is, per se, a merchant, leads Scaccia to recall a further "use" which involved the complete change of one of the well established points of the traditional doctrine (i.e. the right of the merchant, and his right alone, to the interests on the basis of the principle of the loss of gain).

> Collige ... ex hac praxi quod genuenses hac via consequuntur lucra cambiorum et recambiorum, *sine cambio;* quia supposita negotiatione cambiorum pro licita ... *creditores omnes* in vim illius negotiationis consequuntur lucra cambiorum per viam lucri cessantis[12].

The problem of the interest on money (like that already mentioned of the interests calculated on interests) implied facing a long and consolidate tradition of opinions. Scaccia was certainly very prudent and did not strongly oppose well established positions, but offered, through this use of the

---

[9] Scaccia, p. 300.

[10] See for instance for Cremona the remarks by *G. Politi,* Il banco cremonese di Gianfranco Amidani negli ultimi anni di attività (1569 - 79), in Atti del Convegno Istituzioni e attività finanziarie milanesi dal XIV al XVIII secolo, Milano 1977 (duplicated): "the reference to the "Besançon" fairs has the only aim, as admitted in a moment of confidence by the notary, to settle the rate of interest of his bank". *A. P. Usher,* The Early History of Deposit Banking in Mediterranean Europe, Cambridge Mass. 1943, p. 123: at Lyon fairs "each national group . . . agreed upon a rate of interest on fund payable at the next fair . . . This rate is described in the contemporary documents as a rate of exchange, but it is more accurately described to a modern reader as a rate of interest". See also *R. De Roover,* L'Evolution de la Lettre de Change, XIVe - XVIIIe siècles, Paris 1953, pp. 61 - 62; *J. G. Da Silva,* Banque et crédit en Italie au XVIIe siècle, Paris 1969, vol. I, p. 212.
The book by *M. Cassandro,* Le fiere di Lione e gli uomini d'affari italiani nel Cinquecento, Firenze 1979, is mainly a compilation.

[11] ASG, Rota civile 1, cc. 510r - 511v.

[12] Scaccia, p. 301 (my italics).

Genoese "habit", conceptual instruments to liberalize the doctrine from the restrictions imposed by the prohibition of usury.

In the previously mentioned judgement[13], there is a very significant passage in this respect: "consideravi ... quod secundum morem regionis Genuensis nummus nummum parere solet." Scaccia, evidently, appreciated the concept, and repeated it, in a similarly significant way in the treatise, wherein he affirms that, on the basis of a certain reasoning, "salvatur, seu excusatur, Genuensium vulgare illud contra Aristotelicam doctrinam dictum, *denà fa denà*". A proverb of a merchant town is, in this case, opposed to the formal (and authoritative) Aristotelian tradition[14].

Moreover, more than one century before, a Dominican of Genoese origin, Theophilo Giustiniani, had already considered the problem in similar terms, giving an answer which did not appear too different:

> queritur ergo come stano insieme che il denaro non facia denaro et tamen in li cambij el denaro fa denaro.

The answer had been that "through business" (i.e. through lawful contracts, like permutation or sale and purchase) "il denaro fa denaro"[15].

If, at this point, we wished to recall this quotation from Giustiniani's work, it is to underline how Scaccia has found a very fertile ground, full of ideas to be discussed when he arrived in Genoa, a town in which the debate

---

[13] See note 6.

[14] Scaccia, p. 219. On the theme of the Aristotelian tradition see the interesting conclusions drawn by *O. Langholm*, Wealth and Money in the Aristotelian tradition, Bergen 1983, p. 53, and *Id.*, The Aristotelian Analysis of Usury, Bergen 1984, passim.

[15] T. Iustiniani, Tractatus cambiorum, BAV, Vat. Lat. 6434 c. 316v.

The information about Giustiniani is very scarce: from the Vatican codex it appears that the treatise was made in Chios (probably in the period between the end of the XV and the first years of the XVI century: the work by De Vio is not, for instance, mentioned). Evidently Theophilo descended from some branch of the Giustiniani of Chios, on which see *Ph. P. Argenti*, The Occupation of Chios by the Genoese and their Administration of the Island, 1346 - 1568, Cambridge 1958, in which some notes regarding the settling of Dominicans can be found, and *A. Rovere*, Documenti della maona di Chio (sec. XIV - XVI), in ASLSP XIX (XCII), vol. II (1979). He belonged to the congregation of Observants of Lombardia and is mentioned with words of appreciation by Matteo Bandello who remembers him in his role of deputy Prior in the Genoese monastery of S. Maria di Castello in 1504 (M. Bandello, Opera latina inedita vel rara, ed. *C. Godi*, Padova 1983, p. 179) and for the same monastery he is also remembered, may be wrongly, as the Prior (*E. Pandiani*, Un anno di storia genovese, in ASLSP XXXVII, 1905, p. 441 and, *contra*, *R. A. Vigna*, Storia cronologica del Convento di Santa Maria di Castello, in ASLSP XXI, 1889). Giovanni Salvago in the Historie di Genova, ms. Archivio Doria Genova, nº 1912, c. 8r, remembers Theophilo as "grecho cresciuto ne la izola di Scio" and mentions the fact (even if he will then delete the sentence in question) that, the "populari" merchants gathered in his room during the rebellion of 1506.

In 1512 De Vio ordered him to leave Chio; the following year he had a quarrel with the monastery of S. Maria di Castello of Genoa (see *A. De Meyer*, Registrum Litterarum Fr. Thomae de Vio Caietani O.P. Magistri Ordinis 1508 - 1513, Roma 1935, pp. 275 - 277).

on the different aspects of the problem of exchanges had been present for more than a century.

Recent and not so recent contributions have focused the attention on some texts written by Genoese, or in the Genoese circles, in the second half of the 16th or the beginning of the 17th century[16]. However if we follow the specific indications by the Roman jurist or if special themes or bibliographic indications are investigated, we realize how this subject can be examined further.

Obviously Genoa was not an "unicum" in the Italian and European scenario. From Florence to Venice, from Milan to Rome, from London to Antwerp, from Lyon to Medina del Campo bankers and businessmen bartered on money and exchanges, and discussions on the exchanges were going on. But if we wish to consider a dominant image in the general conscience and in the literary transposition, this image reflects the Genoese businessman.

2. We will justify later the further reasons for which, in this essay, an observatory like that of 16th Century Genoa is privileged. Let us just recall how the debate on the problem of exchanges, within the more general one regarding usury, finds in this very century its maximum development at a European level. This is a debate which is constantly renewed with changing economic and institutional reality; in which the intersections of different disciplines are numerous and entangled. As always Scaccia synthetizes, with great accuracy, how "haec cambij materia apud omnes Theologos et Jureconsultos reputatur obscura, difficilis et intricata."

But the debate involved not only theologians and jurists, even if their opinions are the best known and the most widely studied. There were also those (rarely expressed and spread through printed works) of merchants (as we will be reminded by the Theatine Leonardo Duardo) "audentes de justitia cambij disputare ac determinare, cum litteras ignorent; et recusantes theologorum et canonistarum judicium se submittere"[17]. And even if today it is rather difficult to stick completely to the opinion by Lattes according to which "businessmen did always strongly oppose the canonic prohibitions"[18], it is sure that the debate on exchanges (and usury) was a debate

---

16 *G. Cassandro,* Un trattato inedito e la dottrina dei cambi nel Cinquecento, Napoli 1962 (reprinted without the work by Palescandolo, in Saggi di storia del diritto commerciale, Napoli 1974) and *D. Maffei,* Notizie su alcuni trattati cinque-seicenteschi in tema di cambi, in Ricerche storiche ed economiche in memoria di Corrado Barbagallo, Napoli 1970, II, pp. 329 - 347.

17 L. Duardo, Commentaria in Extravag. Pii Papae Quinti de Cambiis, Naepoli [sic], Apud Octavianum Beltranum 1641, p. 147.

18 *A. Lattes,* Il diritto commerciale nella legislazione statutaria delle città italiane, Milano 1884, p. 147. – The image of the merchant is well represented in T. Wilson, A discourse upon usury, with an historical introduction by *R. H. Tawney,* London 1925,

grouping several opinions simultaneously, and in which – also – the role of the Courts, like the Genoese or the Roman Rota, was fundamental in the acknowledgement and the formalization of the new economic and social realities.

The doctors "antiquiores" could ignore the "cambium Bezenzonense ... cum hoc cambio non sit multum antiquum"[19], but it was up to the Rote to decide and find the conceptual means to set contract regulations and obligations.

The "doctores" did not contribute to the development of new theories, only in their role of judges at the courts. Jurists, canonists, theologians were continuously called, through the 16th Century, to express their opinions: the request came either from the Pope, or the local religious authorities, or from the secular authorities or even the merchants themselves.

Let us recall, by way of example, some dates and events:

- 1513 - 1515: debate in the German Universities and in that of Bologna on the problem of interest[20];
- 1515: the "Inter Multiplices" bull establishes a well-defined point on the problem of the "monti di pietà"[21];
- 1517: statement of the doctors of the University of Paris on exchanges[22];
- 1517 and following years: debate in Lucca on exchanges[23];
- 1532: the Spanish merchants of Antwerp again press the University of Paris for an opinion on exchanges[24];
- 1554: in Lisbon cardinal Henry of Portugal submits doubts to Azpilcueta about the problem of loan and usury[25];

---

see, e.g., at p. 251: "you may aswel forbidde bying and selling, as forbidde taking interest for money; for, I pray you, what difference is there betwixt the one and the other?"

[19] Scaccia, p. 150.

[20] *H. A. Oberman,* Werden und Wertung der Reformation, Tübingen 1977, pp. 160 ff.

[21] See the recent interpretation by *P. Prodi,* La nascita dei Monti di Pietà: tra solidarismo cristiano e logica del profitto, in Annali dell'Istituto Storico italo-germanico in Trento VIII (1982), pp. 211 - 224.

[22] *L. Vereecke,* La liceité du "cambium bursae" chez Jean Mair (1469 - 1550), in Revue Historique du droit français et étranger, IV serie, XXX (1952), pp. 125 ff., with the recall and the discussion on the famous passage by D. Soto, De iustitia et iure, L. 6, q. XII, art. 5 (ed. Antverpiae, apud Philippum Nutium, 1567, c. 215 r and v).

[23] Girolamo [Frediani] da Lucca, De Cambiis, Papiae, Apud Jacobum de Burgofranco, s.d. [1517 - 1518] (and in Tractatus universi iuris, Venetiis 1584, VI, I, cc. 408 r - 410 v); and Orpheus de Bononia, Tractatus de marchiis, BAV, Vat. Lat. 7720.

[24] *J. A. Goris,* Études sur les colonies marchandes méridionales (portugais, espagnols, italiens) à Anvers de 1488 à 1567, Louvain 1935, pp. 503 ff.

[25] M. Azpilcueta, Enrichidion sive manuale confessariorum, Romae, Apud Victorium Romanum, 1573, c. 242 v.

- 1554: in Genoa the Archbishop Vicar promotes a debate (involving theologians, jurists and merchants) on the legality of exchanges[26].

We will now stop at this date, being aware of the fact that the most important moments of debate are still to come.

The more specifically doctrinal contributions, as we said in agreement with de Roover, are numerous: let us just call to mind, at the beginning of the century, the *De cambiis* by Tommaso de Vio O.P. (the famous Cajetanus), precisely for its great influence and for having been the first work published and dedicated specifically to the problem[27].

Closely linked, even if more widely autonomous, is the collection of works on usury and interest; from the 30s to the 50s we note a real explosion of interests in Europe: from Du Moulin, Hotman, Doneau, to Azpilcueta, Soto and all the Spanish works. Catholic and reformed countries, Mediterranean and Continental Europe: everywhere the problems of money, its market, and of the contractual forms ruling its traffic are constantly debated[28].

It has often been put forward as an objection that all these discussions effectively involved neither merchants nor bankers, and that the prohibitions by the Church did not effectively influence the reality of economic and commercial life. Referring to a period before that considered, C. Bec was able to affirm that "ne parvenant pas à definir une doctrine unique et claire, les docteurs n'exercent que peu d'influence sur les marchands contemporains. Leurs traités sont stériles"[29].

If such a statement can, I suppose, be discussed for the period of the 14th and 15th Centuries, both the theory and practice of exchange contracts in the 16th and 17th Centuries show its extremely simplifying and partially deviant character. Interest loans, also with high rates of interest, were effectively used; the fact remains, however, that specific forms of contracts were adopted just to avoid being condemned or criticized. De Roover was not the

[26] See in the sequel, § II.

[27] Written at the monastery "delle Grazie" in Milan in 1499, published several times during 1500; a "critical" edition of the same exists in T. De Vio, Scripta philosophica: Opuscula economica-socialia, ed. *P. P. Zammit,* Romae 1934, pp. 91 - 133 (from which we quote); in addition to the editions examined by Zammit, we indicate: the first one (see Indice generale degli Incunaboli delle Biblioteche d'Italia, V, Roma 1972, nº 10332), and a further one, included in a collection of philosophical writings by De Vio, In praedicabilia Porphyrii . . ., Venetiis, Impensis Luceantonij de Giunta, 1519, probably not noted as in the frontispiece no indication about the De cambiis appears).

[28] Recent contributions, in Handbuch der Quellen und Literatur der Neueren Europäischen Privatrechtsgeschichte. II B: Neuere Zeit (1500 - 1800). I: Wissenschaft, hg. von *H. Coing,* München 1977 (particularly the contributions by *H. E. Troje* and *K. O. Scherner*) and in *J. Day* (ed.), Études d'Histoire monetaire, Lille 1984.

[29] *C. Bec,* Les marchands écrivains à Florence. 1375 - 1434, Paris - La Haye 1967, p. 255.

only person who submitted contributions of prime importance to this sector: the remarks made, long ago, by G. Mandich, have to be considered: "Les principes tenaces de la doctrine canonique ... expliquent sans doute, l'emploi si compliqué de la *ricorsa* qui substitue à un prêt manifeste, à échéance assez éloignée, une série de changes réitérés"[30]. These remarks, along with vast documentary support, confirm the studies made by Nicolini[31].

The promulgation of the bull *In eam* of 1571 had effects which were certainly not of secondary importance on the European market of exchanges – from Spain to Lyon[32], to Italy and to Genoa itself, as we shall see.

The process through which the market system came to be accepted, and thus also that of money, was, effectively, extremely complicated; it was a process in which the role played by theories was certainly not secondary to the economic, real one. Herbert Lüthy summed it up with keen insight: "le marché, en effet, constitue une socété abstraite qui ne distingue ni personne ni rang, juridiquement égalitaire parce qu'anonyme et fondée uniquement sur le do ut des, régle de tout échange et de tout contrat". But this was, in fact, a result. "L'alchimie mysterieuse du change" to use Lüthy's words, may also have represented "une régression"[33], but it is also true that, as A.P. Usher judged, "the more we learn of the early history of commercial paper, the more evident it becomes that the evolution of these seemingly simple concepts involved a singularly complex process"[34].

For the most different reasons, during the 16th century, we note, from certain aspects, a profound dichotomy between market practices and theological, juridical and moral theories. This does not mean, however, that the study of doctrines is less interesting and advantageous than that of facts[35].

All the more so when we are in the domain of juridical doctrines and of those regarding commercial contracts. Market economic relationships (even that of money), are mediated by *forms* of contracts; which are elaborated

---

30 *G. Mandich,* Le Pacte de Ricorsa et le marché italien des changes au XVIIe siècle, Paris 1953, p. 4.

31 *U. Nicolini,* Studi storici sul pagherò cambiario, Milano 1936, particularly pp. 46ff.

32 *H. Lapeyre,* Une famille de Marchands: Les Ruiz, Paris 1955, pp. 134ff., 319; see also *M. Venard,* Catholicisme et usure au XVIe siècle, in Revue d'Histoire de l'Eglise de France LII (1966), p. 66, who, erroneously, dates the bull at 1572.

33 *H. Lüthy,* La Banque Protestante en France de la Révocation de l'Edit de Nantes à la Révolution, Paris 1961, II, pp. 764, 768 - 769.

34 *Usher,* p. 109.

35 See *R. H. Tawney,* Religion and the Rise of Capitalism, London 1948, p. 11: "because doctrine and conduct diverge, it does not follow that to examine the formers is to hunt abstractions. That men should have thought as they did is sometimes as significant as that they should have acted as they did, and not least significant when thought and practice are at variance".

(and justified) in the 16th Century not only by the important "hombres de negocios" but also by the school jurists, the judges of the Rote and the theologians.

3. Sometimes the rigidity of the juridical forms of contracts is far greater than the changing reality. Again in the first half of the 18th Century, on the Genoa financial market, when entering into a foreign loan, not only was the word "cambium" still employed, but also the clause "by which the debtor promised to return the capital within eight days from the date of the contract, and, only in case of delay, committed himself "quale creditore moroso et in mora legittimamente costituito" to pay the creditor the interest agreed upon, to refund him for the expenses suffered and the damages for the lack of profit and the deriving damages"[36]. We have to consider that these kinds of contract formulas had already been applied since the 15th century[37]. Why, then, are they still used? Why does this traditionalism persist?

According to an authoritative historian of economics "Genoa was a monetary market exceptionally free from every intrusion by non commercial elements. Practically no relevant pressure by the Church on the financial activities ever existed"[38]. Even if it is true that the Church never did succeed in hampering in Genoa the development of S. Giorgio, or in cramping the financial propensity of the Genoese patrician class, it is however true that a constant pressure always existed, and had the same essential importance as elsewhere.

Already Sieveking had noted, in his avant-garde study, that some forms of payment by S. Giorgio gave rise to certain problems[39]. The recent studies by Kirshner widely demonstrated that in Genoa too, as in Florence and elsewhere, the matter of the interest on public debt titles (S. Giorgio or "Monti") was not accepted passively by everybody[40]. But it is of great interest to under-

---

[36] *G. Felloni,* Gli investimenti finanziari genovesi in Europa tra il Seicento e la Restaurazione, Milano 1971, pp. 363 - 364.

[37] *W. J. Ashley,* An Introduction to English Economic History and Theory, I, II, London 1898, pp. 399ff. (with clear reference to the theorization made by Paolo di Castro).

[38] *C. M. Cipolla,* Note sulla storia del saggio d'interesse. Corso, dividendi e sconto dei dividendi del Banco di San Giorgio nel sec. XVI, in Economia Internazionale V (1952), p. 256, nº 1.

[39] *H. Sieveking,* Studio sulle finanze genovesi nel Medio Evo e in particolare sulla casa di San Giorgio, in ASLSP XXXV (1906), I, pp. 55 - 56, and II, p. 27.

[40] *J. Kirshner,* Conscience and Public Finance in a Questio disputata of John of Legnano on the public debt of Genoa, in *E. P. Mahoney* (ed.), Philosophy and Humanism: Essays in Honor of Paul Oskar Kristeller, Leiden 1976, pp. 434 - 453; *Id.,* The moral problem of discounting genoese *paghe,* 1450 - 1550, in Archivum Fratrum Praedicatorum XLVII (1977), pp. 109 - 167; *Id.,* An opinion of Raphael de Pornassio O.P. on the market in Genoese *Lire de paghe,* in Xenia Medii Aevi Historiam Illustrantia oblata Thomae Kaeppeli O.P., ed. *R. Creytens / P. Kuenzle,* Roma 1978, pp. 507 - 517; *Id.,* Reading Bernardino's sermon on the public debt, in Atti del Simposio Internazionale Katariniano-Bernardiniano, ed. by *D. Maffei* and *P. Nardi,* Siena 1982, pp. 547 - 621.

line that everyone who expressed his opinion to defend the lawfulness of the "luoghi", of the "paghe" (and of their discount) try to bring the contract in question back under the more general form of the "contractus emptionis et venditionis" which, as Bartolomeo Bosco stated, "constat esse licitum, omni iure Divino, Canonico et Civili"[41].

We shall later examine the effective meaning of the adoption of the category "emptio-venditio" for the exchange contract. For the moment let us just underline that this was one of the main ways, even if traditional in type, to justify contracts that could have been included in the category of the „mutuum", and for which interest was prohibited.

Let us briefly make a digression: even in the famous work by Johannes Aepinus (Höck) *In Psalmum XV Davidis Commentarius* which is considered to be one of the key works for an understanding of the "new" attitude of the reformed world with respect to interest and usury, the concept of "emptio" is used (even if not alone, as we will see later):

> Domini praecepta de beneficentia et mutuo non debent opponi emptioni reddituum, quia Dominus in his praeceptis ne quidem verbo attingit emptionis contractum ... empti redditus a non indigentibus pro usura haberi non possunt, quia redditus sunt emptionis lucrum, non mutui[42].

Let us go back now to our main issue. Genoa was not free from moral and religious tensions and the connection between faith and business was far from being simple. Still in 1515, according to a use of long respected tradition, Battista Spinola, when making his will, stated that the Augustinian Stefano Zoagli should examine his account books, judge the lawfulness of the operations and decide, then, whether any amount had to be returned[43]. But if this use is, to some extent, traditional (and, moreover, demands an *ex post* judgement) another case is interesting, traces of which remains in a judgement by the Roman Rota (and this judgement has been frequently mentioned by Scaccia). According to this decision, Father Vipera S.J. (who was the author of a treatise on exchanges) had been asked to express a previous judgment on the lawfulness of a certain contract on "money"[44].

---

[41] B. Bosco, Consilia, Lodani, Apud Franciscum Castellum, 1620, p. 419 (n° 262). About Bosco, in addition to the bibliography quoted by *Kirshner*, see also *V. Piergiovanni*, Lezioni di storia giuridica genovese, Il Medioevo, Genova 1983, pp. 181 ff.

[42] I quote from the edition of Argentorati, Iacobus Cammer Lander, 1543, c. 27 r and v. On this text, widely used by Du Moulin, see *H. Hauser*, Les idées économiques de Calvin, in La modernité du XVIe siècle, Paris 1963, pp. 121 - 122; *P. Nelson*, The Idea of Usury, Princeton 1949, pp. 73, 91; *J. L. Thireau*, Charles Du Moulin, Genève 1980, pp. 359 ff.

[43] One copy of the will in Archivio di Stato, La Spezia, Fondo Lamba Doria, 1.

[44] Decisiones Rotae Romanae in causa ianuensi pecuniaria ... Coram Reverendiss. P. D. Lancellotto, Genuae, apud Iosephum Pavonem, 1611. The fact that Vipera is the author of a treatise on exchanges (which remained in manuscript form) is asserted by the Theatine B. Giustiniani (see infra note 144). An opinion by Vipera on the "libranze" and other contracts made by the noble Genoese is contained in ARSI, Opp. NN. 258, cc. 98 ff.

By this we do not want to state that the ecclesiastical and religious presence was particularly penetrating and univocal. We want to say that it existed and conditioned, under certain aspects, but it was, in turn, conditioned in other respects. In 1567 some judges, following a mandate by the Roman Inquisition, prosecuted a Benedictine monk, Ambrogio da Milano: among the questions put to the witnesses (who included some of the most distinguished Genoese patricians) there was the following:

> item si aliquibus nobilibus dixerit eos posse mutuari sub usuris ad rationem triginta pro centenario regi Catholico, quia ipse Rex onerabat Januenses in extractione bladorum plus iusto[45].

The depositions were all in favour of the poor monk, but probably the "informant" had noted, to his surprise, these accents of economical war aimed at justifying the profitable business of the Genoese with the Spanish Crown.

In 1588 the Archbishop Vicar issued a document in which, in order to face the financial problems of the Genoese curia, he proposed a pardon for all persons who had speculated on the exchanges after the bull by Pious V, and that "potessero quei tali fare una compositione con la Sede Apostolica"[46].

This is an essentially laxist attitude, of a person who tries to make at least some profit from a situation which was, evidently, extremely difficult to control; an attitude highly similar to the one of an anonymous compiler of a draft on the fiscal problems of the Republic in the middle of the 16th Century:

> Trovo che si fanno in la Città ... molte qualità di negotij *dove il denaro fa denaro,* senza alcuna gravezza, si come sarebbero cambii di Corte e de Signori, contri fermi, depositi sopra la fede e sopra oblighi di case, vendite di paghe e di lochi non scritti in San Georgio e similia, sopra tutti li quali vorrei poner gravezza di mezzo per cento [47].

Apart from the interest for the "anti-Aristotelian" notion of money which generates money (and apart from some aspects of fiscal policy in the Republic of Genoa, which will be discussed later) this evidence is quite a good introduction to the multiform world of business which Genoa was in the mid 16th Century, and which never failed to astonish and even perhaps inspire admiration in foreign judges and jurists who came to take part in the Civil Rota, like Scaccia, or an unknown predecessor of his who, in a judgement, wrote: "Genuae, ubi vivitur super interessibus"[48].

In the previously quoted sentence, we find "molte qualità di negotij". Almost all these "negotii" passed through the hands of the notaries. It is superfluous to mention the importance of the Genoese world of notaries, and

---

[45] ASG, Notaio G. B. Procurante, sc. 409. f. 1.

[46] Biblioteca Corsiniana, Roma, ms. 682 (35. B. 11), cc. 419 - 420.

[47] ASG, Senato, Sala Senarega 1276 (my italics).

[48] Decisiones Rotae Genuae, cit., c. 143 v (n° LXVIII).

the extraordinary wealth of documents which it has left. We just wish to call attention to one listing that a clerk of the Board of Notaries made, at the request of the Rector, wherein the agenda were noted, a kind of memorandum for office use:

De notarijs usurarijs ...
De contractibus qui fiunt in ecclesiis.
De illis qui in diebus festivis et dominicis de praecepto conficiunt continue instrumenta.
De instrumentis et contractibus feneratitiis[49].

Who, better than the Rector or the Clerk, could be aware of the enormity of the problem? We are at the end of the 60s, and from a privileged observatory, such as was the Genoese world of notaries, comes precious evidence on a kind of "gold fever" which had infected the whole town and, therefore, the notaries themselves. There are not only those notaries who loan money directly (at what rate of interest?) but also those notaries involved in certain activities bordering on illegality; these are, evidently, so numerous as to cause some concern to the Rector of the Board.

The worries concerning the "negotij dove il denaro fa denaro", and specially the exchanges, were not only of ethical-religious character. There is also a further aspect of the opposition to the diffusion of the financial activities, which needs an albeit short description, also because of some repercussions it will also have in the literature. In an anonymous treatise on exchanges (very probably written by a Genoese Augustinian at the beginning of the 16th Century) at the end of the discussion in which the "ricambi" are considered to be lawful, even if with certain conditions, we find this statement:

His non ostantibus non consulo nostris civibus quod omissa mercatura se dent penitus et perdite cambijs, sed potius cambia ordinent ad mercaturam[50].

---

[49] Manuale diversarum notularum qui in dies occurrunt . . ., ASG, Notai Ignoti, 434.

[50] This anonymous treatise on exchanges is contained in the quoted codex BAV Vat. Lat. 6434, cc. 197r - 222v (the mentioned quotation at c. 215r). This codex is a collection of interesting handwritten and printed documents on the subject; it is certainly of Genoese origin and, probably, it was collected by the Franciscan Angelo Giustiniani, Bishop of Geneva (among other documents there is also a further copy of the treatise by Palescandolo, which confirms its local diffusion: see *Maffei*, p. 338). Of great interest are the letters (contained in this codex) of the Franciscan Arcangelo Botticino, addressed to Giustiniani, in which all problems and doubts of a confessor with respect to the merchant world are expressed: "si enim numquam liceret vendere ultra rigidum precium, esset damnare fere omnes mercatores . . . quia et Genuae et Clavari et fere ubique locorum vix est mercator qui non aliquando vendat precio credito et maiore quam numerato". Botticino was a reader of several authors: he not only mentions Raffaele da Pornassio, but in the monastery of S. Francesco in Chiavari he had works to hand like the Summa Rosella or the De Contractibus by Summenhart (the copies BUG: Rari A. VII. 22 and H. VI. 11 come from that monastery and contain handwritten notes by Botticino). About Angelo Giustiniani first information in J. A. Besson, Memoires pour l'histoire ecclesiastique des diocéses de Genève, Tarantaise . . ., Nancy 1759, pp. 68 - 71; *G. Cantini*, I francescani d'Italia di fronte alle dottrine

And also in Theophilo Giustiniani, belonging to the same period, we find this consideration, regarding the lawfulness of "ricambi":

> così como quelli cambij [reali] si fanno per fine d'implicare in merce, o fare pagamenti in li lochi per ove si danno, et hanno il mercatare per fine loro; cossì questi [ricambi] sono facti et ordinati, perchè essi denari dati a cambio siano remandati per recambio et stare sopra queste volte de cambio et recambio per più guadagno senza altra necessitade[51].

We find here, in nuce, one of the themes recurring in a large part of the literature of the 16th Century, i.e. the opposition between "effective" trading and financial activities, and this theme had enormous repercussion, obviously, also in Genoa. In this town, in fact, from the middle of the century on, we find ample evidence of an ever increasing opposition to the new role assumed by the finance inside the town economy; and the correlative of which is, among other things, the political importance of financers in the government of the Republic. Some of these texts have already been studied from a different viewpoint to reconstruct the political and institutional debate existing in Genoa between the 16th and the 17th Century[52]. Let us consider them, now, in the light of the debate on exchanges.

Giovanni (Cibo) Recco, commercial entrepreneur, silk-merchant, officer of the Republic and, in his free time, historian, returns several times, in his *Historie di Genova* to the problem of the economic-political transformation of the town, accusing the "privata avarizia di cittadini potentissimi" who became rich through "illeciti cambi", and exclaiming, at a certain point:

> in verità sono più lecite le prede de Turchi che degli Cristiani e di più sicura conscienza vi sarebbero che i denari dati a cambio[53].

Recco is echoed by an anonymous dialogue (the author of which was, certainly, very close to the political positions of our entrepreneur) wherein the opposition to the financial oligarchy is no less violent:

> hanno con le grosse usure havuto grandissimi guadagni da 25 e 30 per cento l'anno ... et indebitato tanto quel potentissimo Re [of Spain] che, oppresso da tanti interessi, sarà sforzato far come la corona di Francia[54].

---

luterane e calviniste durante il Cinquecento, Romae 1948, pp. 99 - 101; *C. Fichera*, Registrum Provinciae Ianuae 1520 - 1641. Primo registro della provincia francescana ligure dell'osservanza, Genoa 1978, p. 73. A book of sermons by Giustiniani, in BNF, Tordi, 277; the moltiplicity of interests of our churchman also comes from the legacy of Greek manuscripts which is, partially, kept at the Escorial; or from the books left to the monastery of the Annunziata of Genoa (ASG, Notaio G. B. Cangialanza, sc. 582, f. 1).

[51] BAV, Vat. Lat. 6434, c. 296v; and at c. 297r: "la honestà vorria quelli cambij si facessino quali fuseno utili et necessarij al mercante, et così exorto".

[52] *R. Savelli*, La Repubblica oligarchica: Legislazione, istituzione e ceti a Genova nel Cinquecento, Milano 1981, pp. 40ff.; *Id.*, Tra Machiavelli e S. Giorgio: Cultura giuspolitica e dibattito istituzionale a Genova nel Cinque-Seicento, in Finanze e ragion di Stato in Italia e in Germania nella prima Età moderna, ed. by *A. De Maddalena* and *H. Kellenbenz*, Bologna 1984, pp. 284ff.

[53] G. Cibo Recco, Historie di Genova , BCB, mr. VII. 3.9, p. 452.

The person who summed up the terms of this position in a certainly more representative literary form, was Paolo Foglietta, a poet, who, in his play, *Il Barro* has one of the protagonists speak as follows:

io vedo che i mercatanti di tutto il mondo sono venuti cambisti, che quasi vuol dire usurari, se bene per honestare questa disonestà, quando d'ebrea fecero cristiana l'usura, le cambiarono il nome e la chiamarono cambio ... vorrei fare mercantia reale ... e non pur è lecita, ma di merito grande apresso Dio, perch'ella da inviamento al popolo suo, al quale lo levano i moderni cambisti, poichè non degnano più di far mercantia, perchè temono di imbrattarsi le mani ... ma non temono già d'imbrattarsi l'anima facendo cambi illeciti, li quali in somma fanno più volentieri che la giusta mercantia per due cagioni, l'una perchè sono di minor fattica, che basta una piccola poliza, le quale fanno girar in ogni parte del mondo come il sole; l'altra perchè sono di maggior guadagno[55].

Foglietta's play was not published until the 19th century, but the positions adopted by him must have been widely known, and not only in Genoa, since we find practically identical concepts in Botero[56]. We are now far from the times in which Luca Pacioli could, optimistically, write that the exchange "è veramente laqua [sic] de la nave mercantesca, perchè senza lui serebbe quasi impossibile ben traficare"[57].

The reason is that between the time in which Pacioli was writing, and that in which Foglietta and Botero were treating the "polizzino" ironically, a profound transformation took place in the fairs of exchanges (with their separation from those of goods) of which Bernardo Davanzati left us an accurate account:

è stato inventato dai Genovesi un nuovo cambio, ch'essi chiamano per le fiere di Bisenzone, ove da principio si andava: ora si vanno a fare in Savoja, in Piemonte, in Lombardia, a Trento, alle porte di Genova e ovunque voglion essi; talchè assai meglio, Utopie, cioè fiere senza luogo s'avrieno da chiamare; né di fiere hann'altro che i quattro nomi, accattati da quelle di Lione; perchè non vi vanno popoli a comprar mercanzie, ma solamente cinquanta o sessanta cambiatori con un quaderno di fogli, a ricapitar i cambij fatti quasi in tutta Europa, e ritornarli con quegl'interessi che quivi convengono[58].

---

[54] Sogno sopra la Republica di Genova, BUG, ms. B. I. 19, c. 39r.

[55] P. Foglietta, Il Barro, in ASLSP XXV/2 (1892), p. 356.

[56] G. Botero, Della ragion di stato, ed. by *L. Firpo,* pp. 78 - 79: "e chi non sa che quei che vogliono arricchire d'usure, lasciando il traffico perchè non si può esercitare senza il risico della robba e stento dell'animo e del corpo, con un polizzino, vendendo parte il tempo, parte l'uso della moneta, fanno fruttare il denaro . . .? . . . Egli è forza che a questo modo, perchè ad ognuno piace il guadagno senza travaglio, si disertino le piazze, si abbandonino le arti e s'intermettano le mercanzie . . . Abbiamo in Italia due repubbliche floridissime: Venezia e Genova; di queste senza dubbio che Venezia avanza di gran lunga Genova e di stato e di grandezza. Se ne cercaremo la ragione, trovaremo ciò essere avvenuto perchè Veneziani, attendendo alla mercatanzia reale, si sono arricchiti, mediocremente in particolare, ma infinitamente in commune; all'incontro i Genovesi, impiegandosi affatto in cambi, hanno arricchito immoderatamente le facoltà particolari, ma impoverito estremamente l'entrate publiche".

[57] L. Pacioli, Summa de Arithmetica, Geometria, Proportioni et proportionalità, Venezia, Paganino de Paganini, 1494, c. 167v.

The passage is rightly famous, as Davanzati succeeded in summing up, in a few lines, that complicated phenomenon of concentration on the one side, and of subjection to the Genoese finance, on the other, which has characterized the history of exchanges and of fairs of exchanges starting from the middle of the century. "Leur ville devient le centre de toute l'économie européenne" – states Braudel[59], in conclusion to a cycle of studies and research which analyzed the connections between Spanish crown, international finance and Genoese *asentistas*.

Nothing can be more eloquent and persuasive than the synoptic tables elaborated by Ramon Carande regarding the contracts made by Charles V[60]. And if Carande dated from 1553 the years of the Genoese predominance in Spain, the same period of years has been identified as the turn-about which took place in the Kingdom of Naples "precisely between 1552 and 1558"[61].

Now, as H. Lapeyre noted, the *asientos* did not necessarily also involve the drawing up of an exchange contract, "mais le cas le plus fréquent était le change"[62]; and not only for technical and military reasons (which means e.g., a transfer of funds from Spain and Italy to the Netherlands, engaged in war)[63], but also because through the different exchange techniques profit was added to profit[64]. Doña Juana, the Princess Regent of Spain, was well

---

[58] B. Davanzati, Notizia de' cambij, in Scrittori Italiani di economia politica, Parte Antica, T. II, Milano 1804, p. 61.

[59] *F. Braudel,* Civilisation matérielle, économie et capitalisme, XVe - XVIIIe siècle. T. 2: Les jeux de l'échange, Paris 1979, p. 346.

[60] *R. Carande,* Carlos V y sus banqueros. Los caminos del oro y de la plata, Madrid 1967, passim.

[61] *G. Muto,* Tra "hombres de negocios" e banche pubbliche: progetti di autonomia finanziaria nello stato napoletano (secoli XVI - XVII), in Studi storici Luigi Simeoni XXXIII (1983), p. 89.

[62] *H. Lapeyre,* La participation des génois aux "asientos" de Charles Quint et Philippe II, in Atti del Congresso Internationale di studi storici su Rapporti Genova-Mediterraneo-Atlantico nell'età moderna, ed. by *R. Belvederi,* Genova 1983, p. 149. In the same volume see also the essay by *F. Otte,* Sevilla y la ferias genovesas: Lyon y Besançon. 1503 - 1560, pp. 247 - 277.

[63] *G. Parker,* The Army of Flanders and the Spanish Road. 1567 - 1659, Cambridge 1972, pp. 139ff.

[64] For a slightly later period see the remarks by *G. Doria,* Un quadriennio critico: 1575 - 1578. Contrasti e nuovi orientamenti nella società genovese nel quadro della crisi finanziaria spagnola, in Fatti e idee di storia economica nei secoli XII - XIX. Studi dedicati a Franco Borlandi, Bologna 1977, p. 392: "the transformation of the Genoese hombres de negocios from pure asentistas into factores cambistas had stimulated the need for pushing the speculative manoeuvre on exchanges to the maximum level: it was necessary to make more and more productive that system of arbitrations and "resources" due to which the profit deriving from a careful transfer of funds was added to the simple interest on the advance, thus realizing a profit which was higher, more immediate and free from any control by the orderer . . . We can note how the profit coming to the Genoese businessmen in the period under Alessandro Farnese and Ambrogio Spinola for the speculative manoeuvre alone (exchange and "ricorsa") was, usually, between 18 and 20%, while the part of profit coming from the effective rate of interest was close to 10 - 12%."

aware of this fact. She described as follows, in 1554, the situation of the financial market with respect to the *asientos* made with the Genoese:

> acerca de los excesivos intereses que llevan los mercaderes, vienen los cambios de Italia a 26 por 100 del primer cambio y, ademas de esto, se paga acá ducado por escudo que son otro 7 por 100, en la differencia de moneda y, ademas, se pone con ella otro 10 por 100, de manera que viene a costar el dinero a 43 por 100, y despues corre el interés de la dilación de la paga a 14 por 100, y como las consignaciones son de hoy a tres, cuatro, cinco y aun seis años, todo viene a montar tanto que los 339 000 escudos que ha tomado el embajador de Genova, en estos postremos asientos, cuestan 898 000, poco mas o menos[65].

This explains the principal mechanism on the basis of which the usual rates of interest, acknowledged, on loans, varied between 8 and 14% while the Genoese writers either polemics or historians, always report 20 - 30% (and sometimes even more). These are the "concealed benefits" on which the Genoese "hombres de negocios" founded their fortune and their extraordinary profits[66]. These economic gains were then distributed, through a descending chain, to the collectors of savings, to the brokers of the exchange letters, to the medium and small savers[67].

We return now, after this short but necessary digression, to our starting point, i.e. to the discussions in which the "exchanges" were set against the "mercantia reale". The interest of positions like those of Foglietta or of Recco depends on the fact that these people acting as spokesmen for the criticisms of the predominance of the financial activities, writing against the "unlawful exchanges" and the "usury", are also businessmen, certainly not churchmen or "pure", "professional" scholars, strangers to that shining world of trade typical of 16th century Genoa.

The hypotheses which we can formulate to explain this attitude are of two different kinds: the first one is that in these writings we find the echo of a deeper conflict of interests connected to the economic development of the town; i.e. whoever argues against the "cambisti" (exchanges makers) can be cut off from this stream of wealth for many different reasons (family, belonging to one or another noble group); or else being a part of those "middle class" groups of merchants or manufacturers which were – or supposed to be – damaged by the choice made by saving in favour of more profitable investments, like those connected to loans and exchanges (with the connected increase in the cost of money). The second hypothesis (which does not

---

[65] *Carande,* p. 22; and see also the remarks made by *F. Ruiz Martin,* Las finanzas españolas durante el reinado de Felipe II, in Cuadernos de Historia. Anexos de la revista Hispania 2 (1968), p. 114.

[66] An exemplary analysis of this mechanism in *G. Doria,* Consideraciones sobre las actividades de un "factor-cambista" genoves al servicio de la corona española, in *A. Otazu* (ed.), Dinero y Credito (siglos XVI al XIX), Madrid 1978, pp. 290 - 293 (wherefrom I derived the term "concealed benefits").

[67] *G. Doria,* Un quadriennio, cit., p. 384; *Braudel,* p. 341.

rule out the first one but, on the contrary, may coexist with it) is the one of a penetrating influence (even if certainly not uniform) of the traditional doctrine on money and usury (grounded both in Aristotelian tradition and in religious beliefs).

This hypothesis may be confirmed by an interesting document found among the papers of a typical representative of the Genoese "middle class" of the 16th century, Teramo Canevari (1511 - 1592). His father, Matteo, travelled for a long period through Europe, trading and working as broker of exchanges between Besançon and Antwerp. On returning to Genoa he opened a "volta" for silk, for which in the period of greatest prosperity, up to 50 looms were in operation. Teramo became a member on the Board of Notaries (on which he was to hold the title of Rector for several periods) but he was, at the same time, also a member of the "Art of silk"; the sons of Teramo were sent away to study (medicine for the famous Demetrio, and law for Ottaviano)[68]. Matteo and Teramo were not only businessmen, but were also actively present in the life of a famous religious Confraternity, that of "Divino Amore", which we will again deal with[69].

In a codex in which Teramo copied documents concerning both his family and the political life of the time, and literary compositions, all in admirable disorder (but he evidently attributed great importance to these documents), an anonymous undated latter, addressed to a clergyman, is also inserted. In this letter the matter of exchanges is carefully considered[70]. If the author was not effectively Canevari, he very probably was another member of the Confraternity (wherein a high number of notaries were present); a brief mention of the dealings between the Republic and S. Giorgio can be used to set a sure term *ante quem,* i.e. 1562[71]. A further element serving to identify the whole figure of the author is given by one of the final exclamations: "in

---

[68] In addition to the information and sources reported in the foreword to the Catalogo del fondo Demetrio Canevari della Biblioteca Civica Berio di Genova, ed. by *R. Savelli,* Firenze 1974, see also ACG, ms. 1141; ASG, ms. 477, p. 172; *G. Costamagna,* Il notaio a Genova tra prestigio e potere, Roma 1970, p. 285. On the Genoese "setaioli" see *P. Massa,* Un'impresa serica genovese della prima metà del Cinquecento, Milano 1974 (and the bibliography quoted therein); for the contrasted role of the Genoese "setaioli" in the Genoese society of the second half of the 16th Century, see also *Savelli,* Tra Machiavelli e S. Giorgio, cit., p. 292 and foll.

[69] Matteo becomes a partner in 1555, Teramo in 1558. For the sources, the bibliography and a first evaluation on the role of this confraternity in the Genoese society, see *R. Savelli,* Dalle confraternite allo Stato: il sistema assistenziale genovese nel Cinquecento, in ASLSP XCVIII, N.S. XXIV (1984), pp. 171 - 216 (at p. 190 on Teramo Canevari).

[70] BCB, mr. I.1.2, cc. 39r - 42v. The letter was published (without identifying the origins and with several inaccuracies) by M. Rosi in the appendix to Foglietta, Il Barro, cit., pp. 531 - 534.

[71] This date can be advanced, with some certainty, at least to 1554, the year in which there is already a commission of S. Giorgio having the aim of negotiating with the Republic for the return of Corsica and the continental zones under S. Giorgio (see ACG, Ms. 224: Raccolta di tutti i magistrati che si sono fatti nella casa di San Giorgio).

questa nostra republica quanti tiranni sott'al mantel de cittadini", one of the *topoi* of the writings of opposition in the 50s and 60s of the 16th century (the Foglietta brothers, Cibo Recco, the author of the *Sogno*).

Let us now consider the most interesting points of this document, with reference to the exchanges and to the "contratti pecuniari"; which are, in the Author's opinion, a veritable "plague". Women (widows and young women) sell the "luoghi" of S. Giorgio, gold objects, "e fuorsi anco delle vesti, per tenerli sopra cambi"; "alchune ... sono anco partecipanti in quelli 30 per cento, e più et meno, come si fa in li contratti che si fanno con li principi".

Many "non volendo più la servitù della mercatura" turned their hands to mainly financial business (leaving the "poveri gioveni" without work and commissions) and thus have "posto talmente sotto la mercatura, che puochi sono li negocianti di merce che alle volte non stien sotto cambii. Et se alcuno per disgracia non si leva presto, resta facilmente rovinato, perchè ordinariamente il guadagno delle merci non può esser tale che compir possi il denaro de i cambii".

We can see therefore that there were many reasons for the contrast between "mercantia reale" and exchange.

There were, then, people making exchange "senza mandar lettere e ciò fanno per non pagar provigioni né cabella, et per non cambiar il suo debitore che fan qui, et vogliono il medesimo precio che si fa con coloro che pagano queste tali spexe": a typical example of "dry" exchange, in which disapproval for the fiscal aspects of the problem is added to the moral censure ("uzura", "senz'alcuna carità").

No less reproachable then are all forms through which the market of money was manipulated: "quando sentono che Sua Maestà e altri prencipi hanno fatto qualche partito ... sanno ... molto bene stringere e far stringere la moneta". There often appears, then, a not completely clear reference to the "prestare a controfermo": the mentioned rate of interest ("a nove et dieci per cento") and the fact that this is a loan which is made "ai ricchi", to rich persons, (in correspondence with the "partiti con prencipi" in which a 30% interest is usually charged) probably lead us to believe that these contracts were made by the small and medium savers with the great "asentistas" ("si contentono di guadagnar quel meno, per parersi a manco risico per una fera col suo cittadino o cognoscente, che fidare per uno anno un principe che non si può astringere")[72].

---

[72] See what was asserted by Fabiano Chiavari in this respect, in De Cambiis (see infra note 120): "Hoc idem dicendum est [that they are usurers] de illis qui suas aliis dant pecunias nomine depositi, aut (ut dicitur) contrifirmi, aut partiti, aut commodi" (c. 7r).

The letter, addressed to a clergyman, and written by one who used to frequent Piazza di Banchi (the merchant heart of Genoa, where businessmen, "hombres de negocios" and notaries used to meet) seemed to be an interesting proof of some aspects of the economic moral, and a way to introduce a very specific moment of debate, in the problem of exchanges, between theologians and lawyers.

II. The debate of 1554

1. In a judgement of the Genoese Civil Rota of 1588, which settled a complicated controversy between businessmen regarding an *asiento* with Spain[73], we find a certain number of interesting elements: both regarding the history of the diffusion of Du Moulin's work (recalled herein through the intermediation of the successful Cavallini's "reissue")[74] and the history of the Genoese legal tradition on the subject of exchanges[75]. In this judgement, in fact, we find one of the infrequent references to two decisions by the Government of the Republic which seem to call into question the traditional image of a substantially liberal legislation (even if the judgement declares that, in the case in point, they were not applicable).

In fact the act of 1363 ("contra allegantes cambia vel assecuramenta esse usuraria") is well known. It prohibited, "in quocunque contractu mercantiae", to allege "quod ille contractus esset usurarius"[76]; well known are also the rules of the tax on exchanges of 1554 in which an item is dedicated to exchanges "i quali si faranno per le dette fere senza mandare lettere"[77].

---

[73] ASG, Rota civile, 1, cc. 568 - 593.

[74] See *A. Lattes,* Carlo Dumoulin e Gaspare Caballino, in Archivio Giuridico Filippo Serafini s. IV, vol. XI (1926), pp. 7 - 19. About Cavallini see *P. Colliva,* Due studiosi cinquecenteschi delle "Constitutiones" dell'Albornoz: Virginio de' Boccacci e Gaspare Cavallini da Cingoli, in Storiografia e Storia. Studi in onore di Eugenio Duprè Theseider, Roma 1974, pp. 835 - 866, and the article in DBI vol. XXII, pp. 773 - 774.

[75] About which see *A. Lattes,* Genova nella storia del diritto cambiaro italiano, in Rivista del diritto commerciale XIII, p. I (1915), pp. 185 - 199.

[76] The text of the chapter is missing in the Statutes of 1363; as the same title is used for a statute of 1403, then re-used in 1459 in the Statutes of the Padri del Comune, we think that the text remained substantially the same. The reason quoted in the statute mentioned is interesting: "si enim per hec et similia impedimenta instrumenta cambii et alii contractus mercantiarum, facta cum scriptis vel sine, non possent executioni mandari, verteretur in magnum damnum et incommodum civium et mercatorum Ianuensium qui communiter faciunt similes contractus nec aliter possent exerceri mercimonia": see Statuto dei Padri del comune della Repubblica genovese, ed. by *A. Desimoni,* Genova 1885, pp. 14 - 15.

[77] See *D. Gioffré,* Gênes et les foires de change de Lyon à Besançon, Paris 1960, p. 247.
On the problems of the fiscal law see also *G. Felloni,* Asientos, juros y ferias de cambio desde el observatorio genoves, in *A. Otazu* (ed.), Dinero y credito, cit., pp. 347 ff.

Less common are, on the contrary, the two rules to which the judgement in question refers: the first one is of 1467 and in it, among other things, also the "dry" exchanges were forbidden, i.e. those made without mailing the relative letters[78]. The second is dated 1555 and brings us directly to the core of the problem. The text is hardly known, as no memory of it remains in any of the collections of the Genoese laws in the modern age, neither has it been assimilated at the level of *Statuti*[79].

Which were the prohibitions of this decree? Two kinds of contract are condemned by it:

> quicumque ... in civitate Genuae vel districtu aliquam pecuniae quantitatem dederit vel tradiderit alicui ad certum et terminatum lucrum ultra sortem principalem percipiendum et dandum sive sub nomine mutui vel cambij vel cuiuslibet alterius contractus ... cadat ipso iure in penam ...

We face, now, the formal (and traditional) prohibition of the loan with interest, in which the element which generates the condemnation is the "certum et terminatum lucrum", the profit agreed upon in advance, hidden in any form of contract which could be used to avoid the canonical condemnation of usury, of which the one of the exchange had long been the most used[80].

More specific and detailed is what is condemned by the second part of the law:

> non possit quivis civis ... in ferjis Bezensoni dare vel recipere nec in se ipsum cambiare aliquam pecuniarum quantitatem in loco de nondinis ad nondinas vel pro alio termino sub certo et terminato interesse vel lucro ultra sortem percipiendo sive nomini depositi fiat, vel mutui vel cambij ac etiam assecurationum quae fierent ex reditibus nundinarum seu feriarum qui reditus vulgariter dicuntur retorni.

The prohibition, then, did not only affect the Genoese, but also the other merchants that, on the basis of the recent rules on fairs, had been admitted "in ponendis precijs cambiorum". The element which activates the prohibition is always the "certum et terminatum interesse", but the range of the prohibited activities becomes, here, more specific, and concerns the exchanges from fair to fair, the deposits and the "ritorni" (which, similarly to the exchanges had been charged, during the previous year, to the payment

---

[78] The decree of 18th March 1467 is in ASG Archivio Segreto 581, cc. 83v - 85r (a further copy in BCB, mr. III. 4. 13, cc. 186r - 188v). The precedents have been carefully analyzed by *Kirshner,* The moral problem, cit., p. 129 (at pp. 164 - 167 he publishes the minutes of a meeting which took place shortly before the decree in question, decree that he does not seem to know).

[79] Copies of the decree in ASG, Senato, Sala Senarega 1298; BCB, mr. III. 4. 13, cc. 457 - 458v; ACG, Albergo dei Poveri, Ufficio dei Poveri, Atti diversi, 1. The BCB codex also comes from the Canevari family, and the Ufficio dei Poveri was one of the beneficiaries of the sanctions provided for in the decree.

[80] See, for instance, how already in the 14th Century there was, in Genoa, a "gabella cambiorum vel usurarum" (*Gioffrè,* p. 94).

of the relative tax, even in the case of exchange without a letter). Not only were fines imposed, but for the recidivant notaries and brokers also the loss of office and a ban for the period of two years were foreseen.

What were the reasons for this formal rigour, only one year after the issue of a rule which provided for exchanges without the necessity of sending letters of exchange? The most viable hypothesis is that the aim was to punish a single and specific type of contractual behaviour, which could be more evident, i.e. "exchanges" (let us use this term) in which the interest was agreed upon in advance, and not bound, on the contrary, to the fluctuation (and the risk) of the market.

Moreover, from as early as 1552, a Court to repress usury contracts had been set up in Savona, and in the following years similar Courts were found in other towns and communities of the Genoese domain. It may be worthy of note that an ecclesiastic was always called on to be a member of such Courts[81].

I personally believe that in the 1550s, the presence of the Genoese businessmen having been well established on the European scenario, and the Republic having reorganized the internal operation of fairs[82], a debate began on the significance and lawfulness of the financial activities in the town, proof of which had been previously reported. And in an attempt to understand the cultural background of the law of 1555 a debate has been found, the repercussions of which were not restricted to the town alone.

2. Raffaele Soprani, a 17th Century scholar, reports that:

> l'anno 1554 d'ordine di Monsignor Gerolamo Sauli Arcivescovo di Genova, si radunarono per due volte tutti li Teologi e li più celebri Leggisti della città in conferenza sopra la materia de' cambij di Lione, o sia Bisanzone, conforme si costumava anticamente in simili casi di consideratione et importanza[83].

Soprani's account is, on the whole, quite accurate even if it can be partly supplemented and completed by other sources. Let us say immediately that the Genoese public and ecclesiastic sources are, in this respect, completely silent (or completely absent) and that the texts which have been traced are, up to now, only three.

The other evidence which gives some information comes from inside the Society of Jesus: Laínez, on a mission in Genoa in that period, writes, by the

81 For Savona the establishing law is in ASG, Senato, Sala Senarega 1282. News on the existence, in the 70s in Gavi, Pieve di Teco, Levanto, Novi, in ASG, Archivio Segreto 818 - 825 and Senato, Sala Senarega 1393. See also *E. Grendi,* Introduzione all'analisi storica delle comunità liguri: Cervo in età moderna, in Miscellanea storica ligure VIII 2 (= Studi di microanalisi storica), p. 205.

82 Interesting documents on this theme regarding 1552 in ASG, Senato, Sala Senarega 1283 and Camera, Finanze, 25.

83 R. Soprani, Li scrittori della Liguria, Genova, Pietro Giovanni Calenzani, 1667, p. 77.

end of March, to Loyola that the Government of the Republic had promised the Archbishop Vicar (effectively Sauli was in fact at that time, deputy-legate in Bologna) to order:

> que se junten algunos mercaderes á narar sus contratos y proponer las razones que le paresce que los justifican y tanbién se junten á oyr théologos y juristas[84].

This evidence is very interesting as it shows that the debate was not restricted to theologians and lawyers, but that merchants were involved too.

The problem was not only of great concern to the members of the Society of Jesus, but also to the upper echelons of the ecclesiastic hierarchy. A few days later (on 5th April, to be exact) Loyola wrote to Laínez reporting that he had discussed the problem with the Pope and other Cardinals, and that Cardinal Cervini had passed a report to him on the problem, supplied "de una persona de mucho crédito en vida y letras", but who wished to remain anonymous[85]. Now, among the papers of Cervini a document has been found which, almost certainly, is that shown by Cervini to Loyola. Its title is *Contractus quidam qui hac nostra tempestate a quibusdam Christi fidelibus celebrantur* and the author was the Genoese Augustinian Fabiano Chiavari, as can be deduced by the accompanying letter[86].

The letter, undated, poses some chronological problems: it begins, in fact, with this statement "haec ... sunt quae his proximis temporibus Bononiae in primis et subinde Genuae a probis Doctisque viris examinata et decisa fuerunt". The discussion had thus already begun some time before, certainly before the end of March 1554, which is the date of the Laínez's letter: probably near the end of 1553. In fact: Chiavari is certainly in Genoa in 1553[87], but on 2nd March 1554 before leaving from Brussels, Seripando sent a very kind letter to him in Rome, referring to the studies which he was conducting[88].

---

[84] J. Laínez, Monumenta. Epistolae et Acta. I. 1536 - 1556, Madrid 1912, pp. 251 - 252.
On the mission of Laínez to Genoa see *P. Tacchi Venturi*, Storia della Compagnia di Gesù in Italia, II 2, Roma 1951, pp 482ff.; *M. Scaduto*, Storia della Compagnia di Gesù in Italia. L'epoca di Giacomo Laínez. Il governo, Roma 1964, pp. 138ff.

[85] I. de Loyola, Epistolae et instructiones, VI, Madrid 1907, p. 561.

[86] ASF, Carte Cervini, 33, cc. 59r - 60v. About Chiavari, known also as Fabiano da Genova, one of the closest collaborators of Seripando, see the excellent article by G. Fragnito in DBI, vol. 24, pp. 624 - 627 and the bibliography quoted therein.

[87] ASG, Cancellieri di S. Giorgio 288 and S. Giorgio 3039 (PN), cc. 208 - 209: acts regarding the institution by Chiavari of a "colonna" in S. Giorgio in favour of the Monastery "della Consolazione" to support economically two lecturers of theology and philosophy; and see also D. A. Gandolfo, Dissertatio historica de ducentis celeberrimis augustinianis scriptoribus, Romae 1704, pp. 117 - 119.

[88] BNN, Viennese Lat. 61, c. 52r. The letter is dated 2nd March; for the date of the leaving, see G. Seripando, Diarium de vita sua. 1513 - 1562, ed *D. Gutierrez*, in Analecta Augustiniana XXVI (1963), p. 101 (of the offprint). Fabiano Chiavari took part in the initiative for the printing of the works of Egidio Colonna; those edited by him were published in 1554 (Expositio in cap. firmiter credimus, Romae, per Antonium

In addition, Chiavari, in the foreword to his treatise on exchanges, points out expressly that the Archbishop Vicar recommended that all persons taking part in the debate note their opinions. Thus he participated in one of the first stages of the discussion, followed by others, in which Laínez also participated[89]. Who were the others? One of them we know by name only, the Dominican Clemente Serravalle (mentioned in fact by Soprani, but whose writings have not yet been traced). The opinion of another person remained, in addition to the name: this is Nicola Senarega, one of the most authoritative Genoese lawyers of the first half of the 16th Century and one of the editors of the revision of the criminal statutes issued in 1557[90].

Before analyzing these papers, it is perhaps necessary to point out a particular detail, which might help to clarify the cultural situation in which this debate took place.

The settlement of the Jesuits in Genoa in 1553 is advocated by the secret confraternity of Divino Amore (previously mentioned). The doge holding office at that time, Giacomo Promontorio, had long since been a member of such confraternity; in 1555 also the Archbishop Vicar, Egidio Falcetta, Bishop of Caorle, was coopted into the confraternity[91]. We can suppose therefore that among the promoters of this debate on the economic morals there were, surely, some of the most important representatives of the "catholic reform" in the town, on the uppermost echelons of the respective hierarchies.

3. Let us now consider separately, the three contributions still extant, beginning with that of Nicola Senarega. Published posthumously[92] it stands

---

Bladum, and the De charactere, in Liber de renuntiatione Papae, ibid.). A great deal of information about this edition, then interrupted, is contained in the correspondence between Seripando and Chiavari filed in BNN.

89 In May he writes to Loyola that they met three times (Laínez, p. 255). A reference to the fact that the Bolognese Theologians were also consulted on this problem is found in J. A. de Polanco, Vita Ignatii Loiolae et rerum Societatis Jesu historia, IV, Madrid 1896, p. 33, which also recalls the document received from Cervini "a theologo quodam perito".

90 In the years around 1520 he is found among the "sapientes reipublicae" (ACG, Ms. 288) and he will be in the same condition again in 1554 (ASG, Senato, Sala Senarega 1293). He died on 24th March 1563 (ASG, Notaio Marco Antonio Morinello, sc. 348, f. 1); and see *G. Montagna,* Il collegio dei dottori a Genova: la documentazione dal 1541 al 1603, in Annali della facoltà di Giurisprudenza di Genova XVIII (1980 - 1981), p. 97.

91 For the sources see *R. Savelli,* Dalle confraternite, cit.; many are the inaccuracies in this respect of *G. Cassandro,* Un trattato, cit., pp. 31 - 32: speaks of Falcetta as Bishop of Caprile (!) rather than of Caorle (and on him see *D. Cambiaso,* I vicari generali degli arcivescovi di Genova, in ASLSP LXXXVI (1972), pages 44 - 46); he denies Fabiano Chiavari the honour of his family name, as he interprets the latin "Clavarius" as a position in the Augustinian Order. Effectively from June 1554 Chiavari had already reached the important position of procurator of the Order (having already been proposed as general in the previous years).

92 It was edited for the first time by the Cassinese Ilarione da Genova, De latissimo avaritiae dominatu, Brixiae, Apud Damianum Turlinum, 1567, pp. 92 - 94, who

out for its brevity and the inflexible positions of the author. The demonstration of the unlawfulness of the exchanges of "Bisenzone" is based on a series of rather simple and acute arguments: even if the contracts are made "sub nomine emptionis", we are faced, in fact, with a case of loan, "et si veritatem velimus intueri mercatores invenerunt huiusmodi contractum ad evitandum nomen usurae, non ad evitandam usuram".

In fact, to purchase the "scudo di marche" in Genoa with the aim of selling it at the fair is, actually, a loan transaction, "cum emant per anticipatam exbursationem rem minori precio alio tempore consignandam, quam vere sit valitura tempore consignationis". And since the price of the "scudo di marche" varied depending on the shorter or longer variation in time from the date of the fair, this variation is "ob dilationem temporis ... et implicat in se tacituum mutuum".

Senarega comes close to one of the logical and problematic points of the whole question. In fact, the fairs of exchanges regarding the actual activity of exchange and compensation are not under discussion, but rather their purely speculative aspect of hiding other kinds of contracts. The Genoese lawyer judges, in fact, that his fellow-citizens

> nihil ad aliud tendant nisi ut ex suis pecuniis quolibet anno recipiant octo vel decem pro centenario, non habentes animum ad aliquam veram permutationem pecuniarum vel aliquam veram emptionem scutorum de marchis.

The "scudo di marche" (a money of account by which the different monetary kinds were valued)[93] was, in fact, a great problem: how can you purchase something which does not exist? Senarega makes short work of it:

> re vera non reperitur scutus marche, nec est talis moneta in rerum natura.

Rigorists found a logical defect in the sale and purchase of the "scudo di marche" (and, therefore, an unlawful act). Orfeo da Bologna, for instance, had previously ironically remarked:

---

defines Senarega as an expert "in studio sanctarum scripturarum". Ilarione (in the world Giovanni Ambrogio Auricola or Orecchia) took part in the Cassinese congregation in 1533 (see ASG, Notaio Nicolò Pallavicino Coronata, sc. 179, f. 23). Of this very prolific author and preacher it is important to remember also the philological interests, proved by two works which remained unpublished: BAV, Vat. Lat. 6149: In divi Ioannis Chrysostomi Homiliarum in epistolas paulinas recognitiones (in which his connections with Gregorio Cortese are mentioned), and Vat. Lat. 12607: In Theophylacti evangelicarum Enarrationum recognitiones. And see *C. Ginzburg / A. Prosperi*, Giochi di pazienza. Un seminario sul "Beneficio di Christo", Torino 1975, p. 206. – The opinion of Senarega was re-published the following year by F. Chiavari in the third latin edition of the De cambiis (on which see infra note 120) at pp. 86 - 89, without mentioning the name of the author and with an accurate answer. – We remember, finally, how Giovanni Recco (remembered at § I, note 53) in the foreword to his Historie affirmed that Senarega had convinced him to write the history of the Genoese civil wars "mosso dall'amicizia che passava tra noi".

93 See *G. Felloni*, Un système monétaire atypique: la monnaie de marc dans les foires de changes génoises, XVIe - XVIIe siècle, in *J. Day* (ed.), Etudes, cit., pp. 249 - 260.

Scuta marcharum non reperiuntur nisi forte dicas quod sint in concavo lunae et ideo merchatores dicunt quod scuta marcharum sunt (ut secundum ipsos loquar) come li fiorini da 36 qui numquam videntur[94].

It was not by chance that one of the targets of Orfeo da Bologna's polemics was De Vio who, among the theologians was the only one who had made noteworthy progress regarding the theory of sale and purchase (even if the concept of the "scudi di marche" had not yet become fully developed).

However in order to return to the brief opinion expressed by Senarega, some remarks on the doctrinal sources should be made: Giovanni Calderini, Panormitanus, Hostiensis are among the most quoted authoritative sources, and, similarly, Ambrogio da Vignate, Angelo da Chivasso or Boich. What arouses interest, along with a certain amount of surprise, is the use made by Senarega of Summenhart and Du Moulin, authors who, even from different points of view, are recognized as the most "liberal" or, even, "revolutionary" in the theory on usury and interest[95]. For instance, Senarega selects from Du Moulin's vast work, those paragraphs (504 and following), in which the French lawyer criticizes the systems of the fairs of Lyon, the "impiae usurae lugdunenses"[96]; his criticism is based, on the one hand, on a moral/evaluative assumption ("pecunia non tantum parere debet quantum industria"), because the more "shocking" element is that the profit is made, substantially, without performing any kind of activity; on the other Du Moulin still supports the theory of the "quality" of the persons with respect to the lawfulness of the contracts, and on this basis only those persons who work constantly and professionally as merchants can legally make certain kinds of contracts, from which they derive consequent gains.

Obviously Senarega's only interest in discussing the arguments of Du Moulin is to support his own arguments, according to a well known and tested technique. It is, moreover, of great interest that already in 1554 the work by Du Moulin was read and known in Genoa, one of the first indications of the success of this work, notwithstanding intervention on the part of the Index[97].

---

[94] BAV, Vat. Lat. 7720, c. 27r (see § 1 note 23).

[95] *J. T. Noonan,* The Scholastic Analysis of Usury, Cambridge Mass. 1957, pp. 340ff. (especially p. 344 note 18).

[96] C. Du Moulin, Tractatus commerciorum et usurarum, Parisiis apud Ioannem Lodoicum Tiletanum 1546, pp. 224ff.; see also the judgement left by Du Moulin in the Sommaire du livre analytique de contracts, in Opera, Paris, A. Besoigne, 1681, II, par. 74): "quelq'un m' a voulu donner une autre palliation, justifiant par accident la dite tolerance a cause des grandes usures d'Italie, et qu'au moyen d'icelles l'on ne peut mettre bride aux Banquiers de Lyon, car incontinent il porteroient leur argent a Genes".

[97] *F. Reusch,* Der Index der verbotenen Bücher, Bonn 1883, vol. I, p. 442. Very interesting are the reasons on the basis of which Clemente VIII in 1602 renewed the prohibition of the works by Du Moulin: "attendentes, sicut ad audientiam nostram pervenit ... a pluribus et iis praesertim qui utriusque iuris scientiam profitentur, con-

4. Laínez's work, although completed before September 1554, was not published until the end of the 19th Century[98]. If, regarding the opinion expressed by Senarega, we can be almost certain that it was the same as that expressed to the Archbishop Vicar, in the case of Laínez's work (as for that of Chiavari) we have a subsequent re-elaboration of what he expressed during the meetings with other theologians and lawyers, and of the contents of

---

tra huiusmodi prohibitionem dicti Caroli scripta et commentaria, sub variis praetextibus, sive illa examinandi et expurgandi sive corrigendi et emendandi, ut dicunt, sive illis utantur in Iudiciis et Decisionibus causarum et aliis eorum scriptionibus, frequenter legi et retineri . . ." (see Index librorum prohibitorum Alexandri VII . . . iussu editus, Romae ex Typographia Rev. Cam. Apost., 1667, pages 195 - 196). To meet the needs of those who possessed works like the Consilia of F. Decio, with the notes by Du Moulin, the Index printed, in the same year, a thick Censura in omnes Additiones seu Adnotationes marginales Dam. mem. impij Caroli Molinaei, Romae, ex Typographia Camerae Apostolicae 1602 (re-issued in the Indicis librorum expurgandorum . . . Tomus primus . . . per Io. Mariam Brasichellen., Romae, ex Typographia R. Cam. Apost. 1607, pp. 308 - 406). – The diffusion of the Tractatus commerciorum of Du Moulin, due to the "re-edition" by Cavallini, was not restricted to the forensic class only. In 1576 it came into the hands of the Jesuits who, in Germany, were deep in controversy over the problem of the "German contract" and there were people, like Hoffaeus, who posed the problem of revising the traditional theory, without realizing that the name of Cavallini concealed the one of Du Moulin (and not even the careful *J. Brodrick* realized it in The Economic Morals of the Jesuits, London 1934, p. 144): "Si autem vera sunt quae Caspar Cabalinus Venetus nuper de usuris . . . scripsit, nos sane praepropere damnavimus germanos de 5 pro cento" (letter of Hoffaeus to Mercuriano mentioned in P. Canisius, Epistulae et acta, VII, Friburgi Brisgoviae 1922, p. 346). Also the Genoese Angelo Giustiniani (the above mentioned Franciscan Bishop of Geneva) probably made the same error: among his papers (BAV, Vat. Lat. 6434, II, c. 164) we find the note "querendus Filippi Beroaldi liber epitome philosophiae moralis". A book with a similar title has never been written by Beroaldo, while it was the way in which Cavallini concealed the quotations which Du Moulin used make, largely, from another famous Philip, Melanchthon, the author, in fact, of an Epitome philosophiae moralis. The interventions made by Cavallini in the text by Du Moulin are still to be studied (notwithstanding what has been written in this respect by Lattes). On the interest which the French lawyer continued to arouse in Italy, and the connected repression, see also the documents published by *A. Rotondò,* Nuovi documenti per la storia dell'Indice dei libri proibiti, in "Rinascimento" s. II, III (1963), pp. 167 and 175; and *P. Lopez,* Inquisizione stampa e censura nel regno di Napoli tra '500 e '600, Napoli 1974, pp. 199, 216.

[98] On 8th September 1554, in fact, Loyola sends Salmeron a copy of the "librillo de contractibus" by Laínez (Loyola, VI, p. 510).

The Disputatio de usura variisque negotiis mercatorum is in the second volume of the Disputationes Tridentinae edited by H. Grisar (Oeniponte 1886, II, pp. 227 - 321). On this text see *J. M. Gallego,* Diego Laínez y el cambio de Besanzon. Un dictamen del P. Diego Laínez sobre Moral Financiera, in Archivo Teológico Granadino 19 (1956), pp. 5 - 54; *C. Bauer,* Rigoristische Tendenzen in der katholischen Wirtschaftsethik unter dem Einfluß der Gegenreformation, in Adel und Kirche: Gerd Tellenbach zum 65. Geburtstag dargebracht von Freunden und Schülern, Hg. J. Fleckenstein / K. Schmid, Freiburg i. B. 1968, pp. 577ff.; *M. Scaduto,* Storia della Compagnia di Gesù in Italia: L'epoca di Giacomo Laínez, 1556 - 1565. L'azione, Roma 1974, pp. 478ff. The diffusion of the work by Laínez was not restricted to the Society of Jesus alone: Paolo Comitoli, for instance, mentions it several times both in the Trattato de Cambji (BAM, S. 100 sup., c. 356v) and in the Responsa moralia (Lugduni, sumptibus Horacij Cardon, 1609, p. 399); but to Comitoli it had been given by Gian Vincenzo Pinelli, the Genoese scholar settled in Padoa, who acquired one copy of it (BAM, R. 98 sup.) as he did of other works on this subject.

his sermons. In the middle of May, in fact, Laínez informed Loyola of the effects of his sermons ("ya algunos han deliberado de comprar renta y lexar los cambios: otros de hazer mercaderias y no vivir de prestar"), and of the fact that he had prepared a compendium of his opinions, to be submitted to Sauli, a copy of which he also sent to Rome. He could, thus, take advantage of the notes made, on the Pope's request, to the first draft of his work[99].

It was not by chance, then, that he included in his treatise, some paragraphs in which the problem of usury was considered "in venditione ad tempus vel anticipata solutione", a theme connected, although not directly related, to the main problem of the exchanges (and which is, in fact, not found in the works by Senarega and Chiavari)[100].

This is not the case for an analysis of all the aspects of Laínez's opinions in this respect, but it is necessary to try and get to the heart of the problem with reference to the debate which was taking place in Genoa. This is also, probably, a viewpoint which serves to explain not only and exclusively those reasons for which the work was written (as we have seen), but to collocate historically (and therefore in a very definite way) the problem. We are not up against the constant (and immutable) problem of usury and of the lawfulness of the exchange contracts; Laínez (like the others who took part in the debate) was in special historical and social circumstances in which the phenomenon of "exchanges" (if we can term them thus) was undergoing a transformation, and was taking new dimensions, different in quantity and quality. The observation point of Genoa was, as we saw earlier, a privileged one.

We drew attention in the preceding pages to the "utopian" image given by Davanzati of the Besançon fairs, and this was partly a judgement in retrospect, as, by the time, the fairs had already been established in Italy. Laínez, on the contrary, wrote in those very years of the transformation, in full upward acceleration, in which the shadow of the Spanish bankruptcies had not yet appeared. Laínez realized the basic difference between the Lyon fairs and those at "Bisenzone": the Genoese

> transtulerunt cambiorum negotia ad Besansonem ... In qua tamen non nundinae sunt nec magna commercia, ut fiunt Lugduni; sed solum mercatores Januenses ibi in cambiis negotiantur, qui etiam non commorantur Besansone, ut faciebant Lug-

---

99 See the letter of Loyola to Laínez dated 26th May 1554: "si mandano li pareri d'alcuni padri sopra il compendio che V.R. ha cominciato i quali per ordine di nostro Padre si sono congregati et hanno scritto quello ch'ogni uno sente" (Loyola, VII, pp. 59 - 60); the letter by Laínez in Laínez, Epistolae, cit., p. 255.

100 Laínez, Disputatio, cit., pp. 298 - 313, §§ 75 - 86 (from here on the references to the work of Laínez will be made by simply mentioning the paragraph). The insertion of theses problems may have been suggested to him during his stay in Florence (see § 81, e.g.) where the problem had a long tradition and where, even in those years, discussions were still open (see in this respect the many writings of the Dominican Tommaso Buoninsegni).

duni, sed solum tempore nundinarum et solutionis suos juvenes et negotiorum factores illuc mittunt, intra paucos dies reversuros.

And then, to complete the picture, he added:

Besansone autem raro vel numquam fit solutio in numerata pecunia, sed tantum fiunt schedulae seu litterae, ut Januae vel alibi fiat realis solutio et in numerato (§§ 55 - 56)[101].

The separation between the market of capital and that of goods is what creates greater anxiety and doubt. The glowing world of goods (due also to its typical material and tangible aspects) is absent in these fairs. Instead, we find the antiseptic world of written paper (the "polizzini" at which Foglietta and Botero levelled their sarcasm). However as regards these new types of exchange fairs, Laínez, similar to many of his contemporaries, does not consider the more specifically international aspect: he does not evaluate the moment of balancing or transfer of capital. The point which is analyzed is, substantially, the Genoa-fair-Genoa relationship (and not Genoa-fair-Antwerp-Madrid-...)[102].

The judgement and the evaluation are centered, effectively, on what was taking place in Genoa (or in other towns) between the "exchanger" and the "exchangee", even if this event was mediated through these new fairs without goods and without merchants: the interest is focused completely on the local market, on the connections between people (and also on the consequences that these had on the economic reality of the town)[103].

The treatise by Laínez begins with a description of the traditional doctrine of usury ("aliquid ultra sortem accipere vel sperare ob mutuum") and with a discussion on those cases which can justify that "aliquid ultra sortem" (punishment, "damnum emergens', "lucrum cessans", burden to manage the loan, with a clear reference to the question of the "Monti di pietà");

---

[101] See what was written, in this respect, some years later, by the above mentioned Buoninsegni: "In questi luoghi non vi è commerzio di Negozij, ne di traffichi di mercanzie, ma si partono i Mercanti di Genova, di Milano, di Fiorenzia, di Leone e d'altri luoghi, arrivando in quelli alquanti giorni avanti il giorno de' pagamenti, e ivi fanno i loro conti e cambiano fiera per fiera" (T. Buoninsegni, De i cambii, Fiorenzia, Giorgio Marescotti, 1573, c. 13r).

[102] See in this respect the still valid considerations by *G. Mandich,* Delle fiere genovesi di cambi particolarmente studiate come mercati periodici del credito, in Rivista di storia economica IV (1939), pp. 257 - 276.

[103] Usury "est etiam causa penuriae, tum quia usurarii non libenter mutuant pauperibus, qui terram colunt, et ideo agri inculti manent, tum etiam quia artifices et mercatores, ad usuram accipientes, carius merces vendunt" (§ 19); the same takes place with the exchanges: "nocent quoque cambia negotiis et legitimae mercaturae ... quia mercatores, invento hoc securo lucrandi modo per otium, et ex alia parte visis laboribus et expensis et periculis mercaturae, illam relinquunt et cambiis se tradunt ... Illi etiam qui circa merces negotiantur, quia saepe pecunia a campsore accipiunt, quibus merces emant, necessario carius illas vendunt. Pauperibus etiam valde nocent haec cambia, quia mercator valde multos occupat in lana et serico et lino ... et aliis mercibus tractandis, campsor autem vix uni aut alteri ministro prodest" (§ 68).

it also expresses clearly the concept that the principle of the loss of profit cannot be lawfully claimed by those who "non potentes vel nolentes alias negotiari, dum mutuant pecunias suas, aliquid ratione lucri cessantis accipiunt" (§ 30)[104]. In brief the "lucrum cessans" is a principle which cannot be invoked to justify the interest, except on certain conditions, among which that of the quality of the person involved is essential[105].

We enter, then, the problem which is more strictly connected to exchanges, plainly focussing attention on what was happening in Genoa.

There is, in fact, the general aspect, the identification of the abstract categories, and then the discussion on particular questions which emerge. From this point of view the problem of both time and money are of course central; both because if time becomes the measure of the interest we fall into one of those kinds of "dry" exchanges ("principaliter consideratur temporis dilatio, quo pecunia occupata detinetur") (§ 42); and because Laínez remains completely within the theory on the basis of which "pecunia non est merx" and, therefore, "non venditur pecunia pro pecunia ... praesertim quia pecunia, ut sic, pretium et valor aliarum rerum est" (§§ 60 and 43). It is, therefore, clear how Laínez moves away from those conceptions which considered the exchange contract a special type of emptio/venditio, as he regards it as mainly a barter and, secondly, as a "contractus locationis" ("nam campsor suas et ministrorum operas locat, et ab eis, quibus servit, illarum mercedem accipit") (§ 43). The loan (and hence usury) is always there as a snare in all different cases leading back to that one in which the merchant deals, affirming:

> mutuo tibi pecunias meas hoc pacto, ut illas reddas et insuper tantum usurae, quantum lucri reddit cambium Besansonis (§ 47).

In Laínez, obviously, the most specifically ethical-religious (and rigorist) aspect is predominant and tends to demystify all these formalities aimed at transforming a loan contract into one of exchange. This is why we previously considered how the phenomenon of the exchange fairs was analysed, effectively, in a limited perspective, of the town's economic ethics[106].

---

104 This was one of the contracts mentioned as typical in the document sent by Chiavari to Cervini: "quidam nescientes aut nolentes negociari, suas mercatoribus dant pecunias, pacto quod, salvo capitali, singulis annis, eodem in loco, sibi dentur septem vel octo pro singulo centenario datae pecuniae" (ASF, Carte Cervini 33, c. 59r). And thus also Laínez (§ 36) affirms that in such case "usura sine aliquo pallio committitur".

105 See *T. P. McLaughlin,* The teaching of Canonists on Usury, in Mediaeval Studies I (1939), pp. 145 - 147.

106 That Laínez does not realize the objective dimensions of the exchange fairs (putting into evidence the speculative ones only) can be deduced from this passage: "Si quis e. g. dat Januae pecunias campsori, quo illas reddat in Hispania, vel accipit ab eo in Hispania reddendas, quum possent mitti litterae recta via in Hispaniam et ibi fieri solutio, campsores non id faciunt, sed mittunt Besansonem, ut ibi solvuntur cambium et inde alio novo cambio mittunt in Hispanium; quum tamen ille homo nihil negotii

From these preambles it is clear how Laínez, in judging the particular lawfulness of the "cambium Besansonis", is inclined toward the negative ("cambium Besansonis ... claudicare videtur"!) (§ 57). There is not an effective and real exchange of money, as the "scudo di marche" is purchased and sold ("non est realis moneta, sed jus potius ad eam Januae vel alibi recipiendam") (§ 58); time is considered as an autonomous element for evaluation, separate from the effective needs of transfer of the money[107]; "unjust" are the methods used to evaluate the price of the "scudo di marche", which is, often, evaluated in a monopolistic way[108].

Laínez makes an effort, then, to devise some modifications to the exchanges of "Bisenzone", the consequentiality of which derivates from his own moral attitude, which for the local and international financial market was difficult to accept[109]. He left, substantially, only one way out to whoever wished to dedicate himself to changes (not realizing that, by so doing, he was in fact recanting the theory according to which money is not a commodity)[110].

The treatise ends, then, with some suggestions for civil and spiritual fines, to which he also adds an invitation addressed particularly to confessors:

---

habeat Besansone, ac per hoc nullum ei obsequium fiat, si suae pecuniae illuc mittantur" (§ 61).

107 "Quod ut clare intelligatur, supponendum primo, in hoc differre cambium Besansonis atque adeo omnia cambia quae de nundinis ad nundinas fiunt, a cambiis realibus, quae fiunt de loco ad locum, quod in cambiis realibus id temporis tantum a data pecunia in uno loco ad recipiendum in alio, quod commode sufficit ad hoc, quod litterae commode ab uno in alium locum mittantur, et praesententur; in cambiis vero, quae fiunt de nundinis ad nundinas, longe plus temporis statuitur, quam requiratur ad litteras commode ferendas ... His igitur suppositis ... probatur jam in cambio Besansonis ... haberi principaliter respectum ad tempus et expectationem solutionis ... Et si mercatores consulere conscientias proprias voluerint et se ipsos minime decipere, respondebunt se, quum ab eis petuntur pecuniae, statim apud se supputare quantum temporis earundum realis solutio differatur, et quo plus reperitur, plus se velle lucrari" (§§ 59 - 60).

108 Compare with what had been written by Chiavari to Cervini: "Quidam valde tamen raro, nomina locorum pro quibus ineuntur cambia, alijs locis, tantum duobus vel tribus miliaribus distantibus a loco quo inita sunt cambia ... imponunt, nominantes vel ea Lugdunum vel Bezenzonum deinde ... ad praefata proximiora loca, sic ab ipsis ut placuit nominata, campsores se conferunt et conveniunt et ibi fere monopolium facientes cambiorum volvendorum pro libito taxant; quod sane, etiam sine huiusmodi fictione, quamquam et forte pluries fit in ipsis propriis vel veris locis" (ASF, Carte Cervini, 33, c. 59v).

109 The exchanges would have been lawful on these conditions: that whoever sent letters to Besançon, had, in that place cash or real credit (in order to close the circle); that the variations of the scudo depended on the market conditions only (without intervention of the "ratio temporis"); "tertia autem conditio servaretur, si non ipsi mercatores de quorum interesse agitur, taxarent quantum solvendum esse Januae pro scuto marchae e Besansone remisso, sed alii incorrupti et periti mercatores statuerentur judices, qui nullum in ea re haberent interesse" (§ 69).

110 "Solet etiam in loco ubi abundat pecunia, illam ad cambium accipere et mittere alio, ubi est inopia pecuniae ... Hic modus licitus esset si in quovis in eo intervenientium cambiorum non haberetur oculus ad tempus, et justum interesse vel servitium solveretur, et lucrum inde proveniens tribuendum esset industriae campsoris, qui negotiatur circa pecuniam, sicut mercator circa merces" (§ 74).

> Juvaret etiam prohibere confessoribus, ne ab huiusmodi hominibus [merchants and bankers] qui sibi confitentur, aliquid exigant vel oblatum acceptent; quia fortasse blanditiis et muneribus multi confessores corrumpuntur, ut absolvant non absolvendos, praesertim Januae, ubi multi de more solent aureum exhibere confessori, quoties confitentur (§ 88).

We shall now underline some points of the interpretation (which is not particularly original) that Laínez has left on the problem of exchanges, and particularly those of "Bisenzone": money is only a measure, a means for exchange (it is not considered, thus, neither as a commodity nor, even, as capital)[111]; the "taboo of the time" (to use the words of Le Goff) is still fully valid[112]; it is clear, thus, that the problems of the interest on money can only be interpreted in a very limited way.

5. If nothing has been said about Loyola's successor, given the notoriety of the person, something must instead be said about Fabiano Chiavari, the third to intervene in the debate of 1554 (and who will meet again, in Rome, Laínez during the posthumous trial against Savonarola)[113]; there is no better document, to introduce the Genoese Augustinian, than a letter (justly famous) addressed to Seripando, during preparations for the election of his successor to the position of Superior General. Guglielmo da Bologna wrote as follows:

> In Genova ha grandissimo credito appresso tutti gli huomini da bene et inquisitori, né si tratta cosa theologica che lui non ci intervenghi ... et di più ... lui ha scritto a V.P.Rm. che non vorrebbe più stare in Genova per non poter più sopportare le cose indebite che occorrono tra quelli mercanti né gli basta più l'animo di udirli in confessione[114].

The fact that the evidence rendered by Guglielmo da Bologna was not vicious (at least for the role he had in Genoa), can be deduced from what Battistina Vernazza wrote some years later:

---

[111] Only in one passage Laínez deals with the possibility of using money not according to the primary purpose, but the secondary one (theory which is found in a far more problematic way – after De Vio – also in the treatise of Chiavari): "proprius usu pecuniae est servire commutationi ... ultra hunc habet secundarium, nempe lucrum ex commutatione eius cum alia pecunia" (§ 70). The source for this passage is in Aristoteles, Politica, 1257 a. On this theoretical tradition see in addition to the mentioned works by *Langholm,* the remarks by *J. Viner,* Religious Thought and Economic Society, in History of Political Economy 10 (1978), pp. 85 ff.

[112] *J. Le Goff,* Tempo della Chiesa e tempo del mercante, Torino 1977, p. 39.

[113] *R. De Maio,* Riforme e miti nella chiesa del Cinquecento, Napoli 1973, pp. 81 ff.; *M. Firpo / P. Simoncelli,* I processi inquisitoriali contro Savonarola (1558) e Carnesecchi (1566 - 1567): una proposta di interpretazione, in Rivista di storia e letteratura religiosa XVIII (1982), pp. 229 ff.

[114] *D. Gutierrez,* Testi e note sull'ultimo quadriennio del generalato di Seripando, in Analecta Augustiniana XXVIII (1965), pp. 357 - 358. A great burden for the Genoese Augustinian were the problems connected to confession: two years later, in fact, Seripando wrote to him: "et quando pur non potesse soffrire la gravezza del confessare a Genova, la priego che tenghi d'haver in mano soa tutto quel di che posso disporre io" (BNN XIII. AA. 53, c. 2 r).

Io ebbi già stretta spirituale amicizia con un R.P. teologo eremitano che si domandava maestro Fabiano Chiavario, uomo di grandissima importanza che si può dire che consigliava tutta Genova[115].

The fame and prestige of Fabiano da Genova were not restricted to his town: notwithstanding certain suspicion regarding his orthodoxy, he was held in high esteeme by Cervini[116], considered a friend of Morone[117], not to mention his long lasting relationship with Seripando[118].

His opinion was, thus, particularly authoritative, both due to his pastoral experience and the fact that he must also have previously considered those problems connected to the exchanges and economic ethics[119]. In 1556, in Rome, he published the *Tractatus de cambiis* which he dedicated to Seripando[120].

---

115 B. Vernazza, Opere spirituali, Genova 1755, vol. VI, p. 211 (letter of 10th June 1575); other references to Chiavari in vol. VI, p. 205 and vol. V, p. 218.

116 Who in these terms wrote to the Cardinals members of the Inquisition: "religioso di molta bona vita et dottrina" (ASF, Carte Cervini, 46, draft of 16th March 1555).

117 See the letter of Vincenco Ercolani published in the appendix to *B. Aquarone,* Vita di fra Jeronimo Savonarola, Alessandria 1858, vol. II, p. XXV (and on this letter see the remarks by *Firpo-Simoncelli*).

118 To put in evidence the close relationship between the two it is enough to remember what was written by Seripando to Antonio da Padova in 1555: "mai mi è venuto desiderio di tornar a Roma se non dopo che m'havete scritto ch'il p. Maestro Fabbiano vi si è fermato per procuratore dell'ordine", or, how Chiavari in sending him the Index of the forbidden books in January 1559 could comment: "siamo cascati in tempi molto pericolosi" (BNN, XIII. AA. 53, c. 67 r e c. 25 r, respectively), and see also Seripando, Diarium, cit., passim.

119 In the De cambiis he mentions a "quodam nostro alio tractatulo" not yet traced.

120 Romae, in Aedibus Antonii Bladi (there are also some copies with the indication of Vincentius Luchinus); a first and shorter draft is kept in BAV, Ottob. lat. 650. The next year, Blado reprints it, "nuperrime ad unguem recognitus"; and effectively the interventions in the text are rather numerous. In 1561 a translation into Italian of the first edition, by Antonio Maria Venosta, appears in the Compendio utilissimo di quelle cose le quali a nobili e christiani mercanti appartengono, Milano, Giovanni Antonio degli Antonij. He did not stop writing as this subject, even in his late years, and immediately before dying he published in Genoa a third edition (Genuae, apud Antonium Bellonum, 1568; there are also copies dated 1569 with only the frontispiece which differs, but in the colophon it is still 1568). A proof of its success is the inclusion of this third edition in the Tractatus universi iuris (t. VI, I: De contractibus licitis, Venetiis 1584, cc. 410 v - 419 r). In this work we will consider the first edition, comparing the different issues in an another moment (we will only quote the leaf between square parentheses). It is anyhow necessary to remember here how when in 1556 Chiavari published De cambiis, he followed it (without a frontispiece as, evidently, it was also the intention of the editor that it should be considered as a unicum, even if they are now sometimes found separate) with a Tractatus de usuris et restitutionibus attributing it to the Augustinian Gerardo da Siena. As remembered in the dedication of the De cambiis to Seripando, "cum . . . proximo anno ego essem Neapoli, tua singulari benignitate factum est ut huius libri exemplum fuerim assequutus". The interests of Seripando toward Gerardo da Siena are known, see *D. Gutierrez,* La biblioteca di San Giovanni a Carbonara di Napoli, in Analecta Augustiniana XXIX (1966), p. 188, n° 545 and see also nn° 1739 e 2328.

In this case either he or Fabiano made an error in attributing the authorship to Gerardo da Siena, as the work published by Chiavari was not written by him but by the Franciscan Pietro of Giovanni Olivi: see *D. Pacetti,* Un trattato sulle usure e le

The work is clearly divided into two parts: in the first, after a brief explanatory note on the exchange contract, he lists the "pravae adinventiones" of the Genoese businessmen; in the second part he considers the problem of how the exchange of "Bisenzone" may be lawful. If we wished to simplify matters to the extreme we could say that the overall resolution can be summarized in what Fabiano says at the beginning of the work, where he "describes" the "cambium Lugdunense aut Bezenzonense":

> Campsor, spe lucri, congruo tempore, pro singulo scuto de marcha sibi a venditore Lugduni aut Bezenzoni consignando, alio in Regno, puta Ianuae, dat et solvit ipsi venditori precium loco et tempore contractus communiter currens ... secundum varios rerum eventus, puta abundantiam et penuriam emptorum aut venditorum, vel copiam aut inopiam pecuniarum tunc ibi contingentem ... Deinde confectis et missis ipsorum cambiorum litteris, congruo tempore, huiusmodi scuti de marcha, sive potius equivalens eis, Lugduni aut Bezenzoni sibi efficaciter consignantur [c. 4r].

We put "describes" in inverted commas as, under an apparent description, the choice of the terms adopted implies the assumption of a certain kind of hypothesis rather than another, and thus leads to results which are completely different from those of Laínez or Senarega.

It is the banker who *purchases* "scudi di marche" and pays for these "scudi", in cash, a price which varies according to the conditions of the market ("secundum abundantiam et penuriam emptorum aut venditorum, vel copiam aut inopiam pecuniarum"); it is not this commodity (we will use this word even if Chiavari does not, but the concept is completely implicit as will be seen later) but an *equivalent* which will be handed over to him.

The game on forms can be considered complete: a loan contract becomes a contract of exchange, which is then identified with the most traditional (and free from implications) "emptio-venditio" contract.

Fabiano da Genova was certainly not the first to formulate this interpretation of the exchange contract: there is a long tradition both among theolo-

---

restituzioni di Pietro di Giovanni Olivi falsamente attribuito a f. Gerardo da Siena, in Archivum Franciscanum Historicum XLVI (1953), pp. 448 - 457; *A. Spicciani,* Gli scritti sul capitale e sull'interesse di fra Pietro di Giovanni Olivi, in Studi Francescani 73 (1976), pp. 289 - 325 (and at pp. 301, 313 - 314 on the edition); *Id.,* La mercatura e la formazione del prezzo nella riflessione teologica medioevale, in Atti Acc. Naz. Lincei. Memorie. Cl. di Scienze Mor. St. e filologiche S. VIII, vol. XX (1977), pp. 127 - 273. A critical edition was then published by *G. Todeschini,* Un trattato di economia politica francescana: il De emptionibus et venditionibus, de usuris et restitutionibus di Pietro di Giovanni Olivi, Roma 1980 (on which see *J. Kirshner / K. Loprete,* Peter John Olivi's treatises on Contracts of Sale, Usury and Restitution: minorite economics or minor works?, in Quaderni fiorentini per la storia del pensiero giuridico moderno 13, 1984, pp. 233 - 286). About Olivi see also *Langholm,* The Aristotelian Analysis of Usury, cit., passim. The reasons for the edition by Fabiano are to be found (in addition to the editorial policy of recovery of authors of the Order – or so considered) in the contents of the text and particularly in the theory of money, capital and interest as declared by Olivi.

gians and lawyers[121]. The interest is generated by the extension of this concept also to the kind of exchange in question (not even imaginary currency is bought, but its equivalent) and by the place which our Augustinian will give it in the second part of the work.

It is, perhaps advisable to follow his reasoning and hence confront in a more systematic way the problem of the contractual solution reached. In the first part of the treatise, Chiavari does in fact evaluate different attitudes of bankers and businessmen, which, in his opinion, were to be criticized and condemned, even if the reasons were varied and diverse.

The first example used refers to those who pass their riches round between Genoa and the fairs "nullam aliam mercaturam praeter ipsa cambia exercentes"; to which he objects that "laudabilius tamen se gererent si peractis et completis primis aut saltem secundis cambiis, illis pecuniis, aut saltem illarum pecuniarum parte, victualia et merces ad vitam et usum hominum necessaria, et ad publicum commodum opportuna compararent" [c. 5r]. In this case, taking a passage from St. Antonino against those who change the "rectum civitatis vivendi modum", Fabiano comes into line with the town-merchant tradition, ample examples of which we saw above.

The judgements that he issued against those who speculate, for different reasons, on the rates of exchanges are, therefore, of great interest: we have injustice and usury "non quo ad formam contractus, cum sit contractus emptitius, sed quo ad intentionem depravatam". There is always this underlining distinction, in Chiavari, between the "sinful" intentions (which can be condemned "in foro animae") and the formal-juridical aspects of the contracts made[122].

His critical review then moves on to analyze and criticize some concrete aspects of the financial activities "his nostris cupidissimis temporibus": they vary from the exchange contracts without letters to the different kinds of contracts made with "magnis dominis" (substantially the *asientos*), to the very mechanisms which imposed prices on the exchanges:

> quarta prava adinventio est illorum capsorum sive nummulariorum qui aut monopolio, aut colusione, aut quovis alio dolo aut fraude, arte, vel exquisito ingenio iusta cambiorum precia quovismodo augent vel imminuunt [c. 6r].

---

[121] We mention, e.g., Baldo: "Qui contractus fuit iste? videtur pecuniae emptae et venditae" (Baldi Ubaldi, Consiliorum . . ., I, nº 368, Venetis 1575, c. 113r). The partial publication of the opinion of Francesco da Treviso by Battista Trovamalla in the Summa Rosella (Papiae 1489, cc. 408v - 410r) had granted a wide diffusion, even out of the groups of lawyers, of the theory of the exchange as an *emptio-venditio* contract (one full copy of the opinion in BAV, Chigi B.V. 86, cc. 43v - 45v).

[122] See for instance this passage: "Decima prava adinventio est illorum campsorum, qui suas aliis dant pecunias ad cambium pro Lugduno, quos tamen sciunt vel probabiliter credunt scutos illos de marcha, pro quibus praefatas pecunias dederunt, non posse Lugduni solvere vel consignare. Huiusmodi enim contractus, si cessante omni alia quavis fraude celebretur, licet in se iustus sit, iniuste tamen cum paupere et non valente solvere contrahitur" [c. 9r].

Chiavari is both very accurate, and wise, in the description and condemnation of what was actually happening in the exchange fairs at that time: the economic (and also institutional) predominance of the Genoese bankers in the Besançon fairs was such that you could in fact, without moving too far away, use the term "monopoly".

Among the many examples mentioned by Fabiano da Genova (it is not necessary to analyze each one in detail) one final should be recalled, as it is useful to associate with some remarks made by Scaccia at the beginning of the 17th Century. According to Fabiano we must consider as usurers those

> qui suas dant pecunias artificibus sive navigantibus aut mercatoribus, eas in eorum artificiis aut mercimoniis expositaris, pacto tamen aut spe principali, quod salvo capitali, id quod vera cambia pro Lugduno aut Bezenzono eundo et redeundo parient, sibi consignetur [c. 7 r].

The interest of this passage lies not only in the fact that it states how there was, by that time, a certain abundance of capitals in Genoa (compared to the productive – commercial uses); but also because from this we can deduce that the system used to calculate the current rate of interest (acknowledged and legitimized by the Civil Rota) derived from a merchant practice (which was anything but peaceful in the eyes of the churchmen).

The second part of the work by Fabiano Chiavari is completely positive and contains proposals, aimed at legitimizing (and justifying) exchanges and fairs (and always with the addition of the clause "cessante omni quavis fraude"). After describing how the exchanges through letters take place, and how those of "Lione o Besanzone" can be assimilated to them, in chapter 5 he faces the real point of the problem i.e. what kind of contract was the exchange of "Besanzone". The process by which he reaches the conclusion (which we previously saw in the "description" at the beginning of the work) is a typical process of elimination: permutation, is eliminated; the hire of work is eliminated ("quia campsor non suscipit aliquam pecuniarum summam transvehendam"); he goes into detail to explain the reasons for which it could not be considered as a loan contract (the difference in type of currency, in place, the prefixed times according to which the payments are made) and restates:

> huiusmodi Lugdunense aut Bezenzonense cambium ... esse contractum emptionis et venditionis, emptione videlicet se tenente ex parte campsoris, venditione vero ex parte capientis ad cambium [c. 14 v].

Now, as De Roover correctly noted[123], through this definition it was possible to legitimize all exchange contracts (provided that the market conditions

---

123 *R. De Roover,* Cardinal Cajetan on "Cambium" or Exchange Dealings, in Philosophy and Humanism, cit., p. 432: "By defining the *cambium* contract as an *emptio venditio,* Cajetan subjected it to the rules of the just prices . . . The consequences were not immediately apparent, but they almost inevitably led to laxity and to the approval

were respected), and De Roover praised De Vio with having been the first to open this way. De Vio had actually been slightly more prudent: he in fact affirmed that it was a contract "*quasi* emptionis et venditionis"[124]; while he had discussed the "egregii cuiusdam doctoris in theologia opinio singularis", who, even if stating that the exchange was "permutatio pecuniae pro pecunia" however added "vendibile esse pecuniam a campsoribus utpote rem quamdam, et eius pretia variari sicut aliarum rerum, iuxta temporum locorumque diversitates"[125].

The consequence (and the first assumption) deriving from the assertion that the exchange contract is a sale, is that money is a commodity just like any other.

For this reason Fabiano Chiavari not only demonstrates, using different arguments (only partially taken from De Vio), that money is legally subject to sale and purchase, but also that it has an "international" price (which is not identifiable with the domestic legal rate of exchange); the consequence is that it is possible to earn money through money. In a few lines he succeeds in ridding himself of one of the most prickly problems:

> illud itaque dictum Divi Ambrosij ... quod videlicet ex pecunia pecunia non nascitur, intelligendum est in contractu mutui, ut ex ipsiusmet divi Ambrosij verbis clare elici potes. In mutui enim contractu committuntur usurae [c. 15v].

But the exchange is a purchase-sale and not a loan. But the exchange of "Bisenzone" is, also, an exchange (provided that "cessante omni fraude celebratus") and, thus, a purchase-sale;

> si ergo emptio in hoc cambio sic celebrato non iuste fit, nec etiam emptiones aut venditiones omnium aliarum quarumcumque rerum quovis modo fieri possent, et quia hoc est absurdissimum et intollerabile, ergo illud ex quo sequitur ... quod cambium Lugdunen. sive Bezenzonen ... recte ac iuste celebrari possit [c. 17v].

The demonstration, therefore, that time may be a factor changing only the number of buyers/sellers on the market (thereby varying the price of the "scudo") is taken verbatim from De Vio[126].

---

of all exchanges concluded at the just price, leaving out of the picture only fictitious exchanges, because they were based on fictitious or arbitrary rates instead of on quotations set by the market conditions".

On the role of the emptio-venditio concept see also the considerations by *O. Capitani,* L'etica economica medievale, Bologna 1974, p. 18 and p. 44, where, taking a judgement by *Noonan* (p. 317) he affirms that with the theories of De Vio we are "now out of the Middle Ages". But the above mentioned Antonio Merenda (both rigorist and careful) affirmed, by the middle of the 17th Century, that "la dottrina del Gaetano ... è la chiave di questa materia, alla barba del Navarro e di tant'altri scrittori" (see G. D. Peri, I frutti di Albaro ovvero il Negotiante ... Parte terza, Venetia Gio. Giacomo Hertz, 1673, p. 92).

[124] De Vio, De Cambiis, cit., p. 124, § 284.

[125] Ibid., pp. 108 - 109, §§ 234 and 236; on who may be the "egregius doctor" see the subsequent note.

[126] Ibid., p. 127, § 191: "tempus intermedium est occasio quod inveniantur quasi venditores; ita multum tempus intermedium est occasio multorum venditorum com-

Almost everything, now, is subject to the laws of the market (time being the sole exception)[127].

---

muniter, et paucum tempus multorum emptorum. Ac per hoc, multo interiacente tempore, propter abundantiam venditorum, rationabiliter minus datur a solventibus, qui sunt quasi ementes marchas absentes ...". Chiavari: "Intermedium ergo tempus est occasio quod inveniantur venditores sive capientes ad cambium, quo fit ut multum tempus intermedium sit occasio multorum venditorum, et paucum tempus paucorum venditorum et multorum emptorum. Iccirco multo interiacente tempore, propter abundantiam venditorum ..." [c. 19r].

This conception of the role played by time can be found also in two others Dominicans, contemporaries of De Vio: one is the mentioned Theophilo Giustiniani (BAV, Vat. Lat. 6434, c. 309r): "tal varietade de più precio o mancho precio, in tal tempo, non il causa il tempo, ma il causa lo maggior o minor bisogno in tal tempo". The other is the far more famous Silvestro Mazzolini da Prierio who, in the Summa (Bononiae, in edibus Benedicti Hectoris, 1514 - 1515 c. 664r) justified in this way the changes in value and price according to the time of payment: "non est gratia temporis, sed rei in tempore, quae aliquando plus aliquando minus valet, sicut marcha venalis Lugduni valet aliquando plus aliquando minus secundum penuriam et abundantiam venditorum vel emptorum."

Now, in Silvestro da Prierio there is also the theory of the sale-purchase of money even if the word "permutatio" is very often used: the sum of these elements would lead us to identify in him that "egregius doctor in theologia" with respect to whom De Vio makes, very often, critical remarks (op. cit., §§ 234ff., 277); rejecting, thus, the hypothesis formulated by *De Roover* (Cardinal Cajetan, cit., p. 428) according to which, on the contrary, in the passage in question it had to be seen "a reference very probably to Sant'Antonino". Sant'Antonino, effectively, is mentioned expressly by De Vio in the immediately preceding pages; there was no reason to use the expression "post praedictas opiniones, egregii cuiusdam doctoris in theologia opinio singularis occurrit", by which, on the contrary, he refers clearly to the opinions of some of his contemporaries whom he does not intend to name; and De Vio knew Mazzolini well.

At this point some problems arise: De Vio writes the De Cambiis in 1499, while the "editio princeps" of the Summa silvestrina seems to have been the one remembered of 1514 - 1515 (see *A. Serra Zanetti,* L'arte della stampa a Bologna nel primo ventennio del Cinquecento, Bologna 1958, p. 288). But, rather strangely, in the Summa the De Cambiis by De Vio is never quoted (while works which have been diffused only in their handwritten form, like the Tractatus de Pagis, by Raffaele da Pornassio, are remembered).

It is possible to hypothesize, then, that De Vio has seen either a first draft of the Summa or some other work by Silvestro da Prierio, then included in the Summa. Mazzolini, effectively, had already studied "cases" and problems of economic moral in the Quaestiones in the appendix to the Aurea Rosa (of which I could not see the edition of Hagenau 1500, quoted in *Serra Zanetti,* pp. 286 - 287); and moreover there are several elements which lead us to date the Summa earlier: for instance the 17th Century scholar Giovanni Maria Borzino (or Bolzino) in the Memorie genovesi domenicane (BAV, Vat. lat. 9451, c. 109v) remembers a handwritten copy of the Summa kept in the Genoese Monastery of S. Maria di Castello, wherefrom it resulted that the same had been completed in 1506. But far more interesting is the evidence given by another Dominican, Alberto da Castello, who in his chronicle, published in 1506, writes about Mazzolini: "multa praeclara edidit ... summa de casibus valde utilis et notabilis" (see *R. Creytens,* Les ecrivains dominicains dans la chronique d'Albert de Castello, in Archivum Fratrum Praedicatorum XXX (1960), p. 298).

It is thus possible to hypothesize that by the beginning of the 16th Century the Summa silvestrina was already known in the Dominican circles. Did, may be, another edition exist prior to the one of 1514 - 1515, as it could be supposed from the words of Alberto da Castello? Anyhow by the end of the Summa, in the mentioned edition of Bologna, there are strong words of Mazzolini against the "impudentissimos fures, qui etiam me vivente questiones nostras auree rose ... usurpare non verentur" and against the "emulos impressores": in short, the history of the editions of the works by Silvestro da Prierio is, partially, still to be made.

We now have a better understanding of the intellectual and cultural mechanisms on the basis of which in 1555 the Republic of Genoa sanctioned the exchanges made "sub certo et terminato interesse vel lucro": to agree beforehand on interest was to disregard the mechanism of the market and, thus, to completely distort the "purchase" of the "scudi di marche".

III. An antiformalistic reaction

1. Both Laínez and Fabiano Chiavari had expressed the opinion that an official judgement on the part of the Church would have been necessary, which would above all settle the disagreements in interpretation, and would give a unitarian address to a problem which, by that time, had assumed great qualitative and quantitative importance.

The judgement finally arrived: the bull by Pious V *In eam* promulgated in 1571[128]. An historical reconstruction of the works of the Commission of Cardinals that studied the document is still missing. The chairman of this Board was, probably, Cardinal Sirleto[129]. According to a report made by the Jesuit Comitoli, a very important role was performed by another Jesuit, Antonio Possevino, "cuius etiam persuasu, ut mihi is narravit, Pius V constitutionem postea adversus haec recentia cambia edidit"[130]. It is however certain that Possevino, during his stay in Lyon, studied this problem in depth, from a rather rigorist point of view[131].

The bull by Pious V (a source for endless interpretation) stands out for its desire to cut all the various forms of "dry" exchanges which had developed in the meantime. The exchanges were considered "dry" as no letters were sent; because, if mailed, there was a previous agreement to have them sent back, so that "pecunia ibi denique cum interesse reposcitur, ubi contractus fuerat celebratus". Deposit in fairs, exchanges extending from one fair to

---

127 As it has been very synthetically noted by *J. A. Goris* (p. 503) when introducing the chapter on "la morale et les affaire": "Au fond tout se réduit à la question de l'intérêt, à la question de la valeur du temps".

128 Bullarium romanum, VI, Torino 1862, pp. 884 - 885.

129 See the letter of Pedro Afan de Rivera, viceroy of Naples, dated February 1568, addressed to Sirleto, published in G. Poggiani, Epistolae et orationes, t. IV, Romae 1758, p. 459. A summary (again addressed to Sirleto) containing the "Quaestiones cambiorum tractandae in congregationibus futuris" is in BAV, Vat. Lat. 6431, c. 340r; an informative record on exchanges made in Naples, also written in 1568, in ASV, Misc. Arm. II 80, cc. 170 - 172.

130 Comitoli, Responsa moralia, cit., p. 399; in the Trattato de cambij, cit., c. 368 he wrote as follows: "quella constitutione fu fatta dal Romano Pontefice direttamente contra il cambio della ricorsa ad instanza del nostro Padre Antonio Possevino, come egli qui in Padova n'ha poi affermato".

131 G. Dorigny, Vita del P. Antonio Possevino . . . illustrata con varie note e più lettere inedite, Venezia 1759, I, p. 63; II, pp. 133ff. (who published a work by Possevino on deposit).

another, with times longer than necessary, were condemned and, obviously was set down "ne deinceps quisquam audeat, sive a principio sive alias, certum et determinatum interesse, etiam in caso non solutionis, pacisci" (not differently from that which was contained in the decree of 1555 by the Republic of Genoa).

The issue of the bull did however cause some concern in Genoa, mainly because, according to the opinion of the Government of the Republic, it was not clear "qual sia stata la sua [of the Pope] mente in materia de cambij, rispetto al tempo passato, come che la bolla ultimamente uscita non riguardi che l'avvenire". Cardinal Vincenzo Giustiniani, to whom the letter containing the preceding quotation was addressed, answered immediately inviting his fellow-citizens to be very prudent "parendomi esser negotio da non precipitarlo, ma ben maturarlo ... le cose non sono adesso in termine di tal remedio o provisione, ne far questo romore, et a mio giudizio quanto manco strepito si fa è meglio" (also because "*solo* da Genova" remarks had been made to the bull: "possiamo dimostrarle ... quanta durezza per non dire impossibilità in se contenga")[132].

The death of Pious V gave the Genoese a few faint rays of hope, who from November 1572, started again to send out feelers; between the end of April and the beginning of May 1573, it was decided to send a commission comprising three monks (one Augustinian, one Franciscan and one Dominican) to Rome, "come informatissimi del bisogno dei ... Popoli intorno alla materia dei cambij, per esporli a pieno il desiderio che universalmente si tiene d'essere liberati da la Santità Vostra da quelle cose che gli potessero dare scrupolo alla conscientia"[133].

The answer of Gregory XIII is unknown (at the present stage of the studies) also because in the papal brief which accompanied the return of the three holy men, he wrote: "nostram ipsis sententiam exposuimus, eandem his literis iterare non necessarium est; praesertim cum eam facile ab ipsis accipere possitis"[134]. The impression is that all this "negotio" was conducted with the greatest prudence, as recommended by Cardinal Giustiniani from the very beginning. There was however someone who wished to "fare

---

132 ASG, Archivio segreto 2831 (letter of the Republic dated 11th May 1571), and ASG Senato, Sala Senarega, 397 (letter of Giustiniani dated 18th May 1571).

133 From the letter of the Archbishop of Genoa to the Pope dated 5th May 1573, in ASV, Segreteria di Stato, Genova, 1; and see also ASG, Archivio Segreto 1844.

134 ASG, Archivio Segreto 1554 B (Papal brief of 26th May 1573); and see ASV, Arm. 44, t. 21, c. 265r (and at c. 265v the answer addressed to the Archbishop of Genoa). Worried, and also slightly irritated, was the milieu of the Society of Jesus, not included in the dealings: rather interesting, in this respect, is a letter by Possevino addressed to the Rector of the Genoa college, in which he reports what was learnt through Toledo: "mi ha risposto che Sua Santità concedette a quei teologi ogni autorità che poteva per assolvere dispensar et comporre per opere pie in una parte o in più con qualunque havesse trafficato cambij illiciti et questo quando i creditori fossero incerti et non conosciuti" (ARSI, Opp. NN. 257, c. 172r).

strepito" (even if perhaps he did not succeed in creating the repercussions he wanted).

2. While, in Rome, some compromise solution was being sought, a pamphlet was published in Genoa, which represented, in certain respects, a real case. It was the anonymous *Dialogo nel quale si ragiona de' cambi et altri contratti di merci: e parimenti delle fiere di Ciamberi e di Trento*[135], which notwithstanding the abundant research, still remains of uncertain paternity.

It must be excluded that the author was Cristoforo Zabata, the author of the dedication addressed to Agostino Grimaldi on 15th May 1573. And this is not only because there is also another dedication by the anonymous author to the Archbishop of Genoa, Cipriano Pallavicini, but rather because Zabata does not seem to be capable of such an intervention: in 1560 he inherited a bookshop[136], and from then on he continued to work surrounded by books in Genoa, Pavia and Venice, in the role of "gubernator et administrator in apotheca libraria"[137], editing collections of poetry or popular literature, or else writing poetry himself (often signed C. Z. L., i. e. "libraro"-"bookseller")[138]; as happened in April 1573, when he published the *Nuova Scelta di Rime* as always, through Cristoforo Bellone. An interesting character, certainly from the point of view of literary interests, but it is doubtful whether he is the author of the *Dialogo*.

In that very year Cristoforo Bellone took over from his father the only existing printing house in Genoa and found a new partner, Antonio Roccatagliata, who was then Chancellor of the Republic. Three days after the date in which Zabata dedicated the *Dialogo,* Roccatagliata was the sole printer appointed by the Republic, for the whole territory for a period of 35 years, starting from 1575, the year in which the apointment of Bellone expired[139].

Roccatagliata was now the new protagonist in the Genoese publishing world (from the managerial point of view, at least). For the moment (we shall have cause to speak of him again) let us recall that in 1556 as a young man at the beginning of his carreer as a notary, he published a pamphlet in

---

135 The title continues as follows: Ad informatione di tutti colore che trattandone desiderano saper il proprio di tal materia, in Genova, appresso Christoforo Bellone 1573.

136 ASG, Notaio Marco Antonio Morinello sc. 348, f. 1.

137 ASG, Notaio Alessandro Castagnino sc. 398, f. 2.

138 A great deal of information in *N. Giuliani,* Notizie sulla tipografia ligure sino a tutto il secolo XVI, in ASLSP IX (1869), passim; rhymes by Zabata also in the Pallavicino codex in BNF, Fondo Nazionale II. III. 473; interesting is the letter addressed to him by A. Grillo, Lettere, Venetia 1616, I, p. 586. The world of the Genoese booksellers (sometimes also editors, as in the case of Orero) is remembered by Zabata in Diporto de' viandanti, Venetia 1623.

139 ASG, Senato, Sala Senarega 1398; Archivio Segreto 818; Cancellieri di San Giorgio, 339.

the defense of the nobility of the notarial profession[140]. Could he be the author? We have no proof of it, but there again nothing to exclude it. It is certainly difficult to think that, at the same time that he was coming to an agreement with Cristoforo Bellone on the new management of the printing house, Bellone published something with which Roccatagliata did not agree. When, a few years later (after the death of Cristoforo and when his son, Marco Antonio, took his place) an inventory of the printing house was made, the *Dialogo* is always mentioned as being anonymous[141].

Palescandolo, the first (and perhaps the only one) who faced the problem of answering the *Dialogo*, disputed with anonymous "merchants"[142]. Francesco Adorno, a Genoese Jesuit who was to polemically refer to the *Dialogo* (and perhaps could have discovered something) does not say anything about the author[143]. Just as the Theatine Bernardo Giustiniani in the 1620's attributing the pamphlet to a "banchiere o cambista", was not to say anything[144]. In conclusion to this brief premise to the *Dialogo* let us just underline the fact that it came out in the vernacular, in the form of a dialogue, and in printed form. The author, and the editors, consequently, intended to have a widespread circulation: Zabata mentions this, explicitly, in the dedication: "promettendomi di potere, co'l mezzo della Stampa, far giovamento a molti"[145].

---

140 A. Iustiniani Roccataliatae, Scriba, Genuae s.n.t. [1556]. On this text and the connected problems see *G. Doria / R. Savelli*, "Cittadini di governo" a Genova: ricchezza e potere tra Cinque e Seicento, in Materiali per una storia della cultura giuridica X (1980), p. 289.

141 *Giuliani*, p. 520. The retrieval of some documents allow us to rectify the existing information on the dynasty of Bellone (see e.g. Le cinquecentine piemontesi, vol. II, ed. by *M. Bersano-Begey* and *G. Dondi*, Torino 1966, p. 326): Cristoforo Bellone, who worked under his own name in Genoa during 1573 and 1574 is the natural child of Antonio; by Maria Plazia he had Marco Antonio; that Cristoforo Bellone who worked in Turin in the same years is son of a brother of Antonio, and thus a cousin of the "Geonese" Cristoforo (who certainly died before May 1576, but probably already in 1575): see ASG, Notaio Lorenzo Pallavagna, sc. 442, f. 2 and Notaio Gio. Giacomo Merello, sc. 474, f. 1.

142 Palescandolo, Trattato de'cambi, quoted edition (see note 16), chapters 14 - 23 (Cassandro, obviously, did not manage to identify the target of Palescandolo).

143 F. Adorno, An cambium bisuntinum sit licitum, BAM, S. 103 sup., c. 336r (a further copy of the work of Adorno in the often quoted codex BAV, Vat. Lat. 6434).

144 B. Giustiniani, Breve trattato della continuatione de' cambi, Mondovì, Giovanni Gislandi e Gio. Tommaso Rossi, 1621, p. 33. In the first edition of the work (Genova, Giuseppe Pavoni 1619, p. 113) he mentions the treatises "mandati fuori da mercanti" (on these two editions see *Maffei*, art. cit., p. 336). Of great interest is the letter addressed to Cardinal Bellarmino when he sent him a copy, still hand-written, of his treatise: "vedo che mi bisogna lasciar di confessar (in Genova almeno) o aprovar quei contratti ch'io scorgo in coscienza non essere leciti, o prendermela contro gli altri confessori". He invited, then, the authoritative Cardinal to write personally on the problem of exchanges "in lingua però italiana volgare" as the works of the scholars, written in latin, "non vanno per le mani de' negotianti" (ARSI, Opp. NN. 240, cc. 291 - 292; a reference to this letter is found in *X. M. Le Bachelet*, Bellarmin avant son Cardinalat 1542 - 1598, Paris 1911, p. 89, note).

3. The most remarkable thing in this pamphlet, is the "attack strategy" used by the author, even in the dedication to Archbishop Pallavicino[146]: "Il Decretale della felice memoria di Papa Pio Quinto [avrebbe] dovuto ... chiuder la bocca, non che a una qualità di persone, poco intelligenti di tal professione, ma anche a' Predicatori, i quali informati da tali, trascorrono in far conoscere alli audienti loro non haver piena notitia di tali affari" and then adds: "mi è parso ... indirizzarlo a V.S. Reverendissima, con speranza che dove si sarà mancato per chiarir'il fatto, altri vi aggiungeranno a informatione di coloro quali né per pratica né per theorica non arrivano a intendere le qualità de' Cambi" [p. 6].

The controversy was aimed at the clergymen – confessors, theologians – whose opinions "hoggidì sono tali e tanto in sè diversi che confondono (temo) se stessi e il mondo insieme". To understand the attitude of the author of the *Dialogo* (and of his customers) there are no words better than those already mentioned which were to be used, a few decades later, by the Theatine Duardo, to dispute this pamphlet and polemize against those merchants, "qui de hac re tractatus ediderunt et typis dederunt, audentes de justitia cambij disputare ac determinare, cum litteras ignorent. Et recusantes thelogorum et canonistarum iudicium se submittere"[147]. The author was not ignorant of "letters" actually, but he objected to the confused and contradictory intervention by the churchmen in the world of business, mainly because it was confused and contradictory[148].

The first pages in the *Dialogo* are aimed at demonstrating the usefulness of trade (and its necessity, in a town like Genoa) and then indicating the problem of the different practical ways in which it is performed:

> e se direte che i setaiuoli non dovrebbero ... comprare a tempo; io vi rispondo che non si deve così a fatto restringere le forme e i modi con i quali, e con l'*industria* e con il *credito* il mondo si è sempre governato da molti secoli in qua, per volontà elettiva e non forzata[149].

---

145 Dialogo, cit., p. 3 (from now on only the page in square parentheses will be quoted).

146 Even more controversial would be this dedication if we could believe completely what the Barnabite Antonio di Sansalvatore affirmed (some years later), with respect to Pallavicino: "dannava tutti i cambij di fiera e la ricorsa insieme" (A. Sansalvatore, Trattato della ricorsa e continuatione de cambi, Lucca O. Guidoboni 1620; on which see *Maffei*, art. cit., p. 336).

147 See § I note 17.

148 "E' piu' inconveniente che i confessori consentano et assolvino parte tutti e parte parte delli negocianti in cambij, e parte biasmano qualche qualità de'cambij, e parte li biasmano tutti a fatto; e con tutto ciò io vedo che li trattanti in tutte le qualità de' Cambij ordinariamente si confessano e sono assoluti, e che loro Confessori così assentono, e chi potrebbe provedere di qualche digesta e buona risolutione, non provede e perciò si vive con biasmo e risico di tutti, nella confusione che se ne vede" [p. 11].

149 Dialogo, p. 17 (my italics). Testimony of the controversy on the credit to the town manufacturing sector is the Ristretto di quanto disse f. Alessandro Franceschi

Let us stress how this connection between legal credit and freely chosen credit began to appear ("per volontà elettiva e non forzata") as this was to be one of the hinges on which the whole *Dialogo* turned.

As we go on, however, we find further justification of the selling "ad tempus" (or of recourse to credit). A further important theme of the moral-theological debate beginning from the middle ages was, as we know, that concerning the right price (and the ordinary price). Note how elegantly the author combines these two themes:

> dico che il prezzo ordinario et honesto dovrà essere quello al quale la maggior parte di quella merce, in quella stagione, per li trattanti ordinarij in quella merce, in quella città si vende; e però se le sete o lane, o altro che si sia, si venderanno per un prezzo, in pluribus, a tempo due Fere, io chiamerò quello essere il prezzo ordinario [p. 19].

Obviously the Author (not being ignorant in letters) knows that in this kind of contract the question of the sale *of* time (which cannot be sold) might be involved; but it is impossible to distinguish, openly, between those who sell "ad tempus" since they remain within the ordinary procedures of the market, and those who, on the contrary, sell "a più tempo del corso ordinario"; thus "consentendosi la prima forma a dannandosi la seconda, io non vedo che vi si possa fare regola certa, né legge sopra: qual'hora che il caso e le intentioni possono essere diverse, poichè la intentione giudica l'huomo". And it is at this point that the author of the *Dialogo* sets down a further basic principle in his argument:

> Io per me crederei che ciascuno in simili casi potesse o dovesse essere giudice della intentione e della conscienza sua [p. 20][150].

I would say that what seems to be most important in this *Dialogo* (beside the specific theorization on the problem of the exchanges) is, first of all, this will to express secular and individualistic ethics on business matters, duly separated from the restraints of the Church[151].

Secondly, the whole *Dialogo* is permeated by an antiformalistic reaction, which is probably connected to this theory of the supremacy of the individual conscience:

---

attorno al vendere a tempo, predicando nel Duomo di Genova il sabbato avanti la domenica delle palme nel 1572, in BAV, Vat. Lat. 4666, cc. 1 - 4.

150 The concept is stressed also when it exemplifies the more thorny case of the sale "ad tempus" of food-stuffs: if "il vender a tempo grano non habbia altra intentione salvo di smaltire e non per cavarne più prezzo. Mi ridurrei anche in questo a dire che la intentione e la propria conscientia doverebbe essere il vero giudice" [p. 20].

151 "Se voi mi volete stringere a che io vi parli da Teologo per consultare la vostra conscienza meco; io vi dirò, Voi sarete mal cauto a credere a me idiota et io presontuoso a parlarvi fuori della mia professione, e saprei soggiongere che non solo il non trattar de' cambij, né anche in altra sorte di mercantia, né trafichi; ma che lo appartarsi affatto degli affari del mondo, e il ritirarsi in uno heremo, sarebbe molto più cauto; e che neanche in tutto ciò si sarebbe sicuro senza la gratia e misericordia di Nostro Signore; ma volendo stare nel mondo e traficare . . ." [p. 24].

mi torna a proposito per hora brevemente dire la natura de' contratti pecuniari essere molta, però sotto diversi nomi e sotto diverse specie, molti da molti approvati, e molti da molti reprovati; fatti però tutti de denari, con oggetto principale di cavarne, non dirò denari, per mutar vocabolo, ma dirò per cavarne utile e commodo.

As we can see, the author is also capable of subtle irony. But let us follow his reasoning:

Alcuni si chiamano redditi annuali, censi, monti ... cambji con mandare lettere ... altri vi sono senza mandar le lettere, che alcuni dicono secchi; altri che si domandano Depositi et similia. In ristretto, io credo, che mantenere si potesse che il tutto sia pane d'una pasta, e che la intentione e l'effetto sia tutto uno; però sotto diverse forme e vocaboli; e che il nome né la forma, come alcuni tengono, non varia punto l'effetto né l'intentione de li contrahenti [p. 25].

Obviously such an antiformalistic (and also anti-juridical) position could have nothing other than disruptive effects on the whole theorization of the exchange contracts. The Author does not simply limit himself to discuss exchanges in general, he does not try to systemize thing, but directly faces up to one of the most common problems of the time (and one on which tradition was greatly divided): that "cambio usitato da huomini e da donne", by who "ha nella sua casa diece mila scudi, non sa, non può o non vuole far mercantia" and invests them in exchanges. Thus, "non haveva bisogno alcuno de' denari nella Fera; e solo se gli ha rimessi per arbitrio et per oggetto di guadagnare". The "formality" of whether a letter was sent or not would change the exterior characteristics of the contract, but not the will of those involved in it. Now, following the decree by Pious V which permitted the effective exchanges "cum missione litterarum", our keen and intriguing author observes that it will no longer be possible to object "che per via di cambio reale il denaro non possi guadagnare denaro". But, then, perhaps the position on the problem of exchanges "without letters" can be modified:

dico che alcuni argumentano ch'essendo permessa l'intentione e l'effetto dell'altro cambio [with letter], che questo [without letter] differente solo in la forma, si havrebbe similmente a permettere, dato che da Theologi il primo sia chiamato cambio reale, chiamandolo contractus emptionis et venditionis; poichè questo e tutto il resto sono forme, ma alla verità poi lo effetto e l'intentione dicono essere tutt'una [p. 36][152].

The question, and answer, that he puts to theologians and confessors is clear and alarming:

Domando hora a voi se havemo a credere che la intentione e lo effetto sia quella che habbia d'approvare o riprovare il cambio, o pur la forma? So che per ragione mi hareste a dire le intentione e lo effetto; perchè la forma sia scorza et non spirito;

[152] And see p. 39: "et se questo segue e che in Fera non vi accada numeratione alcuna di denari, perchè non vi fu altra intentione ne i contraenti, salvo che per via di cambio il credito e il debito ritorni a Genova; a che serve dicono la forma, che si battezza contractus emptionis et venditionis, poichè non vi è né fine né intentione d'alcuna esigentia, né in l'uno né in l'altro cambio."

anchora che molti moderni vogliono che proceda la forma e che questa basti [p. 37][153].

Perhaps we have made excessive use of quotations, but we thought it necessary to present, as faithfully as possible, the thought of this unknown author (was he a merchant? a lawyer? a clergyman?) who differs so much from the whole tradition and who is, in some aspects, a *unicum* in the Italian scenario of the 16th Century.

A *unicum* both because of his capacity of linking up with the previous doctrinal tradition and because of his capacity of transferring new elements of the theory of usury through this controversy. In this dialogue notwithstanding its simple aspect, of a work which does not intentionally want to give any doctrinal contribution, we do, in fact, enter into the dangerous domain of doctrine. The author states: "io vi ho detto che non so né devo rispondervi da Teologo né intrare a distinguere qual sia precetto di Dio nostro Signore, e qual sia consiglio" [p. 40]; but he has all the same introduced this distinction[154]; and how, then, can we fail to remember the proclaimed and clear supremacy of the individual conscience?

This work, rather strangely, excaped the notice of the Congregation of the Index; otherwise it would have met the same end as those written by Sansalvatore or by Basilio Alemanni, which were certainly far less "heterodox" than this *Dialogo*[155].

The author was well aware of the fact that such a clear and unusual discussion about the exchange contract also obviously implied a confrontation with a consolidated doctrinal tradition on the theme of usury. With great skill he had already made some preliminary statements in describing the normal procedures between the parties involved in an exchange contract:

---

[153] See what was noted by *Palescandolo* (p. 130): "stimano male alcuni marcadanti, i quali donano il tutto all'intentione e dicono che i contratti pecuniarii son ben di molti et varii nomi, ma tutti fatti di danari ... Talchè la diversità tra di loro sarà solo di vocabuli e di forme o modelli, ch'importa solo la scorza della cosa ... Diciamo dunque che dicono molto male, perciochè le diverse forme ne' contratti danno loro diverso essere e diversa sostanza, essendo la forma sostanza ed essere della cosa e non la scorza". And Francesco da Treviso already resorted to this principle (c. 408 v): "contractus debet iudicari secundum eius formam et apparentiam".

[154] This distinction is widely used by Du Moulin (Tractatus, cit., p. 38, § 88) who takes it, identical, from Aepinus (c. 29 v). On the concept (with special reference to Francisco de Vitoria) see *Langholm,* The Aristotelian Analysis of Usury, cit., pp. 18 - 19.

[155] In December 1624 both the quoted treatise by Sansalvatore and the anonymous Discorso e parere d'un theologo intorno al cambio della ricorsa con se stesso (Milano, G. B. Bidelli, 1623) were included in the Index: see *Reusch,* II, p. 848. The author of the anonymous treatise was probably the Jesuit Basilio Alemanni, as it has been indicated on the copy of the Biblioteca Naz. Braidense in Milano (press-mark: F. VII. 272). This is the reason for which *U. Gobbi,* L'economia politica negli scrittori italiani del secolo XVI - XVII, Milano 1889, p. 259, mentioned it under the name of Alemanni, while *De Roover,* (L'évolution, cit., p. 172) affirmed "nous n'avons pas trouvé trace ailleurs" (a further copy has been indicated by *Maffei,* p. 336).

> In pluribus chi dona a cambio fida o crede fidare a persone più ricche o tanto ricche come esso datore, li quali ricchi non pigliano a cambio per necessità necessaria ma per elettione, pretendendo loro di straricchire con il credito et con il denaro del compagno, quale occupano, oltre le loro facultà, in qualche qualità de negocij, dove pretendono guadagnar più di quello credano poter perdere nel cambio che pigliano [pp. 34 - 35].

Any description begins with the assumption of a prospect, and this leads us directly to consider the exchanges as contracts between rich people (between rich people, it must be said, and not only between merchants: here the professional qualification is, replaced by the degree of wealth, by the "credit"); rich people who make investments and trade "in una effettuale mercantia qual si fa di denari". In fact, it can be safely said that:

> per ordinario è vanità parlare che i poveri sentano interesse in detta qualità de' cambij [p. 35].

We thus find ourselves in an autonomous field of contracts which have nothing to do with the "dreaded" loan:

> né si può né si deve chiamare mutuo, né io credo si trovi legge alcuna qual faccia obligato l'huomo a mutuare il suo gratis ad alcuno, quale per bisogno elettivo e per arbitrio, e non per necessità lo ricerchi a chi tal volta possiede manco di lui [p. 35][156].

As we can see the traditional view has now been turned on its head: the borrowers are the rich (and certainly not the poor) and they do it freely and to make money. The separation between those contracts which are typical of the business world and the problems of helping the poor people, is thus put simply:

> mi dirà alcuno, dunque ai poveri costituti in necessità non è provveduto. Risponderò, Messer sì, ma per altre forme delle quali non è di nostro proposito ragionare per hora, e non per via del cambio [p. 35].

Evidently he did not think these considerations sufficient, and then he returns again to the argument, and directly tackles the problem of the difference which, in his opinion, exists between an exchange contract made "tra persone ricche e per elettione di tutte le parti" and usury:

> qui sta la difficultà in conoscere e decidere qual sia usura prohibita: perchè per me ... tengo che il negocio del cambio non sia prohibito dalla legge ... e non manco alla [sic] carità christiana, se si ha da considerare la forma e la intentione [p. 41].

The distinction between the two worlds is now clear: on the one hand business and contracts and on the other the charity and "l'intentione" i.e. the world of conscience[157].

---

[156] Extraordinary is the resemblance with the dialogue by Thomas Wilson (p. 242): "for what reason is it, that I should lende freely to every man a like? . . . I do thinke no reason, nor lawe of god or men, wil enforce me to it". But the possible source in common is perhaps Du Moulin, Tractatus, cit., § 71: "non hoc vult Christus, ut cuilibet quavis ratione petenti demus".

Then what is usury? here the *Dialogo* expresses a view dominated by a limited view of the usury: in "old times" usury was present when the debtor, unable to return the capital, had to give the creditor his own children as servants; in "present times" the examples are different and always concern situations in which whoever borrows money is subject to contractual conditions which impose limits on their own personal freedom[158], or in which the price of goods to be delivered by the harvest time is "tale che evidentemente vi sia il pregiudicio del pigliatore del denaro". But above all usury is:

> il prestare il suo a chi ha bisogno necessariamente a tanto per cento il mese o l'anno, con essere sicuro del capitale e dell'interesse, sopra un pegno equivalente et in sua mano ...
> il vendere le sue vettovaglie a più prezzo di quello che vagliono a denari per ragion del tempo a chi ne ha bisogno per il viver suo e della famiglia [pp. 41 - 42].

Usury therefore involves all forms of loan made to persons who are in need, i. e. to the poor. We are therefore outside the world of business.

But this kind of distinction brings us back to the work of Du Moulin, who throughout Europe had expanded some of the ideas of the German reformer Johann Höck (Aepinus). The latter had grouped men in three different social categories: the poor, i. e. those who own nothing, and to whom alms must be given; the needy, to whom interest-free loans must be made (and according to Aepinus' theory only for this second category was the Evangelic commandment valid: "ad hunc secundum ordinem referendae sunt divinae leges de mutuo et usuris ... quae significanter loquuntur de indigentibus, non de omnibus"); the rich, who make contracts subjected to the Civil Laws ("ea licebit sequi, quia Christus non abolet veteres politicas ordinationes, neque condit novas, nec arrogat sibi politica iudicia, sed committit civilium rerum cognitionem legibus et politicis ordinationibus")[159].

---

157 And continues as follows: "né in modo alcuno questa qualità di trafico pecuniario si può né si deve chiamar mutuo, non che usura; ma neanche io trovo che l'huomo sia obligato, havendo per lui e per gli affari suoi bisogno, mutuare il suo ad altri, dato che ne avessero bisogno, e molto manco quando non per necessità ma per arbitrio piglino in qualsivoglia delli modi soprannominati a cambio".
We have to compare, in this respect, the considerations made by Lüthy on some aspects of the thoughts of Calvino: "De deux choses l'une: qu'on n'admette pour règle de vie économique que la loi de charité, et alors qu'on ferme le marché: ou qu'on admette le marché, mais alors qu'on ne prétende pas qu'il est régi par la loi du don gratuit. Le *mutuum date nihil sperantes* ne vise pas les échanges économiques" (*Lüthy*, II, p. 760).

158 Differently from what happens in case a person goes bankrupt due to the exchanges: "resta in osservanza che un fallito non solo dona né se stesso né i figli per schiavi al creditore, ma fatta conoscere la sua impotenza ... pagando quella poca parte che può et alle volte quella poca parte che vuole per pura malitia; resta per ordinario e dalla cortesia de i creditori e dalla legge assoluto." [p. 42].

159 Aepinus, In psalmum XV Davidis, cit. cc. 27 v - 28 v; and see c. 31 r: "ex praedictis enim fit clarum praecepta Christi de mutuo et elemosyna non pertinere ad tertium ordinem, eaque quae inter homines eius ordinis mutuo dantur, sponte absque necessitate ex officio amicitiae dari, eisque mutuum posse denegari sine conscientiae periculo". But see also, e. g., what Melanchthon affirmed (another author frequently used

Du Moulin adhered exactly to this triadic distinction (admitting however his debt to Aepinus), and confirmed the subordination of the "actus negociationis" to the law and to the civil judges[160].

It is difficult now to hypothesize as to whether some of the ideas of the *Dialogo* reached its author directly from his reading of works like that of Aepinus, or, which seems more probable, through the intermediation by Du Moulin who has by then well known in Genoa, or perhaps they were the result of a fully autonomous elaboration. The similarity is, nevertheless, remarkable. In certain aspects, the *Dialogo* make a further simplification, making a distinction between only two fields of activity: that of charity and the economic one, but the basic sense is the same.

The last pages of the *Dialogo* are, then, devoted to a brief exposition of those problems connected to the "deposit" (this too is "una forma di negocio volontario e non forzato, il quale si faceva effettualmente fra persone ricche e potenti") which had been condemned by the bull by Pious V[161]; and thus, in a rather polemic (and ironic) way, it recalls how following the advice of "Padri theologi" it was decided to hold the exchange fairs alternatively in Chambery and in Trento[162], so that payment did not take place "in eodem loco": "al che fu per molti avvertito ed adherito volentieri, stante che in tal *forma* [!] ubidivano al Decretale di Sua Santità, si come erano obligati, et insieme provedevano al particolar commodo loro" [p. 47].

IV. The "Decisiones Rotae Genuae de Mercatura"

1. Times, however, were not yet ripe for taking such a clear ideological stance. Even Du Moulin, who was considered one of the greatest innovators in the scenario of the 16th Century juridical culture, had been so extremely traditionalistic on the topic of the exchange fairs, the "impiae usurae lugdunenses", that he was used (or rather: quoted) by Nicola Senarega, on rigorist positions. The fact, then, that no detailed answers to the *Dialogo* have been found, is somewhat disconcerting: the number of copies kept in the libraries proves that the book was circulated, and in the right places (one copy was in the library of Angelo Giustiniani, the Franciscan Bishop of

by Du Moulin): "iudicium de contractibus non pertinet ad privatos homines aut docentes Evangelium. Tota res ad magistratus reiicienda est. Is debet pronuntiare, qui contractus sunt probandi ... Itaque non est permittendum concionatoribus, ut sibi sumant iudicium de contractibus ..." (Commentarii in aliquot politicos libros Aristotelis, 1530, in Corpus reformatorum, XVI, Halis Saxonum 1850, p. 430).

160 Du Moulin, Tractatus, cit., §§ 85 - 90, pp. 37 ff.; for the diffusion of this distinction see how Wilson (in his dialogue) made the "lawyer" use it as his own (without mentioning Du Moulin, who is, on the contrary, remembered by the "civilian": Wilson, pp. 236, 242, 343).

161 *Mandich,* Le pacte de ricorsa, cit., pp. 172 ff.

162 On the transfer to Trent see ASG, Senato, Sala Senarega 1393.

Geneva)[163]. References, in printed works, appeared very late and, strangely enough, were hardly controversial. It almost seems as though silence was chosen as the means of answering the provocation. In any case we must give to the anonymous Genoese due credit for having pin-pointed the problem.

The fact of the matter is that such a work served only for cultural and ideological discussions; and in Italy, in the period after the Council of Trent, it had a very limited market. This was also because a numerous and powerful category of potential users would not only have been able to identify with it, but they would not even have appreciated it very much. I am referring to lawyers (both barristers and judges). A book such as the *Dialogo* did not serve any purpose: on the one hand it was antiformalistic and on the other to follow such teachings may not have been wise, as Scaccia was to point out: "est ... haec matéria cambiorum periculosa". Basically barristers, judges and businessmen themselves needed something different.

This "something different" was again provided for them by the printing house managed by Antonio Roccatagliata, which, between the end of 1581 and the beginning of 1582 published the famous *Decisiones Rotae Genuae de Mercatura*. Since different hypotheses have been made both on the "double and simultaneous" edition (Genoa and Venice) and on the name of the editor, perhaps we should now add some order to the certain facts and use them as a foundation to formulate some hypotheses[164].

Let us first consider the more material aspects of the volume: both the text and the indexes are identical in all the copies, and all at c. 270r (at the end of the text and before the beginning of the new quire with the index) have "Genuae M.D.LXXXI.", which is clear proof that the text was printed in Genoa and completed before the end of 1581. The differences are contained in the first four leaves (not present in all copies and not mentioned in the "registrum") which contained the frontispiece, the dedication to Nicolò Doria, the Doge who was about to leave office, and the rights (four for Antonio Roccatagliata and two for Francesco Ziletti, the latter dated 6th January 1582). The basic difference, which has brought about the problem, is the frontispiece: in some copies the frontispiece was printed in Venice by Ziletti, and in others in Genoa by Roccatagliata. As has been hypothesized, some copies of this volume were distributed in Genoa, and some in Venice[165], but the book was conceived and printed in Genoa[166].

---

[163] BAV, Vat. Lat. 6434 (see I note 50).

[164] *A. Neri*, Una società tipografica in Genova nel secolo XVI, in Giornale Ligustico di Archeologia Storia e Letteratura, XIX (1892), pp. 458 - 466 (which is still the best documented article); *N. Calvini*, Una strana cinquecentina genovese: Decisiones Rotae Genuae de mercatura, in La Berio VIII (1968), pp. 24 - 29; *G. Petti-Balbi*, Le edizioni genovesi del Cinquecento, in Società Savonese di Storia Patria, Atti e memorie NS. IX (1975), p. 86.

[165] We do not know exactly, up to now, whether this was a consequence of the disagreement between Roccatagliata and Marc'Antonio Bellone. It is anyhow sure that

But who made and edited it? The first rights of 1578 - 1579 lead us in the right direction: "Antonio Roccatagliata ... nella sua stampa che ha in Genova sotto nome di Marc'Antonio Bellone". The misunderstanding existing about a possible editorship by Bellone arose (as Neri has clearly demonstrated) from the fact that in the right granted him by the Grand Duke of Florence, Bellone is mentioned as "I. U. C.", while the request had been made by Roccatagliata according to the above mentioned formula[167]. We have already considered how Roccatagliata had obtained the appointment as printer from the Republic and how in 1573 came to be a partner of Cristoforo, father of Marco Antonio. We do have a document, however, from 1577, which gives us some information on the structure of the company. The company's capital was composed of four shares: two of which belonged to Roccatagliata, one to Marco Antonio Bellone and one to Luigi Portelli, and "si dovrà stampare sotto nome di Marc'Antonio Bellone"[168].

Roccatagliata's climb appears evident at this point: after obtaining the appointment, previously held by Bellone, he becomes a partner in the company, invests enough in it to hold 50% of the capital and, subsequently, evidently invests more and renovates completely the printing house, so that in the documents we find mention of the *"stamparia di"* [printing house of] Antonio Roccatagliata, even if, up to 1578, the editions were issued (as set down in the contract) "under the name of Marc'Antonio Bellone'[169]. The reasons why the name of Roccatagliata should not appear (or it was more convenient for him not to appear) derive from the fact that he was still Chancellor of the Republic, a member of the patrician class and could, thus,

---

the connections between Genoese and Venetian editors were not infrequent. Already in 1568, for instance, the Stanze di diversi eccellenti poeti (one copy in BAV, Capponi IV. 233) are printed in the printing house of Antonio Bellone, edited by Zabata: though on the frontispiece there are the "Geonese" indications, by the end of the volume we find, printed: "In Venetia ad instantia di Cristoforo Zabata".

Documents still remained, on the basis of which Roccatagliata, in 1585 and in 1586, commits himself not to print in Genoa works published by Giolito and by Giunta, as still in 1596 he commits himself to the heirs of Sperone Speroni (ASG, Notaio Gabriele Pilo, sc. 460, ff. 2 and 4).

166 In some warehouse in Venice a great quantity of copies printed in 1581 must have remained. In fact the Decisiones were put on the market again in 1599 with a new frontispiece (the third one,!): Decisionum perillustris Rotae genuensis; Collectanea fidelissima . . . In quibus ea praesertim tractata et discussa sunt, quae ad mercaturam conferunt, Venetiis Apud Baretium & Socios, 1599 (one copy in Biblioteca Nazionale Roma: 202.10.K.10).

167 *Neri,* p. 465. Also in consideration of the copy BCB, F. Ant. Gen. C. 42, on the frontispiece of which Bellone's name, handwritten, appears, I had hypothesized that he might have had a role in the editorial design of the volume (see *Savelli,* La Repubblica, cit., p. 88, note). But, at this point, I would exclude it.

168 *Giuliani, p. 517.*

169 ASG, Notaio Gio. Giacomo Merello, sc. 474, f. 1; Notaio Alessandro Castagnino, sc. 398, f. 2 (in a document of March 1578, L. Portelli is indicated as "administrator stampariae nobilis Antonij Roccataliatae").

be damaged by the personal exercise of such an activity, due to the existence of those laws which prohibited the "mechanical arts" to such a class.

For this reason his name neither appeared during nor after the break with Bellone: up to 1585 (the year in which he associated with Bartoli) the books printed in Genoa did not bear the name of the printing house. He obtained the appointment for a period of thirty five years, but could not appear as editor.

The work, was, thus, conceived (with remarkable editorial engagement) at this stage (1578 - 1579); it was completed only in 1581 - 1582. In the meantime there was not only the well known breakdown in the relationship between Roccatagliata and M.A. Bellone[170]; but also the plague which raged between 1579 and 1580 and in that period, even if at a reduced pace, the printing house continued to be active[171]. Since no documentary verification on the edition of this volume has so far been found[172], it only remains to make some hypotheses about its compiler and/or deviser.

One element to be considered and, may be, of support is the dedication of the work; this too, unfortunately, is completely anonymous. This fact excludes, however, that the address to Nicolò Doria, the Doge in charge, could be made by a commoner, like Portelli (or Bellone, should he still have been in Genoa). The author of this dedication was certainly a person well known to the addressee, so that he did not deem it necessary to add his signature.

And this fact leads us to consider again, even if only briefly, Antonio Roccatagliata. He had held the position of Chancellor of the Republic for a long time, and had, recently, given up this position (as according to the *Leges novae* of 1576, he could not remain in this position after 17th March 1581). On 2nd October 1581 he was requested to write the annals of the Republic[173]. It is therefore probable that the dedication (dated 1st October 1581) is by Roccatagliata a kind of testimony of his long and fruitful stay in the Chancery, and an expression of gratitude to the Doge, who had also almost reached the end of his mandate[174].

---

170 *Giuliani*, pp. 286ff.

171 "Le cose della stamparia vano a male", wrote Roccatagliata to his colleague Alessandro Castagnino in November 1579, informing him about what was being printed and requesting opinions and suggestions (ASG, Notaio Giudiziari 479). Evidently Castagnino had some role in the partnership, as will happen with another notary, Gabriele Pilo, who was also a collaborator of Roccatagliata (as vice-chancellor), and friend (ASG, Notaio Stefano Sovero, sc. 581, f. 1, from the will of Roccatagliata).

172 I think, for instance, of a contract like the one made on the occasion of the publication in 1594 of the Italian translation of the Mémoires by Commynes, edited by the Genoese lawyer Lorenzo Conti (ASG, Notaio Giulio Priaruggia, sc. 438, f. 13). About Conti see the article I wrote for DBI, XXVIII, pp. 444 - 446 and Tra Machiavelli . . ., cit., pp. 266ff.

173 See the autograph manuscript of the Annali in ASG, Manuscript 63; and ASG, Archivio Segreto 827.

There is, then, a further element which leads us to believe that Roccatagliata did not only sign the dedication of the *Decisiones,* but that he was also one of the devisers, if not "the" deviser, of this collection. Who, in fact, could have access to the judgements of the Civil Rota if not the parties, the judges (who anyhow held the position for such a short period), and the lawyers? Notaries, who, for a long period of their career, performed the role of chancellors at magistratures and offices, including in fact the Civil Rota. The father of Antonio, Girolamo Roccatagliata had already held the position of chancellor of the Rota[175]. It did not appear (on the basis of the acts still remaining) that our secretary had also followed this curriculum.

The study of the so-called *Pandetta combustorum* (effectively an inventory of the files of notaries in the first half of the 17th Century)[176] has informed us about an activity performed by Antonio simultaneously to that of notary: he was chancellor of the deputy "Podestà", of the "Straordinari" and also of the Civil Rota – there were, in the 17th Century, two "foliatia" which covered the period 1557 - 1565. In short, he had a very direct experience of the operation of civil justice and of the Civil Rota.

The access, then, to the Chancery of the Senate opened the last door to him, should he have needed it, to collect judgements. Finally, to this "antiquario benemerito" (according to the definition given to him by the erudite Federico Federici in the first half of the 17th Century) we can also attribute, hypothetically, the merit of collecting and editing the *Decisiones* of the Genoese Civil Rota[177].

---

174 That Antonio Roccatagliata had a prominent role in the organization of the chancery appears evident from the "service orders" dated 30th April 1580, which shares the duties among the chancellors (ASG, Senato, Sala Senarega 1440).
The duty of "custos archivii et scripturarum publicarum" was assigned to him also for a period subsequent to the end of his mandate (see the decree dated 27th January 1581 in ASG, Archivio Segreto 827). The envy aroused by such preference is made evident by an anonymous letter in which he was accused of being a "tiranno" and a "volpe" (ASG, Senato, Sala Gallo, 706).

175 ASG, Notai Giudiziari 123 - 153.

176 ASG, Segreteria. See *M. Bologna,* 1684 Maggio 17: Le perdite dell'archivio del collegio dei notai di Genova, in ASLSP XCVIII (1984), p. 272.

177 The judgement by F. Federici is in Alberi Genealogici, Biblioteca Franzoniana, Genova, Ms. Urb. 128, c. 220r; mention of the relationship between Federici and Roccatagliata in *Doria-Savelli,* Cittadini, cit., p. 343. The edition of the Annali (far different from the quoted autograph) is dated 1873. There is no study on his activity as scholar and collector of the country's memories: his manuscripts were an important source for the Genoese scholars of the first half of the 17th Century. We must also remember that in August 1583 he was called to be a member of the Commission in charge of the revision of the Civil Statutes (which will be published 1587): see G. Pallavicino, Inventione . . . di scriver tutte le cose accadute alli tempi suoi (1583 - 1589), Genoa 1975, p. 9. Rector on the Board of Notaries (five times in the period between 1575 and 1604: ASG Notai ignoti 429, and *G. Costamagna,* Il notaio, cit., pp. 285 - 286) he was appointed in many important administrative and government roles (governor in 1594, procurator in 1597, again governor in 1607). He died on 25th February 1608.

It is hard to establish whether the idea of the collection was essentially one of his own, but it is safe to assume that he elaborated it certainly in the spring of 1575, in the turbulent period of civil conflict in Genoa, when the whole institutional organization of the Republic was called into question; and yet another anonymous writer submitted a project to the Senate to reform the Republic, in which we find also this suggestion:

> Che si debba elleger ... tre ... i quali habbino cura di riveder tutte le decisioni fatte per la rotta dell'anno del 28 in qua, e investigar tutti quelli casi che havessero havuto la esecutione con due sentenze conforme, quale si debbano ponere in stampa, acciò che sempre che capitassi dinanzi alla rota o a qualsivogli magistrato cause conformi a quelle che havessero havuto la loro esecutione, essa Rota e così tutti li altri magistrati habbino da giudicar conforme a quelle[178].

The project, as we can see, is very interesting, both as it underlines circulation through the press and because it proposes an original way of introducing some sort of limitation for the judge analogous to the binding precedent: an obligation not to issue decisions different from a couple of previous conforming decisions.

But if in the dedication made by Roccatagliata to the *Decisiones* we find no reference to this idea that the respect of a previous judgement was mandatory, we find certain other indications which can shed light on the reasons and characteristics of the work. The first one underlines the utility of this edition for the Genoese:

> Utilissimae Genuensibus erunt illae quae de mercimonijs atque de mercatura tractant, nam eam praecipue illos docuit necessitas, qua doctor nullus est praestantior.

The fact that the Genoese had a predilection for the commercial activities was well known; what is interesting is how widespread the *topos* of the "necessitas" was: the Genoese could only do business (due to the sterility of their region). What was the contribution given by the collection of the *Decisiones* to the diffusion of this *topos* (which we have already found in Scaccia)?

We find, then, a reference, very generical in appearance, to the criteria followed in the publication:

> et licet multa fortasse in eis resecari potuissent, et nonnulla tolli, sive quia repetita sint, sive alia ratione, placuit tamen hoc agendum sapientibus relinquere, et ita integras proponere, ut omnes ab omnibus videri possint.

At present it is practically impossible to say which criteria were followed for the selection of the judgements. There no longer exists (if indeed one

---

178 The text published in *Savelli,* La Repubblica, cit., p. 265. Not everybody had the same faith in the judges of the Rota: another anonymous writer of projects in that same period, in fact, recommended taking away from the Civil Rota the commercial judgements, and returning them to an office formed by merchants: "è più conveniente che li fatti mercantili da mercanti siano intesi" (the project in BAV, Barb. Lat. 5303, cc. 49 - 62; and see *Savelli,* pp. 104 - 105).

ever did exist) a unitary file of the Civil Rota, but there are two series which are reciprocally heterogeneous. The first, which we have already mentioned, is composed of the documents filed at the "Notai Giudiziari" of ASG, wherein the trial acts only are kept separate and grouped according to the chancellor who prepared them. The second series (not yet completely put in order) consists of almost forty volumes in which judgements of the Civil Rota are grouped (at an uncertain date).

It is not only a very complicated matter to follow a suit in its entirety, but the judgements which can still be traced are only a collection, and, also, a collection which seems to be completely lacking in material for the first half of the 16th Century. The first volume, in fact, begins in 1563.

The selection criteria which were certainly followed in the edition, are those giving privilege to those issues which can be defined as being closely related to merchant-law (within a wider range of material), and then reproducing the judgements, in their integrity (as stated in the dedication of the *Decisiones*)[179].

But what, and how much, was rejected? Why were certain judgements selected instead of others? Was an ideological-cultural uniformity criterion followed? Were some issues privileged? It is impossible to answer all these questions (unless, of course, new findings complete the scarceness of elements mentioned above). If we ignore what had been rejected, we do have at hand what was chosen.

And, at this point, we return to the problem of exchanges and of interest on money.

2. We have made this long introduction on the publication of the *Decisiones* as it seemed to us that this book represents a rather peculiar way of intervening in the debate on exchanges. Suffice to say that the person who selected the judgements (and we have hypothesized that it was Antonio Roccatagliata) was well aware of the theme of the exchange because of his role as notary, as Chancellor of the Rota, and, more generally, as high ranking officer and man involved in politics. Furthermore the *Dialogo* came from the printing house which would soon belong to him. He was also a Chancellor of the Senate in the very moment in which the discussions between the Republic and the Holy See were being held. He could not, thus, ignore the general and particular terms of the problem. It seems, then, that he selected mainly

---

179 The comparison has been possible for only six judgements (nnº LX, LXXXXVII, LXXXXVIII, CXV, CXXV, CXXVII). Texts are identical; only the amounts have been eliminated. That the volumes which remained in ASG, Rota Civile, are only a very small part of the original material, is evident from the continuous gaps in the oldest page numbers. The interest of some other chancellor for the commercial theme is derived from the fact that, on many (at a later date), the word "mercatoria" was written: was there perhaps a project for another volume?

those judgements issued between 1550 and 1577 (contemporary to him)[180] and which are, thus, subsequent, to the great debate of 1554 and to the law of 1555.

Going through these judgements we have the clear impression of entering directly into the multi-faceted world of the Genoese entrepreneurs of the 16th Century. The spaces: from Alexandria in Egypt to the Canary Islands, from England to the "enemy" Algiers, from Medina del Campo to Messina; the goods: everything circulated in these areas and is exchanged, provided that it generated a profit.

But we also have a further impression: a recurring theme is that of the interest (of the lawfulness of interest), a theme which the judgements deal with again and again (42 on a total number of 215), ending up with rather homogeneous solutions. Tightly connected to it we find the problem of the exchanges (more than twenty deal specifically with this problem, and part of them must be added to those in which a decision is taken on the problem of interest).

Was this redundancy intentional or does it reflect an objective reality? As we previously said, it is impossible to know, today, what these 215 judgements represent in terms of quantity with respect to the totality of the issued ones and, similarly, how often the theme of the exchanges and of the interest occurred. It is anyhow certain that, even if this theme was not stressed particularly, this problem is one of the qualifying points of the whole collection.

Not lower in interest is, the reaction of the judges of the Rota with respect to the Genoese reality, to the commercial and legal procedures there. These judges who lived in the middle of the 16th century were also greatly, and evidently, fascinated by the town's entrepreneurial world. It is not only the full acceptance of the principle of the *consuetudo regionis*[181] or of the *consuetudo mercatorum*, that "consuetudo ... quae proculdubio inter mercatores facit ius" (XXXII § 7) but it is something more: through this principle what, at a purely doctrinary level, would have perhaps been more difficult to accept, is passed to the level of jurisprudence. There is, also, the fact of living in such a very special milieu, that one judge of the Rota exclaimed:

---

[180] The only sure chronological reference is contained in decision XIV (c. 62 r): 1565. The few left, of which one copy is in ASG, Rota Civile 1, can still be dated between the end of the '60s and the beginning of the '70s.

[181] See the decisio LXXVIII § 17 (from now on we will indicate only the number of the judgement and the paragraph). With reference to the *consuetudo loci* there is an interesting reference to Petrus Lusitanus, the Santarem, this being further proof of the interest that this work generated in Italy, and a useful element to date the judgement "post quem". About Santarem and the edition of his work see *D. Maffei,* Il giureconsulto portoghese Pedro de Santarem autore del primo trattato sulle assicurazioni (1488), in Estudos em Homenagem aos Profs. Manuel Paulo Merêa e Guilherme Braga de Cruz, Coimbra 1983, pp. 703 - 728 (Santarem is, for instance, also recalled in judgement CLXVII § 4).

"ita semper fuit iudicatum *Genuae, ubi vivitur super interessibus*" (LXVIII § 9). We will comment further on this connection between judge and the Genoese "peculiarity" (if we can say so). What is clear is that the judge legitimizes, on one hand, and universalizes, on the other hand, this "peculiarity".

Let us go back again for a brief moment to the consideration (which appears as a "statement") according to which "Genuae vivitur super interessibus". In many judgements we find the *topos* of the Genoese who, by nature, has to be considered a merchant: the most famous one, repeated word for word by Scaccia, was remembered at the beginning of this work. In the same one (CXXXIX) we find further elements which concur to form this almost mythological image:

> Cum genuenses soliti sint negotiari et mercari, et nihil antiquius habeant ipsis negotiis et mercatura, iure merito Rota censuit lucri cessantis rationem habendam esse ...[182].

We shall deal later with the principle of loss of gain: we wish, now, to underline this concept that everybody in Genoa may have been considered as being a merchant; they are almost "anthropologically" different (almost a new kind of "Jew" without, of course, the negative notation typically connected with Jews).

In fact, even when referred to women, the judgements contain some ambivalence. In one judgement (XXXVII) there is a more traditional and restrictive consideration: the commercial activity is "proprie officium hominis", "non autem mulieris immiscerese negotiis secularibus mercando et negotiando", and for this reason, even if the complainant used to give money for exchanges, she could not be considered a real merchant ("quem esse mercatorem demonstrat pluralitas negotiorum, non solum respectu cambiorum, sed respectu aliarum rerum") and, thus, had no right to the interests on the basis of loss of gain.

In other judgements, on the contrary, the opinion is more liberal and links up again with the notion of the Genoese/merchant: judgement XXVIII (in which the same complainant is present) for instance, recognizes the right to the interests ("tum ratione damni emergentis, tum ratione lucri cessantis") as "in cambijs negotiari consuevit". In judgement LXXXIV no right for interests in the requested quantity is acknowledged "cum non fuerit probatum hanc mulierem fuisse solitam dare vel accipere pecunias ad cambium" (they were granted at a lower percentage as it was proved that the woman, previously, had her money deposited in San Giorgio, where it gave interests lower than those invested in the exchanges).

---

[182] See also nº CCVI, § 4: "Genuae ubi omnes fere cives sunt mercatores".

Before returning to the main topic we have to consider that the identification between Genoese and merchant is found in many judgements. We emphasize this because according to our opinion, through the use made of quotations in the juridical culture of the 16th and 17th Centuries, the concept had not a simply literary value, but brought about very important logical and juridical consequences: if this was permitted to the Genoese, why prohibit it to others (considering that the Genoese were not like the Jews)[183]?

As we have noted previously, many judgements deal with the problem of interest and, particularly, of interest due to merchants. The doctrine had already elaborated a tradition on this point which was on the whole rather uniform, even if it is still difficult to find a completely organized system. The proof of this statement came from an examination of all sources used by the judges of the Rota when they confirm the right to the interests for the merchant, on the basis of the emerging damage and/or of the loss of gain. The mentioned *auctoritates* are extremely different, but on direct examination we notice that, in the majority of cases, the principle is simply stated, as happens for the *Consilium* XXXIX of Filippo Decio (quoted in at least ten different judgements of those being considered directly in this work), or for the XX of Matteo degli Afflitti. In its whole there are often quotations of quotations, as for instance in the work by Pierre Rebuffi (another author frequently used)[184].

The case of Gerolamo Cagnolî is, on the contrary, different. In it, the work of comment to the *L. unica C. De Senten. quae pro eo* [C.7.47][185] is combined with a consideration on the doctrinal and social evolution of his times ("Nec mirum est quod *hodiernis temporibus* potius permittatur interesse lucri cessantis in solito negociari *indistincte,* quam olim"[186]; so he feels he has the

[183] The problem will be outlined by Scaccia: "Genuae contra debitores morosos rigorose agitur; omnis ratio quae pro interesse concludit, diligenter attenditur iuraque interusurijs faventia inviolabiliter servantur . . . quia sublatis interusurijs, mercatores et mercatura facile ruerent . . . omnis eorum cultura versari debeat in pecunia, et propterea sunt valde prompti ad condemnandum ad interesse, et ad interesse alterius interesse; at Romae alijsque Civitatibus in quibus non viget mercatura . . . odiosum est interusurij et interesse nomen" (p. 298).

[184] P. Rebuffi, L. Unicae C. de senten. quae pro eo quod interest . . . repetitio, Parisijs Apud Carolum Guillard 1548, cc. 127 ff. Still valid in this respect the remarks made, in the XVI century, by Botero (p. 89): "nuoce grandemente la moltitudine de' dottori, che scrivono continuamente, che, sebbene sono alle volte di poco giudicio, fanno però numero, e vince non chi dice meglio, ma chi cita di più".

[185] G. Cagnoli, In Iustiniani Codicem enarrationes. Tomus secundus, Venetiis Apud Haeredem Hieronymi Scoti, 1612, pp. 251 ff. About Cagnoli see the article by *A. Mazzacane* in DBI XVI, pp. 334 - 335, and the judgement made in 1549 by the Venetian podestà Bernardo Navagero: "Alla mattina ho ritrovato il Mantetta et il Cagnolo l'uno et l'altro con bona scola et quasi eguale. Questi dottori . . . sono homeni certo di bon credito, ma non però che di tanto non siano reputati haver in Italia superiori" (Relazioni dei rettori veneti di terraferma. IV: Padova, Milano 1975, p. 25).

[186] Cagnoli, § 30, p. 254 (my italics), and see § 48, p. 256: "quicquid *olim* esset, *hodie* indistincte habeatur ratio interesse lucri cessantis solito negociari".

right to take positions which differ from the doctrinal tradition, to which he can contrast "communis usus mercatorum et practica iudiciorum, quae est optima legum interpres".

It is interesting, taking the cue from Cagnoli, to make a remark on the use of the doctrinal sources made by the judges of the Genoese Rota (at least as far as the published *Decisiones* are concerned). Among the *auctoritates* mentioned by Cagnoli are also De Vio, Thomas Aquinas and Angelo da Chivasso. We never find any trace of these authors in the judgements which, on the contrary, mention far different sources. An equally peculiar use is made of a judgement by Ottaviano Cacherano, mentioned several times[187]. The Piedmontese lawyer uses Du Moulin to justify the principle of the missing gain; the Genoese judges do not take advantage of this authority, even if it could have been of great utility to them. Similarly no mention is found, in these judgements, of the whole debate on exchanges in the 16th Century (there are only four quotations from Lorenzo Ridolfi).

Differently from what takes place in contemporary works (and subsequently: let us consider, even in their *extreme* diversity, Nicola Senarega and Sigismondo Scaccia), these *Decisiones* only use the works of lawyers, and exclude, in my opinion intentionally, theologians[188]. The exclusion does not affect the theologians only, as Du Moulin is also ignored. The impression which we obtain from the whole is that the intention was to avoid all those matters which might, in any way, create problems with the Church. For the judges of the Genoese Rota it was not important to determine what an exchange contract was, but to set the criteria according to which the interest on money was paid[189].

Let us now examine, systematically, which ideology (partly implicit and partly explicit) was the basis for the *Decisiones* with reference to the problem of exchanges and interest, and how this is linked to the problem of the identity of the merchant.

---

[187] O. Cacherano, Decisiones Sacri Senatus Pedemontani, nº CXLIII (Venetiis apud Bartolomaeum Rubinum 1572, pp. 571 - 572).

[188] It is right to acknowledge, anyhow, that there is still a reasonable doubt connected to the role played by the editor of the Decisiones, i. e. that Roccatagliata has made a specific choice of these judgements, excluding, personally, anything which could deviate from a certain cultural line. Therefore, we wish to stress, our study, at this stage, always refers to the Decisiones as to a book, while an overall consideration of the Genoese Rota would imply the use of other sources (which, in part, may no longer exist).

[189] Of a stimulating interest are, in this respect, the notes by Tawney on the contemporary process of secularization in England: "While rival authorities were discussing the correct interpretation of economic ethics, the flank of both was turned by the growth of a body of opinion which argued that economics were one thing and ethics another. The creed of the commercial classes was a doctrineless individualism . . . The significant change which results from that movement is the secularization of the whole discussion" (Wilson, pp. 170 - 171).

One of the main, if not the main element which identifies the merchants is that they are persons "qui non tenebant suas pecunias ociosas" (XXX § 3)[190]; the element which characterizes the specific activity is thus the "movement" of money (even before that of goods). This movement is used to make a profit both on goods in general and on that special commodity which is money: "mercatores solitos lucrari in negotijs mercium et alijs", "solita negotiari et mercari cum pecuniis", "mercatorem et negociatorem solitum dare pecunias cambio" – these are many of the expressions used to characterize the Genoese businessmen[191]. Obviously the simple "movement" of money was not sufficient: as we can see the word "solitus" appears always (or almost always), and this underlines the fact that this activity was performed professionally and continually, as only in this way money gives profit:

> incertum autem lucrum censetur quando expectatur ab homine qui non consuevit negotiari et mercari: talis enim creditur proximus perditioni quam lucro, ut inquit Salicetus ubi subnectit proverbium in his verbis: chi mette denaro in mercantia e non la conosce, li suoi denari diventano mosche (CXXXIX, § 12).

But it has to be stressed that this statement is contained in that judgement in which the identity Genoese/merchant is theorized ("nobiles", "doctores", "mulieres": they are all merchants); and, thus, if this has a limiting function, this function is certainly special and certainly not *ad excludendum*. We must consider, also, that the judges were in a town in which a corporation of merchants did not exist and, consequently, not even a list existed, to be used to identify the persons and their subjective "qualities". The only proof is given by the depositions, and this is an ever requested proof. In the above mentioned judgement XXXVII (in which a woman, Maria Doria, was the plaintiff) the judges did not acknowledge the requested interest, also because the witnesses affirmed "nescire dictam actricem esse mercatorem" (and in the same judgement the problem of the list of merchants is mentioned).

We are, in this case, in a situation in which there is not a separate and distinct *ius mercatorum* as everybody may be a merchant, without any legal obstacle.

The connection between subjective *status* of entrepreneurial type, right to the interests and question of the exchanges can be exemplified in a very clear way by judgement CCVI:

> Cum ... Ioannes Paulus probaverit se fuisse et esse mercatorem et negociatorem solitum dare pecunias cambio, et quod mercatores et negotiatores cambiorum communiter lucrati fuerunt singulis annis prout in dicta exhibita, ita quod si ipse habuisset statuta die pecunias a Bernardo, tantum etiam lucratus fuisset ex ipsis pecunijs, prout in ipsa lista continetur.

---

[190] And see XXXIII § 4: "qui suas pecunias non solent tenere ociosas"; and see also, e.g., XXXIV § 11.

[191] CLXVI § 8; CCII § 4; CCVI § 3.

The list referred to in the judgement is the one of the course of the exchanges, which could be approved by the brokers or by the chancellor of the exchanges tax, which we have already seen mentioned by Scaccia. The reasoning, as it is evident, is extremely simple: if I, who am a merchant, had had the agreed amount at the scheduled date, I could have invested it in exchanges which, in this period, have yielded a profit of a certain amount. "Tenere super cambiis" is one of the ways to invest personal capital, in one of the many possible forms allowed by the financial market of the time. The interest "ad rationem cambiorum quae fierent de Genua ad Bezensonum et de Bezensono Genuam" (CLXXXXIII) is what determined the cost of money in Genoa.

It is also possible to note a certain ambivalence in the judgements with reference to the formula according to which the amount of the interest due is defined: there are cases in which reference is made only, and clearly, to the "lista" without indicating any percentage; then there are other judgements (for instance XXX and LIX) in which the sentence "ad rationem cambiorum scilicet octo pro centenario" is used, or "ad rationem novem pro centenario: constat enim ... cambia redidisse lucrum ad dictam rationem" in which, once more, the reference to the exchanges is explicit. Finally there are judgements (like LXXXXVIIII, CL, CLXXXXIIII) in which, on the contrary, no reference exists on the course of the exchanges, but only the indication of the percentage (and this percentage is not far from the others, in total: the acknowledged interests varies from a minimum of 6% – in the case of a "non-merchant" woman – to a maximum of 10%).

Still more or less linked to the market of the exchanges is also the problem of interest on interest (and of its calculation); from judgement LXXXVIII we take some information:

> actores petierunt interesse ad rationem cambiorum probando se esse mercatores in cambijs negotiari solitos, et cambia rediisse pro ut in lista exhibita, in qua interesse moltiplicatum in unaquaque feria continebatur.

In this case the Rota decided that the simple interest was due, and not "compound" "ad similitudinem usurarum, quarum usurae non debentur". In another judgement we find that, on the basis of the principle of the missing gain, the interest on interest is denied (also in this case paralleled to the "usurae usurarum"), but on the basis of that of the emerging damage the interest was acknowledged "non solum immediatum, sed mediatum, multiplicatum et quomodocumque calculatum" (LXXXVII § 9).

It was, on the contrary, considered as being lawful in two judgements (LXXVIII and CXXXIIII) with clear mention to the above-quoted Girolamo Cagnoli:

> non solum tenetur de primo interesse sed etiam ad interesse cuiuslibet feriae et ad interesse etiam alterius interesse[192].

This recourse to the quotation of the exchange also allowed the judges of the Genoese Rota to avoid the difficult problem of the interest agreed beforehand, despite the fact that, for example, Cagnoli himself had stated that it could have been requested:

> interesse peti semper poterit uniformiter, puta ad rationem decem per centenario singulis annis. Sed secundum practicam et doctrinam aliorum praeall. interesse non posset peti nec deberetur uniformiter, sed iuxta contigentiam factorum ... sed esset valde difficilis probationis ... Ideo praecedens practica melior est et securior[193].

According to one judgement (CLXXXXIII) the fact that in a contract the quantity of interests is "expressa et determinata", "continet dictus contractus usurariam pravitatem", and, viceversa, "reus [non] potuit opponere de usuraria pravitate ... cum interesse non fuerit certum" (CCX § 8).

There is also, anyhow, a judgement which collocates itself in a quite different perspective (the XXXIIII), meeting the difficult problem of the deposits at the fair. In this case (in addition to a contract for the sale of alum) a payment of interest had also been agreed, at the rate of 9% per annum, from the beginning. To the objection that the contract might have been usurious in character, the judges answered:

> respondetur id procedere quando mutuum in stipulatione deduceretur cum spe habendi illa novem pro centenario, ultra sortem, quia in huiusmodi contractu quicquid accedit sorti, usura est ... mutuum enim debet esse simplex et purum.

Different was the contract made, in which the interest was due "loco interesse lucri cessantis" (as money had to be kept "super cambijs realibus Bezensoni"): the agreement of a set interest had been made "ad evitandam difficultatem probationis interesse, quod aliquando in illis ferijs plus est, et aliquando minus".

This judgement is the only one which takes such an anomalous position with respect to the others also because both the decree of 1467 on dry exchanges and that of 1555 which prohibited "certum et terminatum lucrum" were still in force (and references to these decrees are found in judgements XXXVII, LXXVIII, CCX). Above all to acknowledge the right to agree on interest from the beginning of the contract (before the defendant is "constitutus in mora": a further basic principle of the *Decisiones*) would have meant bypassing the whole legal and formal structure built around he problem of the sterility/non sterility of money; just as it would have involved a radical devaluation of the world of exchanges. And this would have meant, also, to adhere to a point of view identical to that of the author of the *Dialogo*.

---

[192] Cagnoli, p. 196: "quod de interesse alterius interesse multi credunt quod non debeatur, nec peti possit, sed veritas est ad oppo. et ita saepe consului, obtinui et vidi iudicatum", and see also p. 255.

[193] Ibid., p. 196.

But whoever issued judgements in his role of judge of the Civil Rota in Genoa certainly did not have the intention of creating ideological controversy; he could, as a maximum, offer subjects and reasonings for other lawyers (as certainly happened with Scaccia, whose use of the *Decisiones* is certainly very interesting from this point of view).

We must however acknowledge that in the *Decisiones*, while on one hand, there is a substantial uniformity in thought on the problem of interests, we can on the other hand note some differences in the definition of the exchange, and this is the sign of a higher or lower ideological autonomy with respect to the doctrinal tradition. The "alchemic" nature of the exchange, then, implied that the definitions were necessarily also different[194].

Judgement IX reminds us of one of the original functions, which, anyhow, was still in force:

> facile pecunia potest et sine periculo ex longinquis locis ad alia loca transferri per viam cambiorum.

Others, following Lorenzo Ridolfi, define the exchange a contract "ad instar emptionis et venditionis" (I § 41 and XXXVII § 15). This definition is found also in decision XXXII § 5, to which also the one of "contractus innominatus", similar to the "contractus bonae fidei", is joined.

Less caution emerges in those cases in which the "pecunia mutuo et cambio data" is mentioned (LVII § 2), as if loan and exchange could almost pacifically coexist[195]. Then somebody, with apparent nonchalance, reveals the secret:

> cambium et mutuum idem [sunt], quia postquam hodie mutuo, et sic gratis, pecunias invenire non possumus, inventum est cambium quod facit ut pecuniae credantur citra usurarum nota (XIV § 88).

The whole problem is summarized in a few lines: today no money can be found on a no charge basis (as the loan would prescribe); to claim interest would be to be called a usurer, and thus "inventum est" the exchange. This opinion is concealed among the folds of a very long and complicated judgement, and is only, substantially, a parenthesis. But it reveals how reality pressed against the formal structures of the juridical and theological arguments.

---

194 For the use of the word "alchemy" connected to the exchanges, see Scaccia, pp. 153 - 154: the merchants "lucri causa cambiorum negotiationem tanquam novi alchymistae invenerunt". The passage, which is also beautiful from a literary viewpoint continues comparing the alchemists and the merchants, and in this comparison the merchants turn out to be the winners: "brevissimis circularibus litteris ex fictis marcharum scutis veros aureos scutos conficiunt". The word "alchemy" has also been used by Lüthy (see supra § I, note 33).

195 See also n° L. Also Scaccia sometimes use this wording (p.110): "pecuniam mutuo seu cambio accepit".

Moreover, this ambivalence of the judges of the Genoese Rota has been noted also with respect to the subject of the connection existing between the personal quality of the parties and the right to interest. In the *Decisiones* it does not seem to emerge as a problem the fact that only the merchants are able to make exchanges[196]. It has been noted that the same percentage of interest is not granted to everybody, and this in consideration of the subjective (professional) qualities. But, at the same time, also the concept that all Genoese were "mercatores" became firmly established; there was, then, the possibility of not considering the personal "qualities" of the parties[197]. In a judgement (LXXXXVIIII) it was stated that even the poor had to pay interest on the basis of the principle of the emerging damage. The "auctoritas" invoked is, in this case, Matteo degli Afflitti[198], perhaps a sign of the predilection for the decisions of the great Courts; but what is sure is that (irrespective of the invoked principle or authority) the interest had to be paid (and in this case it was 10%).

The *Decisiones*, thus, did not discuss the principles, and did not expose themselves to doctrinal criticisms. They formalized and generalized, within the schemes of the juridical doctrine, what was newly emerging from the social reality of the time; in this case it was the existence of a market, that of money and capital.

(Translated by Gabriella Rasoli)

---

[196] See for instance Girolamo Da Lucca, De Cambiis, in Tractatus universi iuris, VI, 1, c. 410r: "tantum mercatoribus permittitur"; or J. de Medina, De Penitentia, Restitutione et Contractibus, Ingolstadii ex Officina Typographica Davidis Sartorii, 1581, II, p. 305: "non omnibus cambire convenit".

[197] On this theme see also the considerations made by *Capitani*, pp. 10 - 12.

[198] M. De Afflictis, Decisiones Sacri Regii Concilii Neapolitani, nº XX (Venetiis, apud Iuntas, 1635, p. 48).

W. D. H. ASSER

Bills of Exchange and Agency in the 18th Century Law of Holland and Zeeland

Decisions of the Supreme Court of Holland and Zeeland

1. Introduction

The Low Countries, being well-placed as far as communication was concerned, played in important part in international trade since the later Middle Ages. During the 15th century Bruges was one of the commercial and financial capitals of Europe and in the following century this role was taken over by Antwerp[1]. In both cities merchants from all over Europe and in particular from the more sophisticated mediterranean countries had established their branchoffices or had their correspondents and agents. This brought along frequent and continuous trading between the leading houses of business through their offices, correspondents or agents in those two cities.

In 1568 a serious revolt broke out in the Netherlands (Belgium and The Netherlands were not yet separated countries) against the royal government of King Philip of Spain. Eventually this revolt – known as the Eighty Years War, because it was regarded as such and was ended by the Treaty of Munster in 1648 – caused the seven Northern provinces (Guelders, Holland, Zeeland, Utrecht, Overijssel, Friesland and the City and Country of Groningen) to become independent, as united in the Republic of the Seven United Provinces.

In stead of empoverishing the North, the period of the Eighty Years War was marked by a vast economic expansion[2]. Shipping and trade flourished on an immense scale. New markets, both in Europe and elsewhere, were explored and particularly the colonial trade became a very important factor in economic development. This was the period in which the trade with the

---

[1] Cp. the general survey by *H. van der Wee,* Handel in de Zuidelijke Nederlanden, in: Algemene Geschiedenis der Nederlanden (AGN) 6, Nieuwe Tijd, Haarlem 1979, pp. 75 - 83.

[2] Cp. *J. R. Bruijn,* Scheepvaart in de Noordelijke Nederlanden, in: AGN 7, Haarlem 1980, pp. 142 - 144 and *L. Noordegraaf,* Nijverheid in de Noordelijke Nederlanden 1580 - 1650, in: AGN 7, pp. 82 - 85.

East Indies was monopolized by the Dutch and the basis was laid for what was to become the vast colonial empire in that aerea.

Forced to return to the Spanish royal camp in 1585 and cut off from international shipping by the continuous blockade of the Scheldt by the Dutch since that same year, Antwerp lost its dominant position to Amsterdam. The North also gained enormously by the large scale immigration of merchants from the South. They took with them, apart from their experience, their large financial resources and their worldwide commercial interests and contacts. Their role in the development of the young Republic cannot easily be overestimated[3].

In the Republic Holland was the most important and influential province, because of its economic power and great wealth. Its shipping and trading flourished during the 17th and a large part of the 18th century. Its economic and financial heart was, as we have already pointed out, Amsterdam, which still had an open connection with the North Sea, going through the former Zuiderzee.

Being a country governed by free citizens and a nobility, which had lost its feudal nature and had accomodated itself to the new situation without king or emperor to pay allegiance to[4], Holland did not experience any important conflict of interests as to economic development and its organisation. The local, provincial and federal governments recognized the importance of international trade and the power that could be displayed, when all its forces were combined. "*Eendracht maeckt macht*", union or unity is strength, and "*Concordia res parvae crescunt*" were the mottoes of the young Republic.

One of the first examples of this conviction was the creation (in 1602) of the Combined East India Company, the Verenigde Oost-Indische Compagnie (V.O.C.), by amalgamating several of such companies which previously had been established in different cities. This company was not only invested with a monopoly regarding colonial trade, but also endowed with political power in the colonies in the East, although it was and remained a private company.

In those days international trade suffered not only from unstable exchange rates of foreign currencies, as it does today, but also from forgery

---

[3] Especially in Zeeland these merchants settled in the period following 1585. Cp. *Bruijn*, op.cit. (n. 2), p. 143; *F. S. Gaastra*, De geschiedenis van de V.O.C., Haarlem/Antwerpen 1982, p. 26; *the same*, De V.O.C. in Azië tot 1680, in: AGN 7, p. 185; *J. van Roey*, Enkele Antwerpse aantekeningen bij het oudste aandeelhoudersregister van de kamer Amsterdam der Oost-Indische Compagnie, in: Liber Amicorum Jhr. mr. C. C. van Valkenburg, 's-Gravenhage 1985, pp. 251 - 254; *Noordegraaf*, op.cit. (n. 2), pp. 68 and 83.

[4] See on the position of the nobility in Holland during the 16th and 17th century, *H. F. K. van Nierop*, Van ridders tot regenten, de hollandse adel in de zestiende en de eerste helft van de zeventiende eeuw, diss. Amsterdam 1984, with a summary in English.

of coins on a large scale. Consequently traders and governments, aiming at a solid financial basis for commercial activities, looked for means to avoid, or at least to reduce the risks incidental to cash payments. In this respect one should bear in mind that in many countries like the United Provinces all sorts of coins, also many foreign ones, circulated freely and were used for payment, even between the inhabitants of the same city or country.

In 1609 the government of Amsterdam established a municipal exchange bank[5] after the example of the exchange bank of Venice. Its purpose was first of all to regulate the monetary chaos (in which it did not succeed) and to provide merchants with cash in valuable coins in order to stabilize the exchange rate of foreign currencies used in the Dutch staplemarket of those days. Furthermore, merchants used the bank to deposit with it their cash to be credited to newly opened accounts. The bank served also as a clearing-bank for bills of exchange. Its reputation was solid and well-known all over Europe[6].

2. The sources of exchange law in Holland[7] during the 17th and 18th century[8]

The continental jurists, trained in the *ius commune,* tried, of course, to develop the law dealing with bills of exchange in accordance with the principles of the ius commune. It appears, however, that the exchange law was

---

[5] A decree of the *schepenen* of Amsterdam of 31 January 1609, which can be found in: H. Noordkerk, Handvesten der stad Amsterdam, II, Amsterdam 1748, p. 673 (II, 4, 1). The bank was supervised by a board of commissioners, appointed by the local government. Most of them were members of the ruling elite and former *schepenen* or former members of the city council. See Jan Wagenaar, Amsterdam in zyne opkomst etc., III, Amsterdam 1767, p. 401.

[6] All bills of exchange, negotiated in or drawn on Amsterdam and amounting to 600 guilders (by decree of 11 December 1643 this amount was reduced to 300 guilders) or more had to be paid in the bank. A great advantage for the clients of the bank was that no account with the bank could be made subject to seizure of any kind, thus being absolutely safe against claims of any creditor. The city guaranteed the value of the money paid by the bank in cash. See for further information Wagenaar, op. cit. (n. 5), II, Amsterdam 1765, pp. 537 - 542; *J. G. van Dillen,* Een boek van Phoonsen over de Amsterdamsche Wisselbank, a reprint of his article in: Economisch-Historisch Jaarboek, VII, 's Gravenhage 1921, pp. 12 - 18; *the same,* Van Rijkdom en Regenten, Handboek tot de economische en sociale geschiedenis van Nederland tijdens de Republiek, 's Gravenhage 1970 [the book was completed and published by *W. M. Zappey*], pp. 256 - 269; *H. Klompmaker,* Handel, geld en bankwezen in de Noordelijke Nederlanden 1580 - 1650, in: AGN 7, pp. 123 - 124.

[7] Here and elsewhere in this article we mean with "Holland" the province of that name, to which also belonged West-Friesland, a region in the northern part of the present province of North-Holland. It should be noted that every province, town or region had its own laws, although the ius commune was, of course, generally applied.

[8] We shall not deal with the general history of the development of the bill of exchange. A short survey is given in *H. Coing,* Europäisches Privatrecht, I, älteres gemeines Recht (1500 bis 1800), München 1985, pp. 537 - 543 (§ 110). Books we consulted in particular are: *R. de Roover,* L'évolution de la lettre de change XIVe - XVIIIe

developed mainly by the merchants themselves and that the professional lawyers merely tried to adapt the customary law to fit in with the ius commune[9].

In Antwerp rules of customary law were codified during the period between 1547 and 1608[10]. The most influential version of this codification, as far as the northern provinces were concerned, was the printed version, the Impressae. Being completed during the short interval of protestant government[11] in Antwerp and, of course, written in the common language of the flemish and northern part of the Netherlands, the Impressae were easily accessible to the people in Holland. We submit that its growing influence was also due to the Antwerp emigrants who had settled in Holland and Zeeland, because they will have introduced their own laws in the places where they decided to live and work. This would not have been very difficult in those fields of the law, in particular, where the law had not been developed to the extent it had been in Antwerp[12].

Thus Antwerp exchange law was introduced in Holland, evidence of which we can find in Grotius' Inleidinge[13] and in the customary law of

---

siècles, Paris 1953; *H. Lévy-Bruhl,* Histoire de la lettre de change en France aux XVIIe et XVIIIe siècles, Paris 1933; *W. S. Holdsworth,* A history of English Law, VIII, London 1925, pp. 113 - 160; *C. Freundt,* Das Wechselrecht der Postglossatoren, I, Leipzig 1899; II, Leipzig 1909; *L. Goldschmidt,* Handbuch des Handelsrechts, I, Universalgeschichte des Handelsrechts, I, Stuttgart 1891, pp. 403 - 465.

[9] Fine examples of how this was done can be found in *Freundt's* above (n. 8) mentioned study.

[10] See on the Antwerp codification of private law: *M. Gotzen,* De costumiere bronnen voor de studie van het oud-Antwerpsch burgerlijk recht, in: Rechtskundig Tijdschrift voor België, 39 (1949), pp. 3 - 16; 105 - 124; 191 - 208. The codification has known several versions: the Antiquissimae (1547), the Antiquae (1570/1571), the Impressae (1582) and the Compilatae (1608).

[11] This lasted from 1578 until the surrender of the city in 1585 to Alexander Farnese, Duke of Parma, governor of the Netherlands. Almost half of the population of Antwerp during that period was protestant. See *Van Roey,* op. cit. (n. 3), p. 251. *Gotzen,* op. cit. (n. 10), pp. 105 - 113, regards the Impressae as being full of the spirit of independence from the Roman Catholic church and as the fruit of the rebellion *("kind van de opstand").*

[12] As to the Antwerp codification the law of exchange was laid down in the Antiquae (tit. 28), the Impressae (tit. 55) and the Compilatae (IV, tit. 3). The first edition of the Impressae is: Rechten ende costumen van Antwerpen, Antwerpen 1582. A modern edition can be found in G. de Longé, Recueil des anciennes coutumes de la Belgique, Coutumes du pays et duché de Brabant, Quartier d'Anvers, II, Bruxelles 1871. The Antiquae were published in the same work, I, Bruxelles 1870, and the Compilatae in IV, Bruxelles 1874.

[13] Ed.: *F. Dovring, H. F. W. D. Fischer* and *E. M. Meijers,* Leiden 1952. Cp. *H. F. W. D. Fischer,* Het oudvaderlandse handelsrecht en Hugo de Groot, in: Rechtsgeleerd Magazijn Themis 1952, pp. 598 - 610, in which a survey is given of the ancient Dutch law merchant laid down in the Inleidinge and other works of Grotius. See also *W. F. Lichtenauer,* Geschiedenis van de wetenschap van het handelsrecht in Nederland tot 1809, in: Geschiedenis der Nederlandse rechtswetenschap, V, I, Amsterdam 1956, pp. 85 - 104; the edition of the Inleidinge by *S. J. Fockema Andreae* (4th ed. by *L. J. van Apeldoorn*), II, Arnhem 1939, p. 255 (on Inl. 3, 13).

Amsterdam as compiled by Gerard Rooseboom[14]. Apart from this, exchange law had been laid down already in several statutes of the Emperor Charles V in his capacity of sovereign of the Netherlands[15]. They deal with various matters but do not give a complete body of law. The same can be said of the local statutes of Amsterdam and Rotterdam of the 17th and 18th century[16].

An outstanding authority on the exchange law of Amsterdam was Johannes Phoonsen (1631 - 1702), whose book on the customary exchange law and practice in that city[17] became so famous that it was even translated into German and French. A great deal of the exchange law of Holland can be learned from Phoonsen's book.

Apart from these sources, to which we can add the compilations of legal opinions, as e.g. that by Barels[18], and, of course, the writings of several authorities on private law in general and exchange law in particular, both from Holland and from other countries[19], we can find valuable information in the judgements of the higher judicature of Holland and Zeeland, to which we shall now proceed.

---

14 Gerard Rooseboom, Recueil van verscheyde keuren en costumen midtsgaders maniere van procederen binnen de stadt Amsterdam, Amsterdam 1656, cap. 50, "Van Wisselbrieven ende wissel-banck". See also *W. F. H. Oldewelt,* De pogingen tot "codificatie" van het Amsterdamse recht, in: Verslagen en mededeelingen der Vereeniging tot uitgaaf der bronnen van het Oud-Vaderlandsche Recht, XIII, no. 1, Utrecht 1967, pp. 71 - 72. To the judgement of the Court of Appeal of Holland, mentioned by Oldewelt, we can add a judgement of the same Court of as early as 1579, concerning joint and several liability of partners and referring to Antwerp customary law (the Impressae had not yet been compiled). See *W. D. H. Asser,* In solidum of pro parte, Leiden 1983 [Rechtshistorische studies nr. 9], p. 102.

15 Statutes of 1537, 1541, 1546 and 1551. See *S. Lammel,* Die Gesetzgebung des Handelsrechts, III, Niederlande, in: Handbuch der Quellen und Literatur der neueren europäischen Privatrechtsgeschichte (Handbuch), II, 2, München 1976, pp. 776 - 777.

16 See the survey by *Lammel,* loc. cit. (n. 15).

17 Wissel-styl tot Amsterdam. We used the edition by Isaak le Long, Rotterdam 1755. Le Long wrote a sequel to it: Vervolg van de wissel-styl tot Amsterdam, Rotterdam 1755. See on Phoonsen: *Van Dillen,* Een boek van Phoonsen cit. (n. 6), pp. 1 - 11. Cp. *O. Scherner,* Die Wissenschaft des Handelsrechts, III, B, 8, Niederlande, in: Handbuch, II, 1, pp. 982 - 984.

18 Jeronimo Matthaeus Barels, Advysen over den koophandel en zeevaert, I, Amsterdam 1780; II, Amsterdam 1781. Another compilation is: Verzameling van casus positien, voorstellingen en declaratien betrekkelijk tot voorvallende omstandigheden in den koophandel, van tyd tot tyd binnen deeze stad [sc. Amsterdam] beoordeeld en ondertekend, Amsterdam 1793 - 1804 (two parts in one volume). It consists of legal opinions by lawyers, each opinion being followed by a confirmation by a number of Amsterdam bankers and merchants. Of course the *Hollandsche Consultatien* also contain legal opinions regarding the law merchant.

19 As e.g. Heineccius (translated into Dutch by Reitz) Scaccia, Dalla Torre (De Turri), Franck, Du Puy de la Serra, Savary, Pothier. We refer to the article by *Scherner* (above, n. 17).

3. The administration of justice in commercial matters in Holland and Zeeland during the 17th and 18th century

A body of judicature, exclusively competent in commercial matters, did not exist in the united provinces. Both commercial and ordinary civil cases were brought before the ordinary local and provincial courts. In some cities, e.g. Amsterdam, Rotterdam and Middelburg, the local magistrates had established special benches for maritime matters and matters of insurance, but from the judgements these benches rendered, one could appeal to the ordinary local magistrate court *(schepenbank)*. In Holland and Zeeland appeals from the local courts lay to the Court (of Appeal) of Holland and Zeeland *(Hof van Holland en Zeeland)* and from this court to the Supreme Court of Holland and Zeeland *(Hoge Raad)*[20].

The reason why there was no separate judicature in commercial matters may be found in the structure of society itself. Particularly in Holland and Zeeland feudalism and its dominant position of the nobility had dwindled and the cities with their free population of craftsmen and merchants played by far the most influential role in the provincial government. The guilds in the towns had lost almost all their influence[21], whereas the local government was for a great deal in the hands of a relatively small group of "regents", who were, in many cases, members of important business houses themselves. From this it becomes clear that there was little need for a separate judicature where matters of commerce were concerned. There was, so to speak, no mercantile class, well distinguished from the nobility or other classes, as there was, for instance, in France. A judicature established by and reserved

---

[20] The Court of Holland, Zeeland and West-Friesland, as it was called (we shall refer to it as the Court of Appeal), was established by Philip of Burgundy on 13 August 1428. Its code of instructions was given by Charles the Bold in 1462 and was renewed by Charles V in 1531. See *W. G. Ph. E. Wedekind,* Bijdrage tot de kennis van de ontwikkeling van de procesgang in civiele zaken voor het Hof van Holland in de eerste helft van de zestiende eeuw, Assen 1971, pp. 24 - 43; see also *A. S. de Blécourt* and *E. M. Meijers,* Memorialen van het Hof (den Raad) van Holland, Zeeland en West-Friesland, van den secretaris Jan Rosa, I - III, Haarlem 1929, pp. I - XVIII. From judgements by this court one could appeal to the Grand Conseil (Grote Raad) at Mechelen (Malines). After this had become practically impossible as a result of the outbreak of the revolt, the Estates of Holland decided to establish a new Supreme Court in The Hague. It was given a code of instructions in 1582, in which year it started functioning. The Estates of Zeeland did not accept this court as Supreme Court until after 1585 when Mechelen was taken by Parma and it became totally impossible to go to the Grand Conseil. In 1586 Middelburg and in 1587 the Estates of Zeeland accepted the jurisdiction of the Supreme Court, now of Holland, Zeeland and West-Friesland. See *A. S. de Blécourt,* De geboorte van den Hoogen Raad van Holland en Zeeland, in: Tijdschrift voor Rechtsgeschiedenis 2 (1920/1921), pp. 428 - 459.

[21] See Simon a Groenewegen van der Made, Tractatus de legibus abrogatis et inusitatis in Hollandia vicinisque regionibus, Lugduni Batavorum 1649, ad C. 3, 13, 7: "Mercatorum sive artificum collegia (Gildens) perexigua apud nos auctoritate pollent". Cp. *W. F. Lichtenauer,* Burgerlijk en handelsrecht, in: Rechtskundige opstellen, aangeboden aan Prof. Mr E. M. Meijers, Zwolle 1935, p. 351.

for the members of that class was therefore out of the question. Moreover, the local courts were manned for a great deal by the "regents", who themselves, in many cases, would be acquainted with the merchants' customs and perhaps even sometimes, due to their business experience, with the customary law.

However, some cities, as we have noticed, established specialized courts in certain matters (e.g. maritime, insurance and bankruptcy cases[22]). The reason was, that in these fields the law was relatively specialized, which required more or less specialized judges in order to cope with sometimes rather complicated questions arising from these matters. Yet the level of specialization was, presumably, not very high. For, the surviving lists of judges in the maritime and insurance bench of the Amsterdam municipal court[23] show, that most judges were on the bench for a period of one to two years or perhaps a little longer, and that only a few remained on the bench for a relatively longer period (more than 5 years). Furthermore, the judges who changed quickly appeared to be members of other specialized benches as well, apart from becoming sooner or later members of the board of *schepenen,* the ordinary court in all civil and criminal matters, and also of the city-council or even burgomaster.

Claims concerning bills of exchange have never been subject to a specialized court in Holland and Zeeland. Phoonsen, however, advocated in his book[24] such a court, to be established in Amsterdam by appointing the commissioners of the municipal exchange bank as judges in all matters of exchange, bills included. Yet the city government did not agree. We do not know why Phoonsen's proposal did not meet with any response, but clearly the city magistrates found no need for such a court, although even judges in the Supreme Court of Holland and Zeeland considered questions arising from bills of exchange often intricate and difficult[25].

A few words should be said about some specialities of the law of procedure in matters concerning bills of exchange. Anyone liable under a bill of exchange was subject to seizure of his property and to personal imprisonment *(gijzeling).* If the signature on a bill was acknowledged by the debtor

---

[22] See the survey by *Lammel,* op. cit. (n. 15), pp. 779 - 782 and *Lichtenauer,* Burgerlijk en handelsrecht cit. (n. 21), pp. 351 - 356.

[23] In Wagenaar, op. cit. (n. 5), pp. 296 - 306 (burgomasters), pp. 329 - 349 (schepenen), pp. 355 - 360 (members of the city council), pp. 428 - 469 members of the special benches (commissarissen).

[24] Wissel-styl cit. (n. 17), pp. 235 - 236; his treatise on the exchange bank: Berichten en vertoogen raackende het bestier van den omslagh van de Wisselbank tot Amsterdam, edited by *Van Dillen,* Een boek van Phoonsen cit. (n. 6), pp. 142 - 145. See also Lichtenauer, Burgerlijk en handelsrecht cit. (n. 21), p. 353.

[25] In his OT 1609 Bynkershoek exclaims "de literis cambii intricatae saepe et difficiles solent esse quaestiones" and his son-in-law Pauw says the same in OTN 1544: "difficiles et intricatae plerumque sunt lites quae de cambiis aguntur".

(either the drawer, endorser or anyone else liable under his signature on a bill), a provisional decision, executable by anticipation, could be obtained against him *(provisie van namptissement)*[26]. Thus, a bill of exchange could give cause to immediate and effective action.

4. Judgements as historical sources

In Holland and Zeeland (as well as in the other provinces) judgements did not contain their grounds. It was a well established rule of law that judges should keep secret their consultations in chambers[27]. By publishing the grounds of the judgement they were believed to violate their obligation to secrecy, apart from the fact that it was considered to be unwise to reveal the grounds, upon which the judgement was given. The idea that judges should account for their decisions by giving its grounds in the judgements they render, would not be introduced as a fundamental rule of law until the Constitution of the Kingdom of the Netherlands of 1815[28].

However, as to the judgements of the Supreme Court and the Court of Appeal of Holland and Zeeland books, in which reports of the deliberations in chambers were compiled, have been preserved in the Dutch National Archives *(Algemeen Rijksarchief)* in The Hague. Especially in the collected reports *(resolutieboeken)* of the Supreme Court one can find valuable information, as we shall see below.

These reports were meant for Their Lordships' eyes only. For even more private use were the notes in two collected works, which were published quite recently: the Observationes tumultuariae by Cornelis van Bynkershoek and the Observationes tumultuariae novae by his son-in-law Willem Pauw[29]. They contain the personal accounts of the discussions in chambers

[26] See Grotius, Inleidinge 3, 13, 6 and 3, 45, 10; cp. Dionysius van der Keessel, Praelectiones iuris hodierni ad Hugonis Grotii Introductionem ad iurisprudentiam Hollandicam, edd. P. van Warmelo [and others], IV, Amstelodami/Promunturii B. S. in urbe, 1966, pp. 170 - 172 (on Inl. 3, 5, 7) and pp. 334 - 336 (on Inl. 3, 13, 6); see also by the same author Theses selectae juris Hollandici et Zelandici ad supplendam Hugonis Grotii Introductionem ad jurisprudentiam Hollandicam et definiendas celebriores juris Hollandici controversias, Lugduni Batavorum 1800 (our edition: editio nova, Amsterdam 1860), nr. 624.

[27] Cp. *U. Wagner* in his article on compilations of judgements (Rechtsprechungssammlungen) in the Netherlands in: Handbuch, II, 2, pp. 1404 - 1406. See also *Wedekind,* op. cit. (n. 20), pp. 127 - 130.

[28] Articles 172 (criminal judgements) and 173 (civil judgements). In Belgium the obligation to express the grounds of the judgement was introduced in 1795, see *Wagner,* op. cit. (n. 27), p. 1406.

[29] Observationes tumultuariae, edd. *E. M. Meijers* [and others], [I - IV], Haarlem 1926 - 1962; Observationes tumultuariae novae, edd. *H. F. W. D. Fischer* [and others], [I - III], Harlemi, 1964 - 1972. See for a study of the way the Supreme Court applied the law *L. J. van Apeldoorn,* Theorie en practijk van de rechtsbronnen in Holland in den tijd van Cornelis van Bynkershoek (1673 - 1743), in: Tydskrif vir hedendaagse Romeins Hollandse reg, 1 (1937), pp. 4 - 33.

(both authors were successively justice and president of the Supreme Court) and they cover a period of 83 years (1704 - 1787). They show us how the court dealt with any particular case and for which reason a certain decision was reached. The names of the parties and judges are practically never revealed, but by combining a particular report with that of the same case in the court's *resolutieboek* (if this particular report survived) one may find these names back. Sometimes this will enable us to find more backgrounds and facts of the case concerned in other documents or other archives.

All together the official sources and the observations of Bynkershoek and Pauw may give us a complete impression of a particular case and the judgement rendered in it[30].

5. The cases concerned

In both the Observationes tumultuariae (OT) and the Observationes tumultuariae novae (OTN) reports may be found on decisions regarding bills of exchange. We shall pay specifically attention to four decisions dealing with problems arising from bills, drawn or negotiated (i.e. "bought") by agents. The first two cases, which we shall examine, are concerned with a type of agent who was more or less an employee of his principal, whereas the second group of two cases is about agents who were independent merchants, acting on behalf of their correspondents in another town. As far as the law of agency is concerned, this difference is of less importance. We have made the distinction between those two groups of cases, because in the first it is the principal who is being sued, whereas in the second group the agent himself is sued by the principal.

6. The first two cases. Acceptance of bills in general

Both decisions are concerned with a principal, refusing to honour a bill, drawn on himself by his agent. It appears, as we shall see in due course, that in neither of the two cases the principal was successful in avoiding liability and refusing payment, although he had not accepted the bill. On first sight this seems to be in contrast with the rule, already accepted in those days, that only by accepting the bill the drawee would become liable under it. We shall not go deeply into the development of the acceptance of bills of

---

30 *E. M. Meijers,* Uitgegeven en onuitgegeven rechtspraak van de Hoogen Raad en van het Hof van Holland, Zeeland en Westfriesland, in: Tijdschrift voor Rechtsgeschiedenis 1 (1918/19), pp. 400 - 421, already advocated the publication of compilations and reports, which are still unpublished and being kept in the archives. *H. W. van Soest,* Hoe vervaardigde Raadsheer Willem Pauw zijn observationes tumultuariae novae, in: Satura Roberto Feenstra oblata, Fribourg 1985, pp. 585 - 607, shows how Pauw compiled his observationes.

exchange in general, but it is necessary to say something in this respect, because it will help to understand the rules which were applied in both decisions[31].

Presumably the acceptance of a bill was originally not an act necessary to create the obligation of the drawee to honour it. The acceptance, which could very well consist of simply keeping the bill after it had been presented by the holder[32], was probably in most cases only a confirmation of the drawee's obligation, already existing as a result of the transaction between the drawer and the person who paid the value to the drawer (which person we shall call "remitter", because the payee or holder of the bill was usually the fourth person concerned and the agent or correspondent of the remitter). This would have been the case, for instance, when the drawer had borrowed money from a person to whom he subsequently gave a bill drawn on his associate abroad. The latter, being an associate of the drawer, was jointly and severally liable for the repayment of the loan. Whether or not he accepted the bill, was of no consequence to his obligation to repay the money which the drawer had received[33]. Often a drawee, refusing to honour a bill, did so because he was not an associate of the drawer, or at least used this argument in order to escape liability[34].

Gradually it became practice that holders kept the bills for reasons of evidence until they were paid by the drawee. This, however, required that the bills be accepted or dishonoured explicitly in order to ascertain whether the bill would be paid. The drawee, therefore, would place his acceptance in writing on the bill and consequently the rule was developed that the drawee, who had not accepted the bill, could not be forced to pay it.

As to the relation between the drawee and the payee[35], the former was perfectly free to accept or to refuse the bill[36]. This is not without meaning, even

---

31 We refer to the works mentioned in n. 8.

32 This could be based on the lex Si filius familias (D. 14, 6, 16). See *Freundt,* op. cit. (n. 8), I, p. 102.

33 See on the liability of partners my above mentioned (n. 4) book.

34 If such an underlying relationship between the drawer and the drawee did not exist, the acceptance of the bill without any objection implied that the drawee committed himself to pay the amount mentioned in the bill. Cp. *Freundt,* op. cit. (n. 8), I, pp. 104 - 106.

35 It was generally accepted that between the drawer and the drawee a contract of mandate was concluded. See e.g. Grotius, Inl. 3, 31, 1 and 2. The acceptance of the bill by the drawee made him liable towards the drawer to honour the bill. Of course, the holder could not claim payment by the drawee if the latter had not accepted the bill.

36 See Grotius, Inl. 3, 13, 3; Phoonsen, Wissel-styl, 10, 5; Johann Gottlieb Heineccius, Elementa iuris cambialis, Amstelodami 1743, 3, 11 and 12; 6, 6. The rule that the drawee was free to refuse the bill could be based on D. 3, 3, 8, 1: "invitus procurator non solet dari", and on C. 2, 12, 17: "invitus procurationem suscipere nemo cogitur". See also Van der Keessel, Praelectiones, on Inl. 3, 13, 5 (ed., pp. 322 - 325) and Theses Selectae, nr. 616.

As to the rights of the holder, it was difficult to find a basis in the Roman law. See for the different views which were defended, *Freundt,* op. cit. (n. 8), I, pp. 111 - 112.

when the drawee was liable on the strength of the contract between the drawer and the remitter which gave cause to the draft. For by accepting the bill the drawee became subject to the special remedies the payee was entitled to under the law governing bills of exchange, as explained before. However, the drawee who had not accepted the bill could not be sued at all or only by the ordinary action arising from the underlying contract, e.g. the *condictio* or the *actio venditi,* in which case the full burden of proof as to the liability of the drawee rested on the payee, being the claimant.

The drawee who refused to accept or to pay a bill would have some reason or another to do so. Often he would not accept if he had no funds in his hand for payment, because the drawer either did not provide him with the necessary funds or was not his creditor to an amount equal to the sum to be paid under the bill. Another reason to dishonour the bill may have been that the drawer did not have sufficient capacity or authority to draw a bill on the drawee, as e.g. an agent who had neither an explicit nor an implied mandate to draw bills of exchange on his principal[37]. Whether a principal could effec-

---

Van der Keessel, Praelectiones, on Inl. 3, 13, pr. (ed., p. 298) explains it in this way: "Trassatus, postquam litteras cambiales acceptavit, obligari incipit remittenti tamquam emptori eius iuris, quod trassans ex suscepto mandato in eum habebat, uti quoque obligatur exactori et indossatariis tamquam mandatariis remittentis; vel si soluto valore indossatio facta sit, tamquam procuratoribus in rem suam", after which he refers to Heineccius, Elementa, 3, 17 and 15; 6, 5. He recognizes, however, that others think that the drawee becomes liable *ex stipulatu* or *ex constituto* and he does not object against that view. He refers to Jacques du Puy de la Serra, L'art des lettres de change, Paris 1690, 16, 2. It appears that Scaccia held that the drawee was liable on the strength of a *promissio* and that Dalla Torre was of the opinion that the liability was based upon a *constitutum,* see *Freundt,* loc. cit. (above).

[37] According to a *"turbe"* in Amsterdam of 11 July 1601 (*Noordkerk,* Handvesten cit. (n. 5), II, p. 542) a special mandate was required. See also Johann Christoph Franck, Institutiones iuris cambialis ... cum praefatione Henrici Brokes, [I - II], Francofurti/Lipsiae 1751, 2, 1, 1, 3; Phoonsen, wissel-styl, 23, 2; 3; 5; 6; Karel Koenraad Reitz, in his edition of Heineccius' Elementa: Grondbeginselen van het wisselrecht, in 't Latyn saamgesteld door wylen den Heer J. G. H. naar de zevende uitgaaf vertaald en met de noodige aanmerkingen verrykt en opgehelderd, Middelburg 1774, n. 47 to 2, 19; Gottlieb Gerhard Titius, Juris privati Romano-Germanici ex omnibus suis partibus compositi, libri duodecim, Lipsiae 1709, 10, 5, 25 and 50 (acceptance and endorsement); in 10, 5, 11 he deals with the institor. Whether a general mandate implied a mandate to draw, accept or endorse bills on behalf of the principal depended on the circumstances of each case. Franck, Institutiones, 2, 1, 1, 25, says: "merus institor non cambiat", referring to a judgement of the Rota Genuensis (Decisio 14, nr. 88). The Rota decided that always an explicit mandate was required: "regulariter uni merci praepositus non potest aliam exercere, 1. habebat in princ., *ff.* de inst. [D. 14, 3, 13, pr.], sed capere cambio est quid diversum et negotiatio separata est appaltu, ergo praepositus appaltui, negotium capiendi pecunias cambio exercere non poterit, maxime quia, ut dicit *Bal.* 1.2. C. de usur. rei jud. [C. 7, 54, 2] cambium est contractus separatus a mutuo et in cons. 349, n. 6, vol. 1, dicit esse negotium pecuniae emptae et venditae, et sic licet posset mutuo accipere, non potuit cambio capere, praesertim quia secundum *Alber.*, disp. 1. ult. *ff.* de exer. [D. 14, 1, 7] procedit in solo mutuo, non in aliis contractibus et sic cambium videtur excludi, adeo ut nunquam permittatur institori tacite et necesse esset expresse hoc permittere" (we quote from the edition De Mercatura [...] [cura] Benevenuti Stracchae aliorumque juris-consultorum, Amstelodami 1669). In some places publication of the mandate is required, see

tively refuse to accept a bill drawn on himself by his agent, who was in fact authorized to do so, is a question we shall deal with hereafter.

In short this was the law in Holland during the 17th and 18th century, as it was in the other principal nations on the continent.

7. The first two cases. Facts and decisions

a) Supreme Court, 27 July 1709, Romburg v. De Groot, OT 535[38]

Caspar Romburg, managing owner ("boekhouder") of a ship called Edinburg, sent his ship in december 1699 to Lisbon with a cargo consisting of ropes, ivory jars, gunpowder, beer, cheese and boards. He instructed the ship's master, Willem de Grijse, to sell the cargo and to apply the proceeds to buy returncargo (mainly citrus and sugar). Furthermore he told De Grijse not to leave debts unpaid and to settle the account existing with the Portuguese business house Pedro Emaus & Comp. in Lisbon. Romburg had sent a letter to Emaus on November, 23rd, 1699, in which he announced the voyage and arrival of the Edinburg and asked the Portuguese to assist the master by word and deed and to settle the existing account. Romburg also gave a letter for Emaus to the master, in which he introduced De Grijse as the master of the vessel and asked again to assist him and also to provide him with money, if he needed some. Moreover he allowed Emaus in this letter to draw on him for the money provided and promised to honour all drafts. On 28 December 1699 Romburg wrote a letter to Emaus confirming that he had ordered the master to settle everything and that he had given him a letter for Emaus, in which he requested the latter to assist the master.

Having arrived in Lisbon, the master sold the cargo and received some money from Emaus to buy returncargo. Before leaving again for Flushing, where he came from, De Grijse settled the account with Emaus and drew a bill on Romburg to the amount of 2060 crusados, being the balance in favour of Emaus, at least according to the latter.

Franck, Institutiones, 2, 1, 1, 26; Reitz, n. 21 on Heineccius' Elementa, 5, 12 and also Phoonsen, Wissel-styl, 34, 10 and 11. In Holland only Rotterdam required that a mandate to draw, accept and endorse bills be filed at the local exchange bank (statute of 27 August 1720, see Reitz, loc. cit. above). Phoonsen, Wissel-styl, note to 23, 8, advocated publication of such mandates in Amsterdam, which, however, was never introduced.

[38] Ed. I, pp. 297 - 298. The judgement of the Supreme Court is still kept in the Algemeen Rijksarchief (ARA) in The Hague, 3.3.02. (HR), inv. nr. 801 (this is a *"geextendeerde sententie"*, i.e. a document in which not only the decision ("dictum") is given but also a summary of the allegations of both parties). The report of the deliberations in chambers is also kept in the archives, ARA 3.3.02 (HR), inv. nr. 608 (minuutresoluties) and inv. nr. 664 (resoluties). The decision *("resolutie")* was taken on 11 July 1709 by Justices Admirael, Verbrugge, De Vries, Schaep, Keetlaer, Bynkershoek, De Roovere, Sluijsken (judge-reporter) and the President of the Court, Rosenboom.

During her returnvoyage the vessel and her cargo perished. "Hinc illae lachrymae", as Bynkershoek explains, for Romburg subsequently dishonoured the bill, which had been endorsed to an Amsterdam merchant, Willem Loot, and presented by his agent, Jan de Groot.

Sued before the court of Flushing, Romburg tried to escape liability, arguing that the master had exceeded his powers by buying more returncargo, than the proceeds of the cargo sold by him allowed him to do, and by drawing the bill. Moreover Romburg disputed the balance of the account, as compiled by Emaus, and finally put forward that Emaus and the master had colluded against his interests. The claimant, De Groot, repudiated these arguments, pointing out that neither the limits of the master's powers, as set out in the instruction to him, nor the disputation of the account with Emaus was of his concern.

By interlocutory and provisional judgement the court of Flushing condemned Romburg to pay the bill and this provisional judgement was upheld by final judgement of the same court of 20 December 1701, being confirmed by the Supreme Court by its judgement of 27 July 1709. From the report of the deliberation in chambers it appears that all judges of the Supreme Court were of the opinion that Romburg had to honour the bill because not only the account and the bill were signed by the mandatary of Romburg (i.e. the master) but also Romburg himself had written letters to Emaus asking the latter to provide the master with money and promising payment (of the bill); everything Romburg had argued was ineffective, but the law of exchange was clear[39].

b) Supreme Court, 30 September 1744,
Van der Giesen v. the Directors of the V.O.C., OTN 71[40]

Willem Maurits Bruynings, governor and director of the V.O.C. colony on the island of Colombo (i.e. Ceylon, nowadays Sri Lanka), drew a bill on the defendants in favour of Van der Giesen, the claimant, to an amount of 10500 guilders, which money Bruynings had received and paid into the coffers of the V.O.C. The defendants, however, refused to accept the bill, arguing,

---

[39] From a dicision by the local court of Middelburg, Flushing or Veere one could appeal immediately to the Supreme Court. See Joannes van der Linden, Verhandeling over de judicieele practijcq of form van procedeeren voor de Hoven van Justitie in Holland gebruikelijk, I, Leyden 1794, pp. 337 - 338.

[40] Ed. I, p. 52. The "*dictum*" is kept in the ARA, 3.3.02 (HR), inv. nr. 918 (register geresolveerde dictums) and inv. nr. 955 (register van gepronuntieerde sententiën). The report of the deliberations in chambers is also kept, ARA, 3.3.02 (HR), inv. nr. 674 (resoluties). The decision was taken on 18 September 1744 by Justices Van der Does, Van den Santheuvel (both judge-commissioners), De Grande, Mollerus, Pauw, Van Nispen and Keetlaer.

when sued immediately before the Supreme Court[41], that they were not liable, since they had not accepted the bill, and putting forward that the money in fact had gone to the former Governor General of the colony in the East Indies – Adriaan Valkenier –, who owed money to the Company. Therefore, the bill should be regarded as drawn by Valkenier[42].

The Supreme Court rejected this argumentation. There was no evidence that the money was received by Valkenier, whereas it was established that Bruynings had paid the money into the Company's purse. Moreover, Bruynings had acted in his capacity of governor of the colony. Hence the bill should be regarded as being drawn by the V.O.C. itself and needed not to be accepted in order to make the Company liable for payment, because bills of this kind are never presented for acceptance but always for payment only. It is pointed out that the bill was drawn by the *praepositus* of the company, who was authorized to bind the Company, and that the money was used *in usum* of the Company. Non-acceptance was, therefore, of no consequence. The judge-reporter referred to D. 14,3,1, Grotius' Inleidinge, 3,13,4, the notes of Groenewegen to that passage, Voet, Ad Pandectas, Tit. De nautico foenore (D. 22,2), nr. 6, and Hollandsche Consultatien 1,283.

8. The first two cases. Review

As to the first case, one may wonder which legal basis the decision was based on. The Supreme Court mentioned, as we have seen, two arguments: (1) the fact that the bill had been drawn by a mandatary, i.e. an agent, of the drawee, (2) the letters Romburg had written to Emaus by which the latter was authorized to lend money to the master and to draw a bill on Romburg, and in which Romburg promised to honour such a bill[43]. Did the Court consider a promise by the drawee to accept and to pay a future bill, to be an acceptance in advance, to the effect that the drawee would be bound to pay the bill, the moment it would be presented by the holder? Probably the Court did not go that far, because it would be in contrast with the leading opinion in Holland in those days. A promise to honour a bill was not equal to accep-

---

[41] The Supreme Court was competent in first instance when the parties concerned had agreed upon bringing the case immediately before this court. Presumably this is what happened in this case, because, as we have seen (n. 40) two judge-commissioners were appointed and it was apparently practice to appoint judge-commissioners, before whom the case was prepared for trial, when it had been brought directly before the Supreme Court. See Van der Linden, op. cit. (n. 39), I, p. 84.

[42] The governor-general of the East Indies, Valkenier, created a scandal by imprisoning and sending back to Holland some members of the Council of India (among whom the future governor-general Van Imhoff). The directors of the Company accused Valkenier of abuses and criminal behaviour and claimed money from him. They sent him back to Holland, but he died during the homeward journey. Pauw refers to him also in OTN nrs. 26, 40, 72 and 111, calling him "Titius".

[43] In fact the arguments were put forward by the judge-reporter Sluijsken.

tation of that bill, although it could give cause to an action *"in id quod interest"* based upon the promise itself[44]. Such an action, however, would only be granted to the person to whom the promise had been made and not to any holder of the bill[45].

We submit, therefore, that Romburg's letters were mentioned in order to show that the master had not gone beyond his powers. This was important, because if he had so, the first ground for the decision would have been invalid. This leads us to the second case.

The decision in this case was, as we have seen, based on the view, that a bill, drawn by an *"institor"* or factor of the Company – the governor of Colombo was, in terms of the law, regarded as such – should be considered to be drawn by the Company on itself. A bill of exchange, in which the drawer and the drawee were the same person, was not considered to be void in Holland[46]. Unlike the promissory note *(promesse)*, this kind of bill, as all other bills of exchange, could lead to immediate execution *(parate executie)*.

The bill, drawn by the drawee himself, needed no acceptance, but made the drawee immediately liable for payment[47]. Therefore, if the bill in this particular case was rightly regarded as such a bill, the directors of the Company were bound to pay it, even without having accepted it previously.

In contrast to this view seems to be a legal opinion, given by Simon van Beaumont about 1605[48], curiously enough quoted by the two judge-commissioners.

Beaumont was dealing in his legal opinion with a bill, drawn by an admiral of the V.O.C. on his principals, the directors of the Company's chamber in Amsterdam[49]. They, however, refused to accept it – on futile grounds, if

---

[44] See Phoonsen, Wissel-styl, 10, 6; Barels, Advysen cit. (n. 18), 2, 46 (a legal opinion of 1715); Van der Keessel, Praelectiones, on Inl. 3, 13, 5 (ed., p. 322). Cp. Robert-Joseph Pothier, Traité du contrat de change, in: Oeuvres de Pothier, VII, Paris 1818, nr. 9[3] (ed. pp. 51 - 52), to whom Van der Keessel refers (using the translation into Dutch by Joannes van der Linden, Verhandeling van het wisselrecht, Leyden 1801, 4, 44, p. 85).

[45] Pothier, Traité cit. (n. 44), nr. 121 (ed. p. 68) (in the translated version 4, 72, p. 112), suggest that the holder of the bill might sue the drawee with the action of the person (the drawer) to whom the promise was made.

[46] See Phoonsen, Wissel-styl, 36, 12; Van der Keessel, Praelectiones, on Inl. 3, 13, pr. (ed., p. 281). Also in France this kind of bill was accepted. See *Lévy-Bruhl*, op. cit. (n. 8), pp. 73 - 74. It should be noted that in France there existed also "billets de change", promissory notes against which the maker had received one or more bills of exchange, and "billets à ordre", promissory notes which are almost the same as bills drawn by the drawer on himself. Cf. Pothier, Traité cit., nrs. 207 - 222 (ed. pp. 122 - 132).

[47] Phoonsen, Wissel-styl, 36, 12.

[48] Hollandsche Consultatien, I, Amsterdam/Utrecht 1728, nr. 283.

[49] The Dutch East India Company consisted of "chambers" in Amsterdam, Middelburg, Rotterdam, Delft, Hoorn and Enkhuizen. The chamber in Amsterdam was by far the most important. See *Gaastra*, De geschiedenis van de V.O.C. cit. (n. 3), pp. 17 - 19.

we may believe Beaumont[50]. The payee abandoned the idea of commencing proceedings against the drawer, who was at the time apparently still in the East Indies or on his way home. So, the payee decided not to make or instruct for a formal protest, which he did not have to, if he did not want to sue the drawer, but to start proceedings against the directors of the Company on the basis of the *actio institoria*. They were, after all, principals of the drawer and could, therefore, be sued on the strength of the obligation, which arose from the underlying contract between the remitter/payee and the drawer, i.e. the loan, taken up by their admiral.

Beaumont pointed out that the payee, of course could use the *actio institoria* against the directors *in solidum,* but also made a parenthetic remark, that there was no action under the bill against them, since they had not accepted it.

Although the opinion was quoted by the judge-commissioners, but probably only to stress that the directors could be sued in any case, the Supreme Court clearly did not follow Beaumont's view. This was, it is true, nearly 150 years later, but it seems that Beaumont's remark did not even reflect the law of his own time. For according to Antwerp customary law (to be found in both the Impressae and the Compilatae), a principal was bound under a bill, drawn on him by his factor, on the condition, however, that the latter was duly authorized to bind his principal and the value was received for the benefit of the principal's affairs[51].

---

[50] Probably the reason for refusing to honour the bill was that the bill was drawn in favour of the Admiral of the company of Balthasar de Moucheron. De Moucheron was one of the foremost merchants of the end of the 16th century. He was of Antwerp origin but had settled down in Zeeland after the fall of his native city. The establishment of the V.O.C. in 1602 prevented him from making the profits he had expected from the expeditions and trade he financed. In 1601 he had sent three ships under Joris van Spilbergen to the East Indies. In 1602 a fleet of fourteen ships under the flag of the V.O.C. also went to the East Indies. Wybrand van Warwijck was the admiral of this fleet and drew the bill, the opinion is dealing with, in favour of Spilbergen, who had lent him some money. Although De Moucheron had been director of the chamber in Middelburg, there was obviously a conflict of interests between him and the V.O.C. Due to financial problems he left the country in 1603 and went to France. So, probably he was no director anymore in 1604 when Spilbergen returned and presented the bill. We assume that under these circumstances the V.O.C. simply tried to escape payment. Cp. *Gaastra,* De geschiedenis van de V.O.C. cit. (n. 3), p. 26.

[51] Impressae, 55, 1: "De gene die eenen wissel-brief aen hem gepresenteert sijnde niet en accepteert, en is uut crachte vanden selven wissel-brief niet gehouden, t'en ware dat een facteur (macht hebbende om sijnen meester te verbinden) tot behoeve van sijns meesters affairen eenige sommen van penningen op wissel genomen ende eenen wissel-brief aen sijnen meester gesonden hadde, ten eynde hy den persoon, van wien hy sulcke somme ontfangen heeft, oft sijn gecommitteerde daeraf rembourseren soude". Compilatae, 4, 3, 2: "12. Nijemant en is gehouden eenige wisselbrieven op hem comende te accepteren, noch en mach vuijt crachte van dijen niet aengesproken worden, ten waere dat den selven quaeme van eenen facteur, die macht heeft sijnen meester te verbinden, ende de selve macht te wercke heeft gestelt, oft van den meester op sijnen facteur, die van hem suijvere ende onbelaste penningen onderheeft, sonder te commen [ms.: connen] bethoonen van contrarie ordre oft verboth an den selven niet te accepteren". The texts are taken from the edition by De Longé (n. 12).

Grotius adopted this rule in his Inleidinge, 3,13,4 (also quoted by the judges of the Supreme Court), but in a somewhat different wording. He maintains that the principal has to accept such a bill[52], which is, at first sight, not exactly the same, because one could argue that there would be no obligation under the bill, if the principal nevertheless refused to accept, but only an action of the drawer based on non-performance of the obligation to accept. This interpretation would lead us to Beaumont's view, that in case of non-acceptance there could be no action for the payee under the bill. We submit, however, that Grotius words should be interpreted in a different manner. Van der Keessel, commenting on this passage in his Praelectiones, reads them as follows:

> Docet hic Grotius mercatores non posse recusare acceptationem litterarum cambialium, quas institores in rebus ad negotiationem pertinentibus in eos trassarunt, ut ita ad negotia pecuniam habeant. Quod consentaneum est illis principiis, quae convenienter L. 5 § 13 D. de instit. act. [D. 14,3,5,13] iam tradidimus cum Grotio L. 3 Part. 1 § 31[53].

We submit, that he rightly uses the word *posse*, implying that a refusal to accept is without effect towards the payee, and that this is the way Grotius should be read. Grotius, therefore, went much further than Beaumont, because the latter would, apparently, not admit an action based upon the bill, but only an action based upon the underlying contract (e.g. a loan), whereas Grotius would allow the payee to sue the principal immediately under the bill.

The conclusion, that Grotius did not establish a rule, virtually different from the Antwerp law, may also be drawn from the fact, that neither Groenewegen in his notes on Inl. 3,13,4, nor Voet, Ad Pandectas 22,2,6, nor Van der Keessel in his Praelectio on this passage of the Inleidinge and in his Theses Selectae, nr. 615, give any hint to the contrary. They all mention the corresponding passage in the Impressae, without even suggesting that Grotius deviated from it.

The difference of wording may be due to the framework in which Grotius dealt with the matter. In Inl. 3,13 he treated the bill of exchange in its relation to both drawer and drawee. He regards the relationship between both persons as a contract of mandate, which can only be concluded by accepting the mandate, which means in this respect, by accepting the bill. This is pure Roman law, which leaves every would-be mandatary free to accept or to reject the mandate. Therefore, Grotius formulated the Antwerp rule in such

---

52 Inl. 3, 13, 4: "Doch koopluiden zijn schuldig aen te nemen de wisselbrieven ghezonden by een bewind-hebber haerder zaecken, die macht hadde om sijn meester te verbinden, ende ten behoeve van sijns meesters zaken penningen op wissel neemt".

53 Ed., p. 322. Inl. 3, 1, 31 deals with agency by *"bewind-hebbers"*, i.e. institors, and confirms the rule of Roman law that merchants are bound by their institors and can be sued with the *actio institoria*.

a way, as to have it fit in with the law of mandate. The liability of the principal is based upon his obligation to accept the bill. The conclusion of the contract is not dependent on his discretion. Now the question arises how the liability of the principal/drawee towards the payee was established. Normally the drawee becomes liable for payment by accepting the bill, which is regarded by Grotius as a promise to pay towards the payee (Inl. 3,45,10; cf. Inl. 3, 13, 6). But in case where there is no acceptance, the situation is totally different. Perhaps Grotius found the answer in assuming, that the bill should be regarded as accepted. In that manner one could reach the outcome that the principal was also regarded to have promised payment to the payee.

The Antwerp clause survived in the law of Holland until it disappeared during the time of the codifications of the law (about 1800)[54]. Because the French Code de Commerce did not know a similar provision, it would have been quite natural if the Dutch Commercial Code of 1838 would not have included it either for that reason. But already the draft Civil Code of Joannes van der Linden (1807), which could not be and was not based on the French Code de Commerce, did not mention anything similar, although Van der Linden did deal with it in his well-known book on private and commercial law[55]. Neither did the draft Commercial Code of 1809 by Van Gennep, Asser and – again – Van der Linden contain a similar provision. The same goes for the famous compilation of Amsterdam customary law by Gerard Rooseboom (17th century), who only confirms the rule that a drawee is free to accept or to refuse a bill[56], while Phoonsen even seems to reject it explicitly[57]. The latter however, upholding that a principal is not obliged to accept a bill, drawn on him by his servant or factor in their own name, would perhaps have admitted liability of a principal, in case his agent acted explicitly as such, which means by disclosing his capacity as agent. Van der Keessel, in his lecture on Inl. 3,13,4, interpreted Phoonsen in this way. The Antwerp rule only applies when the agent had acted *institorio nomine*. Karel Koenraad Reitz, however, simply held that Phoonsen deviated from the Antwerp provision[58].

We submit that Van der Keessel gave the right explanation of Phoonsen's statement. There was no valid reason to assume that a principal would

---

54 See e.g. Johannes Voet, Commentarius ad Pandectas, [I - II], Coloniae Allobrogum 1757, on D. 22, 2, nr. 6 (ed., vol. I, pp. 949 - 950); Van der Keessel, Praelectiones, on Inl. 3, 13, 4 (ed., p. 322) and Theses Selectae, nr. 615.

55 Regtsgeleerd, practicaal en koopmanshandboek, Amsteldam 1806, 4, 7, 8 (ed., p. 539). He refers to the Impressae, Grotius and Phoonsen 10, 5 (see below, n. 57).

56 Recueil cit. (n. 14), cap. 50, pr.

57 Wissel-styl, 10, 5: "Het staat in de vrye keur van de betrokkene, of hy de wisselbrief op hem getrokken, accepteren wil of niet, zelfs is een meester niet gehouden de wissel-brieven door zyn knecht of factoor op haar eygen naam getrokken, veel min een knecht of factoor de wissel-brieven door haar meester getrokken, te moeten accepteren".

58 On Heineccius' Elementa, 3, 12, n. 26.

always be liable on the strength of a bill of exchange, drawn by his agent (servant or factor). As to the effectiveness of agency, it was generally accepted, that the agent should inform the party, with whom he contracted, as to his capacity, in order to bind his principal immediately under the contract. So, the agent had to act either explicitly in the name of his principal *(in nomine domini)*, or by adding his capacity to his signature, such as "q. q." *(qualitate qua)*. Therefore, if the agent would draw a bill on his principal, making clear that he was doing so in his capacity as agent, the logical conclusion, according to the general principles of agency, would be, that the principal was bound immediately under the bill, because it would be regarded as a bill, drawn by the principal himself[59].

The law of agency being so and as developed during the centuries before Phoonsen wrote his book (but, in fact, even already by the time, the Antwerp clause was laid down in the Impressae), it becomes clear that there was little need for such a clause since it was self-evident. For both the text of the Impressae and the Compilatae and the clause in Inl. 3,13,4 require sufficient authority of the agent to bind his principal, and apparently understand that the agent would act in such a manner, as to bind his principal immediately towards the remitter and payee. It is, therefore, quite logical that Phoonsen stated, that a principal was free to dishonour a bill, drawn by his agent in his own name. And it was equally natural, that neither he, nor Rooseboom, nor the codificators of the beginning of the 19th century, felt any need to introduce a provision to the effect, that a principal would be bound auto-

---

[59] A legal opinion of the Faculty of Frankfurt a/d Oder of 28 February 1679 shows that it was not always clear on whose behalf an agent acted. The criterion was the intention with which the remitter had taken the bill from the drawer-agent. If the remitter intended to deal with the principal he could not recover his loss, incurred by the insolvency of the latter, from the agent. However, if he only wished to deal with the agent himself, he could claim payment from the latter in the case the drawee-principal would not pay. The opinion can be found in Samuel Strykius, Praelectiones Viadrinae de cautelis contractuum necessariis, Francofurti et Lipsiae 1694, 3, 5, 19; Johann Ludwig Uhl (the translation by Isaak le Long:) Frankforter wissel-responsa, I - II, Amsterdam 1750, nr. 12; Le Long, Vervolg cit. (n. 17), 11e beantwoording; Heineccius / Reitz, Grondbeginselen cit. (n. 37), 4, 25; Heineccius, Elementa 4, 25. Cp. however Franck, Institutiones, 2, 1, 1, 29 - 30, who is of the opinion that a principal is always bound to honour a bill drawn by his procurator. He refers to the Impressae and mentions the contrary view of Strykius. Cp. also Gerard Malynes, consuetudo vel lex mercatoria or the antient law-merchant, London 1629, 3, 5, 6, and Antonius Anselmo, Consultationes seu resolutiones et advisamenta diurna ad quaestiones a consultoribus et litigantibus propositas, Antwerpiae 1671, cons. 50.

As to the liability of the agent himself it should be pointed out that in Holland it was generally accepted that an agent who had acted *institorio* or *procuratorio nomine* was not personally liable on the strength of the transaction carried out on behalf of his principal: Van der Keessel, Praelectiones, on Inl. 3, 13, 4 (ed., p. 322) and on Inl. 3, 1, 31 (ed., p. 16). To his references (Voet, ad D. 14, 3, nr. 6; Van Leeuwen, Censura Forensis 4, 3, 10; Groenewegen, De legibus abrogatis D. 14, 3, 19; Coren, Observationes rerum in Senatu judicatarum, Obs. 28, nr. 47) several others could be added, as e.g. Pauw, OTN 1034 and 1544. Cp. in this matter *U. Müller,* Die Entwicklung der direkten Stellvertretung und des Vertrages zugunsten Dritter, Stuttgart, Berlin, Köln, Mainz 1969, pp. 98 - 110.

matically under the bill, when it was drawn on him by his agent in the principal's name.

Returning to the decision of 1744, we should note, that the Court probably followed the same line of thought. The bill was regarded as drawn by the Company on itself and needed no acceptance in order to make the Company liable for payment. There can be little doubt, that the Court's reasoning was the same in the case of 1709, since a master of a ship was, on the basis of the *actio exercitoria* of D. 14, 1, generally accepted as an agent of the shipowner.

9. The second group of cases. Facts and decisions

The two cases, to which we now come, are concerned with the question, whether an agent *(commissionair)*, who negotiates a bill under instruction and for account of his principal but in his own name without disclosing his capacity or the name of his principal, is liable under the bill as an endorser, when he first had the bill endorsed to himself and subsequently endorsed it to his principal.

Generally all endorsers are liable for payment when the bill is eventually dishonoured and not paid. This liability is jointly and severally (in solidum). Endorsement, as a way of delivery of a bill of exchange, was accepted in the continental countries not before the 17th century. According to the general principle, we just mentioned, an agent, receiving a bill, endorsed to himself, and endorsing it subsequently to any third party, would become fully liably as an endorser. Now, the question may be put, whether this also applied to an agent endorsing such a bill of exchange to his principal, according to the instructions given by the latter.

c) Supreme Court, 31 May 1721, Sautijn v. Six, OT 1738[60]

Abraham Sautijn of Amsterdam remitted a certain value to Pieter Six in Middelburg, and asked Six to send him a bill of exchange for the same value. Accordingly, Six negotiated a bill of exchange, drawn on a merchant in Amsterdam, had it endorsed to himself and, after endorsing it to Sautijn, sent it to him. This all happened on the same day. After the bill had been dishonoured and it had become clear that both the drawee and the drawer had become insolvent, Sautijn tried to recover his loss from Six and sued him

[60] The *dictum* is kept in the ARA, 3.3.02 (HR), inv. nr. 912 (geresolveerde dictums) and inv. nr. 953 (gepronuntieerde sententien). The report of the deliberations in chambers can be found in ARA, 3.3.02 (HR), inv. nr. 667 (resoluties). The decision was taken on 13 May 1721 by Justices Van Bynkershoek (judge-reporter), De Vries, Schaep, Keetlaer, De Roovere, Van der Hoop, Van Hees and the president of the chamber Admirael.

before the court of Middelburg. He argued that Six, by having the bill endorsed to himself, had become owner of it and consequently, after endorsement to Sautijn, liable for payment. The court of Middelburg dismissed the claim by judgement of 7 June 1717 and the Supreme Court upheld this decision by its judgement of 31 May 1721[61].

d) Supreme Court, 5 October 1736, Van den Bosch v. Martens, OT 2991[62]

This case is more complicated than the previous one, but may be summarized as follows. Augustin de Bringas of Bilbao instructed Pieter van den Bosch of Amsterdam by letter to acquire for him and to send to him bills of exchange, payable to the order of Dr. Francisco Antonio Gomez of Madrid, and amounting to 2000 ducats de Plata.

Having received this order, Van den Bosch negotiated some bills and in particular one, drawn by Jan Teyler van Sleden in Amsterdam on Giacomo Isidoro Monsagrati of Madrid to the amount of 500 ducats de Plata. After having received this bill, Bringas wrote a letter to Van den Bosch, in which he thanks him for the prompt remittance ("punctuele remise") of the bills on Madrid according to his (Bringas') orders. The bill drawn on Monsagrati was dishonoured by him. In the meantime the drawer, Teyler, became insolvent. Bringas in one way or another in the possession of the bill, sued through his proxy, Pieter Martens, Van den Bosch before the local court of Amsterdam, claiming that Van den Bosch was liable for payment as an endorsee and endorser of the bill. Both this court and the Court of Appeal of Holland agreed with this argument and condemned Van den Bosch to pay the bill of

---

[61] Also in this case the appeal was brought directly before the Supreme Court. See above n. 39.

[62] In the Municipal Archives of Amsterdam the *dictum* of the judgement by the *schepenen* can be found under inv. nr. 5061 - 1962 (geprivilegeerde rol, 14 September 1735). The decision was taken on 3 November 1735 by the *schepenen* Six, Sautyn (cp. the names of the parties in the preceding case; they are members of the same families), Temmingh, Bondaan, Hooft and Geelvinck, and it was pronounced the same day.

In the ARA is kept the judgement by the Court of Appeal of Holland: ARA, 3.3.1 (Hof van Holland), inv. nr. 963. The decision is also mentioned in the compilation of reports, called *"quaetclap"* (i.e. gossip, referring perhaps to its secret character), ARA, 3.3.1 (Hof van Holland), inv. nr. 5767, however without any reference to the opinions of the judges. The decision was taken on 8 June 1736 by De Hinojosa, president of the Court, Slicker, Moris, De Mauregnault, Graafland, Schaep, Van Bochoven, Cau, Muilkerken and Gienhoven, and was pronounced on 13 June 1736.

The dictum of the judgement by the Supreme Court can be found in ARA, 3.3.02 (HR), inv. nr. 916 (geresolveerde dictums) and inv. nr. 954 (gepronuntieerde sententien). The report of the deliberations in chambers is kept in ARA, 3.3.02 (HR), inv. nr. 625 (minuut resoluties) and inv. nr. 672 (resoluties). The decision was taken on 5 October 1736 by Justices Duivkant (judge-reporter), Keetlaer, De Roovere, Van der Hoop, Van Bleiswijk, Van der Does and Bynkershoek, president of the Court. It was pronounced the same day.

exchange (decisions of 3 November 1735 and 13 June 1736). The Supreme Court, however, reversed these sentences and dismissed the claim.

10. The second group of cases. Review

By rejecting, in both cases, the claim the Supreme Court decided on a rule of law, which was not generally accepted. In particular Phoonsen[63], whose authority was, even for the Supreme Court, in matters of exchange almost unquestionable[64], did not share the view which led to both decisions. He was of the opinion, that an agent of the kind we are dealing with in these two cases *(commissionair)*, who does not stand del credere, nevertheless in fact does so – without receiving any reward – by negotiating in behalf of his principal any bill, endorsed to himself. Even if the agent stands del credere on the strength of the agreement with his principal, Phoonsen strongly suggests that the agent must not act in this manner, but must see to it that the bill is endorsed immediately to his principal by the person from whom he acquired the bill. Phoonsen's suggestion is concerned with the apparently widely adopted practice of *commissionairs* to have bills endorsed to themselves before endorsing them to their principals. They did so, because they did not wish to disclose their principal's identity to the brokers in the Exchange Bank, from whom the bills were bought, these people being regarded as gossips ("the echo of commerce"). Moreover, it was felt impractical to have the bills endorsed by the brokers, because it suited the commissionairs better to take the bills home first and then decide to which principal (mostly they had various principals) certain bills should be endorsed[65].

The question arises, whether the principal should profit by this practice, even if he had not agreed upon a del credere-guarantee of the agent (for which, of course, a special fee was to be paid). According to the general rules of the contract of mandate, which applied to the relation between a *commissionair* and his principal, the latter should indemnify the former from and against all liabilities and damages, incurred in the exercise of his functions, provided that the *commissionair* would not have committed dolus or culpa, which included culpa levissima[66]. Phoonsen apparently applied the law of exchange in this respect very strictly and did not appreciate the quality of the *commissionair's* endorsee, i. e. his principal, who was, after all, *dominus negotii.*

---

[63] Wissel-styl, 27, 7 and 8 (cp. 9, 3 and 4 and 36, 17).

[64] See *Van Apeldoorn,* op. cit. (n. 29), p. 26.

[65] Cp. the legal opinion in Verzameling van casus positien cit. (n. 18), 1788, VII, pp. 68 - 74. Phoonsen, Wissel-styl, note on 27, 7, mentions this practice but warns against it.

[66] See e. g. Van der Keessel, Praelectiones, on Inl. 3, 12, 8, v. "anders doende" (ed., p. 270).

In the case of 1721 (c) fortunately a legal opinion survived, published by Barels in his collection of legal opinions in commercial matters[67]. It was given by two advocates from Amsterdam in 1713, A. van den Ende and J. Schrik. From its exposé we learn that the agent, Six, had changed the exchange rate of the bill in order to obtain a fee *("avance")* from Sautijn, upon which they had agreed previously. This fact seems to have been of decisive importance for both counsels, because they used it, together with the fact that Six had the bill endorsed first to himself, as an argument for their conclusion that Six had become owner of the bill and, consequently, liable for its payment[68]. This conclusion, favourable to Sautijn, was in harmony with Phoonsen's view, to whom, as one would expect, reference was made[69].

It was, moreover, not only Phoonsen, who held this view, but also Du Puy de la Serra, an unquestionable authority on the law of exchange in France[70], who, in this respect, refers to a judgement to the same effect, rendered by the *Parlement de Paris* in 1676[71].

The court of Middelburg, as we have seen, dismissed the claim, perhaps because it was not convinced by those "foreign" authorities. Though the Supreme Court upheld the decision, it appears that not all its members shared the same view.

Bynkershoek, who was the judge-reporter in this case, argued that Six had been a mandatary of Sautijn and had acted properly. There was no reason, therefore, why Sautijn should have an action against Six. As to Phoonsen, what he said only applied to third parties, according to Bynker-

---

67 Advysen cit. (n. 18), 2, 41. This legal opinion dates from three years after the protest was made and two years before the case was brought before the court of Middelburg.

68 The opinion continues by pointing out that if one does not accept its view, Six will, in any event, have to prove that he paid for the bill in cash or *"in banco"*, without clearing an old debt to him (owed by the sellers of the bill), and furthermore that the sellers were in good repute. Reference is made to D. 3, 5, 36 (37), 1; D. 35, 1, 111; C. 5, 51, 7 and Joannes a Sande, Theatrum practicantium, 2, 9, 13.

69 Wissel-styl, 9, 3; 27, 8, notes 2 and 3.

70 See above n. 36. Our edition in: Daniel Jousse, Commentaire sur l'Ordonnance du commerce [...] avec des notes et explications coordonnant l'Ordonnance, le commentaire et le Code de commerce, par V. Bécane, Poitiers 1828.

71 16, 11 (ed., pp. 500 - 502): "Ceux qui ont mis des ordres ne sont pas recevables à opposer contre la garantie qui leur est demandée; que ce n'est pas pour leur compte qu'ils ont mis l'ordre, mais par commission ou pour prêter leur nom: car, en cette matière de garantie, l'on s'attache aux termes de la lettre de change". Cp. also Samuel Ricard, Traité général du commerce, [I - II], Amsterdam 1781, 2, 2, 3, 5 (ed., pp. 477 - 478): "Aucuns de ceux qui ont accepté, tiré, endossé une lettre de change, ne peuvent être déchargés de leur obligation, quoiqu'ils n'aient accepté, tiré et endossé que par commission. Les preneurs et les endosseurs des lettres de change, qui en prennent quelques-unes par commission d'un tiers, ont la prudence de les faire à l'ordre de celui pour compte duquel ils l'ont prise, au moyen de quoi ils ne sont plus sujets à aucune responsabilité vis-à-vis des porteurs". This, however, was not practiced in Amsterdam, as we have noticed.

shoek[72], who continued by pointing out, that Sautijn had accepted the bill from Six. Moreover, Sautijn had not returned it immediately after the protest for non-payment was made up, as was required by Phoonsen, but not before a month later. As a result of this Sautijn had lost his right to put forward any claim under the bill.

Justice Keetlaer agreed with Bynkershoek and so did the president of the chamber, Admirael. Justice De Vries held, that Six had been incautious by having the bill endorsed to himself and thus encumbering himself more than he was obliged to, since he was only a mandatary. Apparently De Vries followed the view of Phoonsen. Yet he agreed with Bynkershoek "for the rest", probably referring to the last mentioned argument regarding the returning of the bill after protest for non-payment. Justice Schaep did not agree with Bynkershoek on the first point of his argument, for he held that Six had been owner of the bill and, by endorsing it to Sautijn, had made himself liable to the latter under the strict observance of the law *("naer 't stricte wisselregt")*. Sautijn, however, did not observe the law either by not returning it to Six at once after the protest. So he lost his rights against Six. Justice Van der Hoop shared the views, expressed by Schaep, whereas justice De Roovere in particular agreed with the second argument. Perhaps he was not convinced by either point of view in respect of the first question. Justice Van Hees had doubts as to both arguments. Yet he was of the opinion that Sautijn could not effectively have been interested in whether the bill of exchange had been put in his or Six' name first. Apparently he inclined to Bynkershoek's view. Furthermore, he argued that by not returning the bill in due time the holder would not always be deprived of his rights under the bill, for instance when nothing was lost by being too late. But this should be proved and for that reason he advised an interlocutory judgement.

Considering the various standpoints in chambers we may conclude that in fact the case was decided on the second argument, i. e. that the bill had not been returned in time. For, as to the first argument – whether Six was at all liable to Sautijn on the strength of his endorsement –, three judges (Bynkershoek, Keetlaer and Admirael) would deny any liability of Six, three others (De Vries, Schaep and Van der Hoop) held the opposite view, whereas two judges (De Roovere and Van Hees) at least had doubts about it. The second ground, put forward by Bynkershoek for rejecting the claim, was, however, accepted by seven judges.

Bynkershoek, in his report in OT 1738, provides us with some more and interesting information. As one would expect, he refers to three judges (he does not mention their names, but without any doubt he meant De Vries, Schaep and Van der Hoop), who argued that Six should be condemned to

[72] Reference is made to Wissel-styl 26, 7, but this should be 27, 7.

pay the bill on the strength of his endorsement. Bynkershoek adds to the arguments, we already came across, that, according to their opinion, an agent would otherwise be in the position to commit fraud against his principal. For this he could do by endorsing a bill aquired for his own account to his principal, in case the drawer had become insolvent immediately after the bill had been endorsed to the agent. The explanation of this argument is, we submit, that in such a case the bill would most certainly be refused by the drawee, as a result of which the payee would have to bear the loss, since he would not be able to recover it from the drawer nor from the agent, if the latter would not be liable. Yet the agent, by negotiating the bill to his principal would have received the full value from him.

Now Bynkershoek states that the other five judges *"magis inclinabant in contrariam sententiam"*, because they thought the view of Phoonsen and Du Puy to be applicable only to a mandatary sued by a third party, but not to a principal wishing to seek recourse from his agent. For the bill was at his risk and he could not have been interested in whether the bill had been endorsed to him immediately or to his agent, with either an assignment of the right of action or a further endorsement to himself. Here we recognize the arguments, put forward by Bynkershoek and Van Hees during the discussion in chambers.

Phoonsen and Du Puy, Bynkershoek continues, speak indistinctly[73], but *"ratione consulta"* one should distinguish, unless it is established that the agent committed fraud *("nisi probetur mandatarium mala fide egisse")*. He, furthermore, argues that from the identity of the amount of the bill and the fact that the bill had been endorsed to the principal the very same day the agent had acquired it, it becomes clear, that the agent had acted in behalf and for account of the principal. It is remarkable that Bynkershoek refers to the fact that the amount of the bill had remained unchanged (i.e. the rate of exchange was not changed), because the opinion of Van den Ende and Schrik of 1713 was based on the opposite. If this opinion was produced in the proceedings before the Supreme Court, it probably did not convince the court, which may be easily understood if one takes into account that the fact that a fee was agreed upon would not always influence the nature of the relation between the agent and his principal. Van der Keessel, for instance, also held that the nature of mandatum is not changed by a renumeration for the mandatary, if such a renumeration is usually agreed upon[74]. Apparently

---

[73] One may doubt whether Bynkershoek was right, because Phoonsen made clear that the agent stood del credere effectively, which could only mean that Phoonsen held the view that in any case the principal could sue the agent. For the term "del credere" exclusively refers to the relationship between the principal and his agent. Cp. the opinion of Justice Van Bleiswijk in the case of 1736, as mentioned below in the text.

[74] Praelectiones, V, Amstelodami / Promunturii B.S. in urbe 1967, on Inl. 3, 45, 10 (ed., p. 492) and Theses Selectae, nr. 570.

there was no sufficient reason for the Supreme Court to infer from the fee, agreed upon by Sautijn, that Six stood del credere[75].

We submit that Bynkershoek in his notes especially expressed his own opinion and that, by doing so, gave the impression that the majority of judges fully agreed with him. We now know that this, at least, does not apply to De Rovere and Van Hees.

However, Bynkershoek also deals with the second argument, discussed in chambers, and states that all judges, except one (i. e. Van Hees), agreed upon that and that the decision of the court of Middelburg was upheld on that ground.

As to the case of 1736 (d), the report in the resolution-book shows us that most judges (the judge-reporter Duivkant, Keetlaer, Van der Hoop – who apparently had changed his mind after 15 years – Van der Does and the president, Bynkershoek) found that Van den Bosch had not acted in contravention of his mandate. Hence, according to the ordinary rules of law, he should not be liable to his principal Bringas. With regard to the opinion of Phoonsen, that the *commissionair* by having the bill endorsed to himself before endorsing it to his principal, stood del credere, justice Duivkant pointed out that Van den Bosch stood del credere towards third parties but not towards his principal. Phoonsen could not derogate from the law in this respect, i. e. the law of mandate. So, if Gomez had sued him, Van den Bosch should have been condemned. Duivkant found it absurd if Van den Bosch should suffer any loss, although he had not profited from the bill and was without *culpa*.

Justice De Rovere, in this case, placed his trust in the opinion of the merchants and not in Phoonsen's, who contradicted himself. Presumably De Rovere referred to chapter 25 of Phoonsen's book (also quoted by Duivkant), in which the general rules governing the relation between a *commissionair* and his principal are set out, which rules are in fact the same as those of the law of mandate. Justice Van der Hoop also agreed with Duivkant. He pointed out that the defendant had invoked a rule of customary law (i. e. the passage in Phoonsen's work), but that one should not decide against the Roman law *("'t gemeene rhegt")* on the basis of Phoonsen only. Therefore, Phoonsen's view should not be regarded as a rule of customary law. With this it is implied that, if it would be otherwise, Phoonsen would set aside the Roman law of mandate in this respect. Also Justice Van der Does held that Van den Bosch stood del credere only as far as Gomez was concerned and not towards Bringas.

---

[75] Generally an agent, standing del credere, stipulated a higher fee than usual. Cp. the opinion, quoted above n. 65 and an opinion in the same compilation, 1787, III, p. 29.

Justice Van Bleiswijk was the only dissenting judge. He pointed out that there was no question of an ordinary *actio mandati* in this case, but only the problem whether Van den Bosch had bound himself to his principal by the endorsement. He explained that del credere only concerns the relation between the agent and his principal[76], and that, if one takes del credere in that sense, Phoonsen's saying is perfectly clear. He, therefore, would accept that as customary law *("stijl mercantiel")*.

Bynkershoek agued as follows. Phoonsen only said that the *commissionair,* who did not stand del credere, would stand effectively del credere by having the bill endorsed to himself. This meant that he would guarantee the solvency of the drawer to any holder. Bynkershoek regarded standing del credere as such a guarantee (*"assurantie of borghtoght"*, as he called it in Dutch, according to the *resolutieboek*). From the notes on Phoonsen 25, 8 he inferred that the mere endorsement to the *commissionair* only made him liable to the holders. However, Bringas was in the possession of the bill of exchange, so he might be regarded as a holder. Now Bynkershoek said that, if we regard Bringas as a holder (payee), he would not acquire any right though, because he could always be repelled if his agent (i. e. Van den Bosch) was without culpa, since Bringas was his principal. Thus Bynkershoek chose to let the rules of mandate prevail over the rights of the holder under the bill. However, since Van Bleiswijk might have interpreted Phoonsen in the right way, Bynkershoek probably felt that he would have to find a solution also when Phoonsen was thus interpreted. If Phoonsen, he argued, explicitly stated that a *commissionair* made himself liable by his endorsement towards his principal, *"utique tanti non est ejus auctoritas, ut rationem vincat, aut legem"* (OT 2991). He found that the *ratio* and the *lex* relieved Van den Bosch from liability and that, therefore, it should be established *"ex usu (...) atque adeo ex exemplis et rebus judicatis"*, that his endorsement would cause him to be liable also towards his principal. There was, however, no sufficient evidence (two so-called *"turben"* contradicted each other[77]), Bynkershoek continued, whereas the decision of the *Parlement de Paris,* cited by Du Puy[78], should not be followed, because it must not be applied in this case, which

[76] Referring to Adriaen Verwer, Verhandelinge van 't recht der Hollantsche bodemerijen, in: Nederlants see-rechten, avaryen en bodemeryen, Amsterdam 1716, ad § 24 (p. 200), who confirms that del credere only takes place between a principal and his agent in respect of the debts which the latter incurred in connection with the business of his principal.

[77] Bynkershoek says in OT 2991 (ed., p. 60): "Et nihil quicquam eorum adducit, quin tantum abest, ut de eo constet inter mercatores, ut 15 Amsterdammenses 26 Apr. 1736, in hac ipsa causa responderint, Maevium non teneri, quatuordecim alii 6 Jun. 1735 contra quidem videbantur respondisse, sed advocata sola auctoritate Phoonsen, quem forte non intelligebant, nec etiam illi 14 expressa respondent, dat zo een endossant ook *aan sijn principale* verpligt is, in quo tamen cardo quaestionis versabatur". I have not been able to find these "turben" in the archives, since the papers in the cae have not been preserved.

[78] See above the text at n. 71 and that note.

had to be decided according to the customary law of Amsterdam *("ex usu Amsterdammensi").* Since no rule of Amsterdam customary law in this respect could be found, the question at stake had to be decided by the *ratio* and the *lex* (i.e. the Roman Law).

We submit that in this case the Supreme Court clearly established the rule that the *commissionair* was not liable under his endorsement towards his principal, provided that he had acted in accordance with his mandate.

This ruling was, in any event, accepted in Amsterdam because we have found two legal opinions by lawyers in that city (one of 1787 and the other of 1788[79]) in which its being in force is confirmed[80].

11. Conclusion

The four decisions of the Supreme Court, examined above, give us some valuable information, we submit, on the way the Court dealt with such difficult questions as were here at stake. We may conclude by suggesting that the four judgements show us, that the Court attached much value to the actual situation in which the problems in dispute had arisen and that the formal rules of the law of exchange did not easily set aside the general principles and rules of the *ius commune.*

---

79 See above n. 65 and n. 75.

80 One of the arguments used in these opinions is that the principal immediately acquires the ownership of the bill when it is delivered to the agent. Consequently the agent cannot be liable under the bill. Cp. the above in the text mentioned legal opinion in Barels, 2, 41, where it is said that the agent acquired the ownership of the bill. On the authority of the legal opinions of 1787 and 1788 Van der Keessel, Praelectiones, on Inl. 3, 45, 10 (ed., p. 492) adopted the same view that the agent cannot be held liable because the principal immediately acquires the ownership of the bill.

EVA-CHRISTINE FRENTZ*

Seerechtsentwicklung durch Seerechtsprechung: Der Beitrag des Hamburgischen Admiralitätsgerichts

I.

„Non sibi sed orbi" – diese Inschrift steht auf einem Portugaleser, den die Hamburgische Admiralität im Jahr 1690 prägen ließ. Für die seerechtliche Rechtsprechung der Admiralität, die sie als „Hamburgisches Admiralitätsgericht" von 1623 bis zu ihrer Auflösung durch den französischen Stadtmagistrat 1811 leistete, stellt sich die Frage: Bedeutet diese Inschrift Anspruch *und* Wirklichkeit – oder Anspruch, aber noch nicht Wirklichkeit?

Zweifellos hat das Hamburgische Admiralitätsgericht als gerichtlicher Spezialspruchkörper mit ausschließlicher Rechtsprechungskompetenz in Seehandels- und Seeversicherungsstreitigkeiten schon im 17. Jahrhundert über die Grenzen Hamburgs hinaus Aufmerksamkeit gefunden: Hinweise auf das Gericht finden sich bei Johann Marquard in dessen „Tractatus politico-iuridicus de iure mercatorum et commerciorum singulari" (Frankfurt 1662) und in Reinhold Kuricke's 1667 erschienenem Kommentar zum Hansischen Seerecht „Ius maritimum Hanseaticum. Access. diatriba de assecurationibus et Resolutiones quaestionum illustrium ad ius maritimum pertinentium". In seiner Dissertation „de commerciorum navalium iure singulari" untersucht der Wittenberger Doktorand Hermann Helm schon 1652 den Seeprozeß und einzelne seerechtliche Klagearten am Beispiel der Praxis mehrerer Seegerichte, darunter des Hamburgischen Admiralitätsgerichts und der Rota Genuensis. Franciscus Vasmer promoviert 1674 in Straßburg mit einer Arbeit „de admiralitate", in deren Kapiteln XXXVI und XXXVII er Zuständigkeit und Verfahren des Hamburgischen Admiralitätsgerichts behandelt und vergleichend auf einzelne Verfahrensmaximen der holländischen Seegerichte eingeht. 1709 verteidigt in Helmstedt Johann Friedrich Krüger seine Dissertation „de iudicio admiralitatis Hamburgensis"; die erhebliche Beachtung, die diese Arbeit nicht zuletzt wegen des Abdrucks des Admiralitätsprotokolls in Sachen Dorvill c. Reddeling findet – dieser 1656 vom Admiralitätsgericht entschiedene Fall gilt bis weit in die zweite

* Die Verfasserin dankt den Herausgebern der Reihe, Prof. Dr. Coing und Prof. Dr. Nörr, für die freundliche Aufforderung, zu diesem Band beizutragen.

Hälfte des 18. Jahrhunderts als leading case im Bodmereirecht –, veranlaßt Krüger's Doktorvater Präs. Johann Werlhof 1750 zu einer Neuausgabe der Dissertation unter dem Titel „Commentatio de iudicio admiralitatis Hamburgensis“. Bereits 1707 legt Martin Lucas Schele in Helmstedt die Dissertation „de instrumento assecurationis vulgo polizza“ vor, in deren Rahmen er das Hamburgische Admiralitätsgericht auch als Fachgericht für Assecuranzprozesse vorstellt. Zwei Hamburger Autoren behandeln – neben der Rechtsprechung – das Verfahren des Admiralitätsgerichts: Hermann Langenbeck in seinem Kommentar „Anmerkungen über das Hamburgische Schiff- und Seerecht“ (1727) und Johann Klefeker in Band VII seiner „Sammlung der Hamburgischen Gesetze und Verfassungen“, den er 1769 dem Seehandels- und Seeversicherungsrecht widmet. Schließlich geht Wilhelm Benecke 1810 im „System des Assecuranz- und Bodmereiwesens“ auf den Hamburgischen Admiralitätsprozeß ein und vergleicht ihn mit dem Verfahren der Seegerichte in Frankreich und England[1].

Das Interesse der Zeitgenossen am Hamburgischen Admiralitätsgericht ist damit zu erklären, daß dieses Gericht vor allem vor Inkrafttreten der Hamburgischen Assecuranz- und Havareiordnung 1731 bei zahlreichen Entscheidungen nicht auf vorgegebene Problemlösungen des Hamburgischen Gesetzgebers zurückgreifen konnte und deshalb Lösungsmodelle ausländischer Seegesetze bzw. ausländischer Gerichte rechtsvergleichend heranzog, um auf dieser Grundlage eigene Rechtsfortbildung zu betreiben. Bereits Krüger hat in seiner Dissertation im Abschnitt über die in- und ausländischen Rechtsquellen der Hamburgischen Admiralitätsjudikatur diesen Aspekt der richterlichen Rechtsfortbildung angedeutet; er ist kürzlich an anderer Stelle genauer untersucht worden[2].

Im folgenden soll – entsprechend der Zielsetzung der Arbeitsgruppe „The Courts and the Development of Commercial Law“ – die Frage beantwortet werden, welchen Beitrag das Hamburgische Admiralitätsgericht zur Entwicklung des materiellen Seerechts seiner Zeit geleistet hat und ob diesem Beitrag eine Wirkung „non sibi sed orbi“ beizumessen ist. Ausgehend von der Annahme, daß Rechtsentwicklung durch Rechtsprechung, Rechtswissenschaft und Gesetzgebung gefördert werden kann, bietet es sich an, die unmittelbaren Auswirkungen der Rechtsprechung des Hamburgischen Admiralitätsgerichts

- auf die Rechtsprechung anderer Seegerichte,
- auf die Seerechtswissenschaft,

---

[1] W. Benecke, System des Assecuranz- und Bodmereiwesens, Bände I - V, Hamburg 1805 - 1821, hier: Bd. IV, S. 379, 389ff., 400ff.

[2] *E.-C. Frentz,* Das Hamburgische Admiralitätsgericht (1623 - 1811). Prozeß und Rechtsprechung. Frankfurt/Main, Bern, New York 1985, S. 119ff., 132ff., 248.

– auf die seerechtliche Gesetzgebung

zu betrachten und an einigen Beispielen zu verdeutlichen.

II.

Schon bald nach seiner Gründung genießt das Hamburgische Admiralitätsgericht den Ruf einer „vorzüglichen Rechtserfahrenheit in See-Sachen“[3] und wird deshalb um seerechtliche Gutachten bzw. „responsa iuris“ gebeten. Diese responsa iuris erscheinen in zwei Formen:

Einerseits erstattet das Gericht informatorische oder konsultative Gutachten[4] an Privatleute, die in einem Streitfall "umb was de jure in specie mercantili davon zu judiciren, und daraus vor ein Außgang der Sache zu Erwarten stünde, (sich) bey hochlöblichem Admiralitaet- und zue See- und Handels-Sachen ordentlich gesetztem Gerichte Erkundigen, und eine belehrung deßfalls ... einholen“ mit dem Ersuchen, „über beygelegten Casum und der daraus in fine formirter Frage Ihr unpartheyisches und reiffliches Bedencken zu eröffnen und dasselbe sub Sigillo judicii Admiralitatis ... mit zu theilen“. Das Gericht bezeichnet in diesen Fällen sein Gutachten als „Admiralitäts-Responsum, jedoch ohne jemanden darunter zu prejudiciren“[5].

Während das responsum iuris hier trotz der umfassenden Prüfung des Gerichts, ob „in diesem casu in denen Seerechten und Assecurantz Ordnungen (etwas) Besonderes statuiret, oder durch Kauffmanns-Usance recipiret ist“[6], nicht den Charakter eines verbindlichen Entscheidungsvorschlags, sondern den eines Parteigutachtens hat, gilt Entgegengesetztes für die zweite Form der responsa iuris, die das Admiralitätsgericht anderen gerichtlichen Spruchkörpern im Nord- und Ostseeraum erteilt und die unmittelbar die Rechtsprechung dieser Gerichte beeinflussen. Ein Mitglied des Admiralitätsgerichts schreibt 1743, daß „hiesige Admiralitaet ... von verschiedenen auswärtigen Gerichten um ein rechtliches Gutachten in dergleichen See- und Handlungs-Sachen ... und (um) einen Spruch Rechtens ersuchet“ wird[7]. Bei diesen Gutachtenaufträgen handelt es sich um die

---

[3] J. Klefeker, Sammlung der Hamburgischen Gesetze und Verfassungen, Bände I - XII, Hamburg 1765 - 1773, hier: Bd. I, S. 12.

[4] Zu derartigen privaten Konsilien und informatorischen Gutachten vgl. *H. Gehrke,* Rechtsprechungs- und Konsiliensammlungen (Deutsches Reich), in: Handbuch der Quellen und Literatur der neueren europäischen Privatrechtsgeschichte, hg. von H. Coing, Bd. II, 2, München 1976, S. 1343ff., 1377, 1381ff.

[5] Auskunftsersuchen des Hieronymus Böckell Lt. und Responsum des Admiralitätsgerichts vom 3. 3. 1697, in: Staatsarchiv Hamburg, Senat Cl. VII, Lit. Ca, No. 1, Vol. 2a, Nr. 6, 7, 8.

[6] Responsum des Admiralitätsgerichts vom 3. 3. 1697, in: Staatsarchiv Hamburg, Senat Cl. VII, l.c.

[7] Staatsarchiv Hamburg, Senat Cl. VII, Lit. Ma, No. 6, Vol. 1a.

förmliche „pitte, weill die Parthen selbte acta auff ein Sehgerecht zue transmittire gebeten, dieselbe collegialiter mit fleiß zue verlesen, zue erwegen, undt in der Sachen, was den Sehrechten gemeß, zue erkennen, undt uns die acta nebst der Urthell versiegelt undt wollverschnüret hiewieder zu überfertigen“[8]. Das Admiralitätsgericht verfaßt auf diese Bitte ein responsum iuris mit abschließender „sententia cum rationibus decidendi“[9], die das ersuchende Gericht als für sich und die Parteien des anhängigen Seeprozesses verbindlich qualifiziert und im Text unverändert als eigene Entscheidung mit dem Zusatz „auf eingehohlten Raht der Deputirten Herren und Bürger der Admiralität zu Hamburg“ verkündet[10].

Dieses tatsächliche Procedere entspricht genau dem förmlichen Verfahren der Transmissio actorum oder Aktenversendung an bestimmte Juristenfakultäten, das sich seit dem 16. Jahrhundert bei den erst- und zweitinstanzlichen Gerichten in Deutschland durchsetzte und einen erheblichen Einfluß der Rechtswissenschaftler auf die gerichtliche Rechtsfindung zur Folge hatte, weil die ersuchenden Gerichte die Spruchformel der Fakultäten in der eigenen Entscheidung wörtlich übernahmen[11]. Von den Juristenfakultäten und Oberhöfen, die im Wege der Aktenversendung in Anspruch genommen wurden, unterscheidet sich das Hamburgische Admiralitätsgericht dadurch, daß es seine responsa iuris unentgeltlich erteilt und das Verfahren der Aktenversendung nach Hamburg nicht mit dem formellen Begriff „Transmissio actorum“ belegt[12]. Ein weiterer sehr bemerkenswerter Unterschied ist die Tatsache, daß mit dem Admiralitätsgericht ein erstinstanzliches Gericht um responsa iuris innerhalb einer Aktenversendung gebeten wird; demgegenüber gelten als „klassische“ Adressaten der Aktenversendung – abgesehen von den einzelnen gutachtenden Rechtsgelehrten[13] – die Kollegialorgane der Juristenfakultäten, Oberhöfe und Schöffenstühle, die im zeitgenössischen Rechtsverständnis mindestens die zweite Instanz der Rechtsfindung repräsentieren. Die das Admiralitätsgericht um responsa iuris ersuchenden Gerichte sind ihrerseits in der Regel Appellations- oder Revisionsgerichte in Seesachen, die die seerechtlichen Entscheidungen des örtlichen erstinstanzlichen Fracht- und Seegerichts oder „Segelhauses“ überprüfen[14].

---

[8] Gutachtenauftrag des Bürgermeisters und Rates der Stadt Stettin vom 25. 4. 1629 in Sachen Blume c. Holzen, in: Staatsarchiv Hamburg, Senat Cl. VII, Lit. Ca, No. 1, Vol. 2a, Nr. 16.

[9] So z.B. für die Obergerichte bzw. Senate von Stettin, Emden, Stargard, Stralsund; vgl. Staatsarchiv Hamburg, Senat Cl. VII, Lit. Ca, No. 2, Vol. 1b (Nr. 30, Lit. R, Nr. 31, Lit. W und X); vgl. ferner *Frentz,* S. 31ff. m.w.N.

[10] Vgl. die Nachweise in Fußnote 9.

[11] Vgl. *Gehrke,* S. 1378f.

[12] *Frentz,* S. 33 m.w.N.

[13] Vgl. hierzu *Gehrke,* S. 1377, 1379.

Die Aktenversendung in Seesachen an das Hamburgische Admiralitätsgericht hat in der Praxis offenbar derartige Ausmaße angenommen, daß David Mevius in einem consilium[15] die Zuständigkeit des Admiralitätsgerichts für die Erteilung von Rechtsgutachten prüfte und ablehnte: „Collegium Admiralitatis Hamburgensis facultatem et autoritatem de iure respondendi non habet". Mevius hält die Gutachten des Admiralitätsgerichts für unverbindlich und schreibt demgegenüber der Universität Rostock eine generelle Zuständigkeit für seerechtliche Rechtsauskünfte zu[16]. In der Tat war Rostock neben Frankfurt/Oder die Juristenfakultät, die schon aufgrund ihrer geographischen Nähe zur Schiffahrtspraxis besonders häufig – auch vom Hamburgischen Obergericht in Revisionsverfahren gegen Entscheidungen des Admiralitätsgerichts[17] – um seerechtliche responsa iuris im Aktenversendungsverfahren sowie um Fakultätskonsilien für Privatleute gebeten wurde. Daneben werden die binnenländischen Juristenfakultäten Helmstedt und Halle durch Transmissiones actorum in Seesachen öfter in Anspruch genommen, weil sich die dort lehrenden Präsiden Johann Werlhof und Justus Henning Böhmer der Seerechtsforschung besonders verpflichtet fühlten[18].

Mevius erklärt seine negative Stellungnahme hinsichtlich des Hamburgischen Admiralitätsgerichts damit, daß dessen Gutachten nur auf einem einseitigen Parteivortrag „non informati plene de casu controverso" beruhen. Diese Begründung ist allenfalls für die Erstattung von Parteigutachten schlüssig, denen das Admiralitätsgericht selbst – wie erwähnt – keine Allgemeinverbindlichkeit beimißt. Die Frage der Zulässigkeit der förmlichen, gegebenenfalls prozeßordnungsmäßig sanktionierten Aktenversendung an das Admiralitätsgericht hat Mevius, obwohl er sie im Obersatz seines Consiliums sinngemäß in Bezug nimmt, nicht geklärt.

Ein anderes Problem, das die Parteien der Seeprozesse im 17. und 18. Jahrhundert teilweise so hoch einstuften, daß sie schriftsätzlich entweder eine bestimmte Juristenfakultät ablehnten oder grundsätzlich gegen die Transmissio actorum an Universitäten plädierten[19], ist die Gewährleistung

---

[14] So die Obergerichte bzw. Senate der Städte Stettin, Emden, Stargard, Stralsund, in: Staatsarchiv Hamburg, Senat Cl. VII, Lit. Ca, No. 2, Vol. 1b (Nr. 30, Lit. R, Nr. 31, Lit. W und X).

[15] D. Mevius, Consilia posthuma ... in quibus quaestiones intricatissimae atque utilissimae ex iure publico ac privato, feudali ac canonico discutiuntur et ... deciduntur, Frankfurt / Stralsund 1680, consilium XV, n. 59.

[16] Mevius, n. 58.

[17] Vgl. hierzu *Frentz*, S. 112ff.

[18] Dies ergibt sich aus den Beispielen der Aktenversendung an das Admiralitätsgericht bei Kellinghusen, de discrimine tempestatis marinae, von Seeschaden, Halle 1709, p. 39 - 41, 55, 56.

[19] Beispiel: Instrumentum gravaminum vom 5. 5. 1688 in dem 1683 vor dem Admiralitätsgericht und 1688 vor dem Hamburgischen Obergericht verhandelten Verfahren Thomsen c. Porten, Staatsarchiv Hamburg, Reichskammergericht, T 27.

der seerechtlichen Fachkunde bei der Ausarbeitung der Rechtsgutachten. Das Admiralitätsgericht löst dieses Problem bei seinen Responsen an auswärtige Gerichte, indem der Urteilsentwurf von einem rechtsgelehrten Ratsherrn des Gerichts nach Beratung der Sache mit vier weiteren Gerichtsmitgliedern (einem Ratsherrn, zwei kaufmännischen Admiralitätsbürgern, einem Schiffer) abgefaßt wird[20]; für Einzelfälle geht aus den Akten des Gerichts hervor, daß der Referent seinen Entscheidungsentwurf mit dem sonst an der Rechtsfindung des Admiralitätsgerichts nicht beteiligten Admiralitätssekretär bespricht, wenn der Sekretär über die allgemeine Qualifikation als Lizentiat beider Rechte hinaus als besonderer Kenner des Seerechts gilt. Auf diese Weise werden z.B. Julius Henrich Schaffshausen I.U.L. (Admiralitätssekretär 1693 - 1698) und Hermann Langenbeck I.U.D., der Verfasser des Seerechtskommentars (Admiralitätssekretär 1703 - 1708), an den Rechtsauskünften beteiligt[21].

Bereits aus dieser Verfahrenshandhabung ist erkennbar, daß sich das Admiralitätsgericht der Verantwortung für die Richtigkeit seiner Urteilsentwürfe wegen der unmittelbaren Wirkung auf die Rechtsprechung fremder Gerichte sehr bewußt ist. In formeller Hinsicht wird das Gericht dieser Verantwortung gerecht durch das Zusammenwirken von (See-)Rechtsgelehrten, Kennern der internationalen kaufmännischen Usancen und erfahrenen Kapitänen[22] bei der Gutachtenerstattung. In materiellrechtlicher Hinsicht fällt auf, daß das Gericht mit Rücksicht auf fremde seerechtliche Bestimmungen im örtlichen Zuständigkeitsbereich der ersuchenden auswärtigen Gerichte sein responsum iuris einerseits auf dieses fremde Seerecht, andererseits auf Hamburgisches Seerecht stützt und vergleichend die internationalen Seerechte und Usancen bzw. Assecuranzordnungen heranzieht; im Gutachten spiegelt sich dieser rechtsvergleichende Ansatz in der Formulierung, der Entscheidungsvorschlag sei „den See-rechten und allgemeinen See-gebreuchen gemeß“ oder er beruhe auf „üblichen Seerechten“[23].

Die Rechtsfragen, die im Rahmen der Aktenversendung an das Admiralitätsgericht gerichtet werden, stammen bemerkenswerterweise nur zum kleineren Teil aus dem Seeversicherungsrecht, für das es bis zum Erlaß der Hamburgischen Assecuranz- und Havareiordnung 1731 im Nord- und Ostseeraum sowie in Skandinavien noch keine – in Preußen im Preußischen

---

[20] Vgl. die Nachweise in Fußnote 14.

[21] Responsum iuris vom 28. 2. 1695 an Rat und Bürgermeister von Stettin, responsum iuris vom 4. 6. 1705 an Rat und Bürgermeister von Emden, Staatsarchiv Hamburg, Senat Cl. VII, Lit. Ca, No. 2, Vol. 1b (Nr. 30, Lit. R).

[22] Zum Fachkundeprinzip bei der Berufung der Mitglieder des Admiralitätsgerichts vgl. *Frentz*, S. 46ff., 249.

[23] Blume c. Holzen, Urteilsentwurf des Admiralitätsgerichts vom 25. 7. 1629, Staatsarchiv Hamburg, Senat Cl. VII, Lit. Ca, No. 1, Vol. 2a, Nr. 18; vgl. auch Hupping c. Hübner, Urteil des Admiralitätsgerichts vom 20. 6. 1689, Staatsarchiv Hamburg, Reichskammergericht, H 181, Protocollum Admiralitatis 20. 6. 1689.

Seerecht 1727 Cap. VI nicht sehr umfassende – gesetzliche Regelungen gab. Im Seeversicherungsrecht hätte tatsächlich ein besonderes Bedürfnis für eine Rechtsvereinheitlichung durch Richterrecht bestehen müssen. Die Mehrzahl der Gutachtenaufträge entspringt seehandelsrechtlichen Problemen, die entweder sehr umstritten oder im zeitgenössischen Gesetzesrecht noch nicht legislatorisch gelöst waren. Diese Beobachtung läßt sich an dem responsum iuris demonstrieren, das das Admiralitätsgericht 1629 dem Senat der Stadt Stettin als Revisionsinstanz in Sachen Blume c. Holzen übermittelt[24].

Kernfrage des Rechtsstreits ist, ob die Kosten (Gerichts- und Advocaturkosten) eines für Schiff *und* Ladung erfolgreichen Reclameprozesses im Ausland und die während der Reclame für die Schiffsbesatzung aufgewandten Verpflegungskosten in Avarie grosse oder in Avarie particulière zu rechnen sind. Die Abgrenzung zwischen Fällen der Avarie grosse, in denen die eingetretenen Schäden im Wege der Kontribution über Schiff, Gut und Fracht verteilt werden, und Fällen der Avarie particulière, in denen die Schäden von den betroffenen Eigentümern – Reedern oder Befrachtern – außerhalb der Gefahrengemeinschaft allein zu tragen sind, treffen die älteren Seerechte kasuistisch und ohne dogmatisch durchgeformte Systematik. Im 17. Jahrhundert gilt dies noch für das Hamburgische Seerecht 1603/05 und für das Hansische Seerecht 1614, die wie die älteren Seegesetze nicht die Terminologie der „havaria grossa" oder „avaria grandis" im Verhältnis zur partikulären Havarei verwenden, sondern entweder auf die Rechtsfolge der Kontribution „über Schiff und Gut gehen" oder generell auf das „für Haverey rechnen" verweisen[25]. Unter dem Einfluß der Rechtswissenschaft[26] formuliert das französische Seerecht in Ordonnance de la marine 1681 liv. III, tit. VII, §§ 1, 2 abstrakte und gesonderte Definitionen der Avarie grosse und der Avarie particulière[27], verzichtet aber nicht auf die gesetzliche Regelung der einzelnen Avarie-Konstellationen in Ordonnance de la marine 1681 liv. III, tit. VII, §§ 3 - 8. Im deutschen Sprachraum folgen dieser Struktur der Ordonnance de la marine 1681 das Preußische Seerecht 1727 (Cap. VIII: Von der Haverey) und die Hamburgische Assecuranz- und Havareiordnung 1731 (Tit. XXI: Von Havereyen und deren Dispachirung). Die prägnanteste und gleichzeitig für die deutsche Seerechtswissenschaft des 18.

---

[24] Staatsarchiv Hamburg, Senat Cl. VII, Lit. Ca, No. 1, Vol. 2a, Nr. 18; zu den weiteren Rechtsfragen dieses Falles vgl. *Frentz,* S. 209ff.

[25] Generell zur Bewertung der Hanseatischen Seerechte des 16. und 17. Jahrhunderts als „Recht einer Übergangszeit" *G. Landwehr,* Die Hanseatischen Seerechte des 16. und 17. Jahrhunderts, in: 1667 ars sjölag i ett 300 – arigt perspektiv, hg. von Kjell A. Modeér, Lund 1984, S. 68ff., 119.

[26] Weitere Nachweise bei R.-J. Valin, Commentaire sur l'Ordonnance de la marine 1681, avec des notes par V. Becane, Poitiers 1829, p. 577, 578; B.-M. Emérigon, traité des assurances et des contrats à la grosse, vol. I et II, Marseille 1783, hier: v. I, ch. 12, sect. 41, §§ 1, 2.

[27] Auch der sog. „kleinen Havarie", die hier außer acht bleiben soll.

Jahrhunderts vorbildhafte Definition der Avarie grosse findet sich – nach vorangegangenen Abstraktionsansätzen in Helm's Dissertation von 1652[28] – in der Dissertation „de havaria“, die Paul Gerckens 1721 in Groningen verteidigt: “Havaria extraordinaria sive grossa est communis contributio navis et mercium navi impositarum ad damnum commune sublevandum, quod praecedente voluntate magistri navis eiusque officialium imminente periculo factum est. Huius requisita dantur tria: (1) ut immineat periculum, vel saltem juxta regulas prudentiae metuatur. (2) ut liberato animo, et ex intentione residuum conservandi, voluntaria subeatur amissio. (3) ut navis ad locum destinatum salva pervenerit, quorum si unum deficiat, non erit havaria, sed res amissa perit suo domino“. Diese drei abstrakten essentialia der Avarie grosse werden aufgegriffen unter anderem in der Straßburger Dissertation von Lucas Andreas v. Bostell „de contributione propter iactum marinum, vulgo havaria“ (1735), in Langenbeck's Seerechtskommentar 1727[29], in Klefeker's Seerechtskompendium 1769[30], im 19. Jahrhundert von Wilhelm Benecke[31] und in den 1851 in Berlin erschienenen „Grundsätzen des praktischen Europäischen Seerechts“ von Carl v. Kaltenborn[32]. Sie prägen im geltenden deutschen Seerecht noch die Legaldefinition der großen Haverei in HGB § 700 Abs. 1, 1. Halbsatz.

Die skizzierte begrifflich schärfere Abgrenzung zwischen Avarie grosse und Avarie particulière ist dem Hamburgischen Admiralitätsgericht bei der Erteilung seiner Rechtsauskunft 1629 nicht bekannt; sein Entscheidungstenor, die Kosten des Reclameprozesses (und die während des Prozesses angefallenen Verpflegungskosten für die Besatzung) als Avarie grosse zu qualifizieren, zeigt aber, daß es die genannten drei Abgrenzungskriterien schon damals als Rechtsgedanken für eine tragfähige Analogie zu einem seit langem anerkannten Fall der Avarie grosse berücksichtigt: Bereits die Lex Rhodia de iactu und Consolato del mare, cap. 227, bestimmen, daß die Kosten eines Vergleichs oder Lösegeldvertrages mit einem Kaper als Avarie grosse zu behandeln sind. Entsprechendes sehen Guidon de la mer, ch. 6, art. 1, in Hamburg dann das ältere Seerecht 1497 (P 50) und das Seerecht 1603/05 in Part. II, Tit. 19, Art. 1, Satz 1, vor. In der letztgenannten Norm heißt es: „Würde mit etlichen See=Räubern Composition, oder ein Vertrag gemachet und mit genandtem übergegebenen Gute das Schiff und andere Güter von den See=Räubern entfreyet, den Schaden soll man theilen zu bezahlen vom Schiff und Gute wie oben von geworffenen Gütern gemeldet“.

---

28 H. Helm, de commerciorum navalium iure singulari, Wittenberg 1652, These 9, § 14.

29 H. Langenbeck, Anmerkungen über das Hamburgische Schiff- und Seerecht, Hamburg 1727, p. 163.

30 Klefeker, Bd. VII, p. 176, 177.

31 Benecke, Bd. IV, S. 7ff.

32 Band II, S. 76f.

Der Hansische Seerechtskreis weist zwar weder in den Rôles d'Oléron und im Wisbyschen Seerecht noch – für Stettin maßgeblich – im Seerecht der Hansestadt Lübeck 1586 und im Hansischen Seerecht 1614 eine dem romanischen Seerechtskreis adäquate Vorschrift auf; Kuricke[33] legt aber zumindest Hansisches Seerecht 1614, Tit. VIII, Art. 4, im Lichte der eindeutigen Avarie-grosse-Regelung des Hamburgischen Seerechts 1603/05, II,19,1, Satz 1, aus. Zu dieser Hamburgischen Norm zieht das Admiralitätsgericht in Blume c. Holzen eine Analogie, indem es in Vorwegnahme des Satzes von Loccenius[34] „commune est periculum et communis utilitas" davon ausgeht, daß ein erfolgreicher Reclameprozeß vor dem Prisengericht Schiff und Ladung ebenso begünstigt wie die erfolgreiche Ranzion der aufgebrachten Schiffe und Güter durch den Vergleich mit einem Kaper. Insoweit erscheint dem Gericht eine Erweiterung des Katalogs der klassischen Fälle der Avarie grosse gerechtfertigt, und zwar auch hinsichtlich der während des Reclameverfahrens zusätzlich erforderlichen Verpflegungsaufwendungen für die Besatzung. Deren Einbeziehung in Avarie grosse entspricht dem Prinzip, daß unmittelbare Folgeschäden und -kosten eines Avarie-grosse-Falles ebenfalls von der Gefahrengemeinschaft zwischen Reedern, Schiffer und Befrachtern zu tragen sind. Dieses Prinzip realisiert das Hamburgische Seerecht 1603/05 in Part. II, Tit. 16, Art. 4 unter dem zeitlichen Aspekt (Vernichtung „etlicher Güter *über* der Werffung") und in Part. II, Tit. 16, Art. 10 bzw. in Part. II, Tit. 14, Art. 42 unter dem funktionalen Aspekt (Kosten im Nothafen und Heilungskosten nach Kämpfen mit Seeräubern).

Die vom Admiralitätsgericht in Blume c. Holzen hinsichtlich der Reclamekosten geleistete Rechtsfortbildung ist beachtlich – nicht nur, weil das Gericht in den zeitgenössischen Seegesetzen und in der ihm zugänglichen zeitgenössischen Seerechtsliteratur keine vorbildhafte Havareiregelung für Vermögenseinbußen aus Reclameaufwendungen vorfindet, sondern auch, weil das responsum iuris weiter geht als die ratio legis der bis dahin anerkannten Fälle der Avarie grosse, in denen zwischen der absichtlichen Schädigung bzw. Aufwendung und der tatsächlichen Rettung von Schiff und Ladung ein unmittelbarer Kausalzusammenhang besteht, der allenfalls durch vis maior, aber nicht durch gezielte obrigkeitliche Einwirkung unterbrochen werden kann; im Fall der Aufwendungen für den Reclameprozeß wird die „Salvirung" hingegen durch eine prisengerichtliche Entscheidung bestimmt und bedingt.

Wie umstritten die Rechtsfrage in Blume c. Holzen in der Folgezeit bleibt, zeigt ihre weitere Behandlung in Rechtswissenschaft und Gesetzgebung: Die Analogielösung des Admiralitätsgerichts beherrscht deutlich Art. 29 des

---

[33] R. Kuricke, Ius maritimum Hanseaticum, ad Tit. VIII, Art. IV.

[34] J. Loccenius, de iure maritimo et navali libri III, Amsterdam 1651, hier: lib. 2, cap. 8, n. 5.

Entwurfs für eine Hamburgische Assecuranz- und Havareiordnung, den Hermann Langenbeck 1721/22 formuliert[35]: „Zur Havaria grossa gehören die extraordinairen unkosten und der schade der gethan oder gelitten wird, zum gemeinen besten des Schiffes und der Ladung ... item ranzionirung des Schiffes und der Ladung, sambt allen unkosten dieserwegen angewandt, *processen oder dergleichen freymachungen,* alles dieses gehet über dem Schiff, deßen Ladung, und der Fracht". Konsequent und präzise ist Langenbeck's Differenzierung in seinem Kommentar[36]: „Dieser (Reclame-)Process ist entweder general, um die Freyheit des Schiffs und der Ladung zu erhalten, und in diesem Fall gehören die Reclame-Kosten – so wie die Advocatur- und Procuratur-Gebühren in reclame Fällen – in Avarie Gross, oder Special, wan entweder das Schiff, oder auch die Ladung allein, oder ein Theil der Güter, wie es die Umstände geben können, reclamiret werden, und dann machet sie particulier Avarie zu Lasten des Reclamanten". Auf derselben Linie wie Langenbeck argumentieren Benecke[37] und v. Kaltenborn[38], in Frankreich Emérigon[39] und Pardessus[40]. Andererseits setzt sich die schrankenlose Einbeziehung der Reclameprozeßaufwendungen und deren Folgekosten in Avarie grosse – wie ein beispielhafter Blick auf Ordonnance de la marine 1681, III,7,6/7, auf die Hamburgische Assecuranz- und Havareiordnung 1731, Tit. XXI, Art. 9, Ziffer 4, und auf das Preußische Seerecht 1727, Cap. VIII, Art. 26, zeigt – in der Gesetzgebung nicht durch[41]. Im angloamerikanischen Bereich tendieren Gerichtspraxis und Rechtswissenschaft dazu, die Reclameprozeßkosten nicht in Avarie grosse zu rechnen, sondern im Wege der Avarie particulière der Ladung bzw. den Befrachtern allein zur Last zu bringen[42]. Dahinter steht der Gedanke, daß mit der vom Admiralitätsgericht und von den genannten deutschen und französischen Kommentatoren befürworteten Ausdehnung des Avarie-grosse-Begriffs ein ursprüngliches essentiale der Avarie grosse, nämlich die unmittelbar drohende Gefahr für Schiff und Ladung, vernachlässigt wird. Kent[43] betont: "The jettison must be made for sofficient cause, and not from groundless timidity. A jettison is only permitted in cases of extreme necessity". Der

---

[35] Staatsarchiv Hamburg, Senat Cl. VII, Lit. Lb, No. 2, Vol. 3.

[36] Langenbeck, p. 305, 198.

[37] Benecke, Bd. IV, S. 89.

[38] v. Kaltenborn, Bd. II, S. 117f.

[39] Emérigon, v. I, ch. 12, sect. 41, § 9.

[40] J. M. Pardessus, Cours de droit commercial, édit. III. Paris 1825, tome III., n. 741.

[41] Zur zurückhaltenden Bewertung der genannten Rechtsfrage in Frankreich vgl. Valin, p. 587 - 589.

[42] R. Stevens, Versuch über Havarien und Assecuranz-Gegenstände, enthaltend eine Darstellung des neueren Englischen Rechts und der Praxis in Assecuranz- und Havarie-Sachen (deutsch von F. C. Schumacher), Hamburg 1829, p. 23 m.w.N.; v. Kaltenborn, l.c., Bd. II, S. 117, Fn. 67 m.w.N.

[43] Kent, Commentaries on american law, 2. Auflage, Newyork 1832, part. V, lect. 47, p. 233.

Annahme eines in diesem strengen havarierechtlichen Sinne unmittelbar drohenden Schadens steht in der Tat entgegen, daß sich die Verlustgefahr in Aufbringungsfällen für Reeder, Schiffer und Befrachter erst in der Condemnation, d.h. in der Entscheidung des ausländischen Prisengerichts aktualisiert, mit der Schiff und Ladung zu einer „unstreitigen Prise" (so die Hamburgische Assecuranz- und Havareiordnung 1731, Tit. XVI, Art. 1) erklärt werden. Weiter wird in England befürchtet, daß die Reclameaufwendungen unter Berücksichtigung des tatsächlichen Wertverhältnisses zwischen älteren, abgenutzten Schiffen und hochwertigen Ladungsgütern im Ergebnis nur der Ladung zu gute kämen[44].

Diese Kritik hat man in Deutschland bei der Kodifikation des Handelsgesetzbuches beachtet. HGB § 707 Ziffer 2 bestimmt: „Nicht als große Haverei, sondern als besondere Haverei werden angesehen ... die Reklamekosten, *auch wenn* Schiff und Ladung zusammen und beide mit Erfolg reklamiert werden". Die Gesetzesformulierung läßt vermuten, daß die Abgrenzung der Reclamekosten zur Avarie grosse/großen Haverei bis zur Schlußredaktion umstritten war.

Festzuhalten bleibt am Beispiel des Verfahrens Blume c. Holzen, daß das Admiralitätsgericht in seinen verbindlichen Rechtsgutachten für auswärtige Gerichte einen Beitrag zur Überbrückung von seerechtlichen Gesetzeslücken durch Rechtsfortbildung, damit einen Beitrag zur Rechtssicherheit und weitergehend zu einer ansatzweisen Rechtsvereinheitlichung geleistet hat. Der letztgenannte Gesichtspunkt prägt insgesamt die Rechtsprechung des Gerichts, denn das Gericht will neben dem Hamburgischen Seerecht stets auch die internationalen „Seerechte, in so weit selbe dem Stadt-Buche nicht entgegen", in seiner Judikatur zur Geltung bringen[45].

III.

Tiefgreifend und mit Dauerwirkung beeinflußt die Rechtsprechung des Hamburgischen Admiralitätsgerichts die seerechtliche Literatur und Rechtswissenschaft vom 17. bis ins 19. Jahrhundert.

Eine besonders enge Beziehung zwischen der Rechtsprechung des Gerichts und der Rechtswissenschaft dokumentiert sich in den Personen, die Richter des Admiralitätsgerichts und gleichzeitig führende Seerechtswissenschaftler ihrer Zeit sind. Insofern kann man auch beim Hamburgischen Admiralitätsgericht von einer konstanten „osmosis" zwischen Gerichtspraxis und Rechtswissenschaft sprechen, die Piergiovanni bei den italienischen

---

[44] Stevens, p. 23; vgl. auch *Frentz*, S. 211f.

[45] Vgl. hierzu *Frentz*, S. 119f. unter Hinweis auf die Gerichtsordnung des Admiralitätsgerichts.

Handelsrechtlern Scaccia, Casaregis, Ansaldo de Ansaldis und Rocco als Resultat ihrer wissenschaftlichen und richterlichen Tätigkeit an den Rotae von Genua, Florenz, Rom und Neapel diagnostiziert hat[46].

Ein prägnantes Beispiel für eine derartige Wechselwirkung zwischen Richteramt beim Admiralitätsgericht und Seerechtsforschung ist die Arbeit von Hermann Langenbeck I. U. D., der von 1703 bis 1708 und wieder von 1721 bis 1727 Mitglied des Admiralitätsgerichts war und gleichzeitig Verfasser des 1721/22 vorgelegten Entwurfs für eine Hamburgische Assecuranz- und Havareiordnung sowie des 1727 in erster und 1740 posthum in zweiter Ausgabe erschienenen Seerechtskommentars „Anmerkungen über das Hamburgische Schiff- und Seerecht". Langenbeck's Kommentar ist ein Buch für die Praxis – dies beweist die überwiegend lemmatische Kommentierung des Hamburgischen Seehandelsrechts im Seerecht 1603/05, Tit. 13 - 19 –, gleichzeitig aber ein Buch mit einem weitergehenden Anspruch, der vor allem in den acht Supplementa zum Ausdruck kommt: Langenbeck will darstellen, „was nach meinem Begriff aus denen gemeinen See-Rechten, der hiesigen Praxi und aus eigener vieljährigen Erfahrung observiret, und Anmerckungs=würdig geurtheilet habe"[47].

Unter den „gemeinen See-Rechten" versteht Langenbeck die Gesamtheit des europäischen Seerechts seiner Zeit, das er in Gestalt des Consolato del mare, der niederländischen Seerechte und der Assecuranzordnungen von Amsterdam, Antwerpen, Rotterdam und Middelburg, der Ordonnance de la marine 1681, der Schwedischen und der Dänischen Seerechte sowie der Hanseatischen Seerechte[48] verarbeitet. Damit korrespondiert die Auseinandersetzung Langenbecks mit den zeitgenössischen Seerechtswissenschaftlern, z.B. mit Verver, Weytsen, Straccha, von Aitsma, Loccenius, Kuricke, Surland, M. L. Schele, Grotius, Gail und Pufendorf. Von einer klar definierten seerechtlichen Einheitsidee als Grundlage der Kommentierungsmethode im Sinne Scherners[49] wird man gleichwohl bei Langenbeck noch nicht sprechen können, aber eine vor allem im seeversicherungsrechtlichen Teil des Kommentars weitgehend systematische Rechtsvergleichung ist deutlich erkennbar.

Die „hiesige Praxis" umfaßt das kaufmännische Gewohnheitsrecht und die Observanz, die als Rechtsquellen in der Rechtsprechung des Admirali-

[46] *V. Piergiovanni,* Bericht im Januar 1983 an die Arbeitsgruppe „The Courts and the Development of Commercial Law", Berichtsabdruck, S. 3.

[47] Langenbeck, Anmerkungen . . ., p. 370, § 7.

[48] Gemeint sind hier das Hamburgische Seerecht von 1497 und von 1603/05, das Seerecht im Lübecker Stadtrecht 1586, Buch VI, das Wisbysche Seerecht, die Rôles d'Oléron, das Hansische Seerecht von 1591 und von 1614. Zum Begriff der „Hanseatischen Seerechte" vgl. auch *Landwehr,* S. 68 - 70.

[49] *K. O. Scherner,* Allgemeine Rechtsgrundsätze und Rechtsvergleichung im europäischen Handelsrecht des 17. und 18. Jahrhunderts, in: Ius Commune, Band VII (1978), S. 118ff., 125ff.

tätsgerichts eine nicht unbedeutende Rolle spielen[50] und die Langenbeck in der Ausprägung der Hamburgischen Kauf- und Seemannspraxis juristisch würdigt.

Die „eigene vieljährige Erfahrung" schließlich bezieht sich auf Langenbecks richterliche Tätigkeit beim Admiralitätsgericht. Er zitiert zwar auch Erkenntnisse des Hamburgischen Niedergerichts und Obergerichts sowie bei Assecuranzproblemen die Meinung der Rota Genuensis, vor allem aber Entscheidungen des Admiralitätsgerichts aus den Jahren 1681 bis 1727, aus dem Jahr 1656 die Sache Dorvill c. Reddeling. Diese Nachweise der Admiralitätsrechtsprechung – mit benanntem Rubrum und mit in zwei Sätzen skizziertem Sachverhalt – dienen Langenbeck entweder als nachträgliche Bestätigung seiner Kommentierung oder als Ausgangspunkt für die Weiterentwicklung eines neuen Rechtsgedankens.

Im Sinne der zweiten Variante wirkt der von ihm mitgeteilte Fall Lemvig c. diverse Assecuradeure, in dem das Admiralitätsgericht 1726 für Recht erkennt, daß gemünztes englisches Geld in den allgemeinen Begriff „Kaufmannschaften" einzubeziehen sei und unter dieser Benennung – ohne präzisere Bezeichnung des Versicherungsgegenstandes in der Police – wirksam versichert werden könne[51]. Langenbeck selbst hatte noch in seinem Assecuranzordnungsentwurf 1721/22, Art. 12, verlangt, „Edelsteine, Perlen, Geld, Gold und Silber" als Versicherungsobjekte in der Police spezifiziert anzugeben. Diese Auffassung entsprach den Bestimmungen in der Middelburger Assecuranzordnung 1689, Art. 7, in der Amsterdamer Assecuranzordnung 1598/1603, Art. 17, und in der Rotterdamer Assecuranzordnung 1721, Art. 41, in denen nach dem Vorbild der Florentinischen Assecuranzartikel vom 15. 6. 1526[52] Geld, Gold und Silber nicht unter die „generale benaminge van Waren ende Koopmanschappen" gefaßt werden. Auch M. L. Schele hält in seiner versicherungsrechtlichen Dissertation 1707[53] die exakte „designatio mercium, quae, quales et quantae illae sint" in der Police noch für erforderlich. Gleiches gilt für preußische Geldversicherungen nach dem Preußischen Seerecht 1727 (Cap. VI, Art. 3).

Andererseits fehlt eine entsprechende Verpflichtung in der Ordonnance de la marine 1681. Im französischen Assecuranzrecht – ebenso im englischen

---

50 *Frentz,* S. 128ff. Zur Bedeutung der „mercantile customs" bei der Rechtsfindung der englischen common law courts vgl. *K. W. Nörr,* The European Side of the English Law: A Few Comments from a Continental Historian, in: Englische und kontinentale Rechtsgeschichte: ein Forschungsprojekt, hg. von H. Coing und K. W. Nörr, Berlin 1985 (Comparative Studies in Continental and Anglo-American Legal History, Band 1), S. 15ff., 23f.

51 Langenbeck, Anmerkungen . . ., p. 398.

52 Zitiert nach N. Magens, Versuch über Assecuranzen, Havereyen und Bodmereyen, Hamburg 1753, p. 382.

53 M. L. Schele, de instrumento assecurationis vulgo polizza, Helmstedt 1707, p. 35.

Recht[54] – bedarf es keiner speziellen Benennung edler Metalle oder Geldmünzen in der Police; diese gelten unter der generellen Bezeichnung „sur facultés“ oder „sur marchandises“ als versichert[55]. Die französische Rechtsauffassung beeinflußt das Admiralitätsgericht; an dem Verfahren Lemvig c. diverse Assecuradeure wird besonders deutlich, daß sich das Gericht im Assecuranzrecht vornehmlich mit den französischen und den niederländischen Regelungsmodellen auseinandersetzt und – wie auch andere Urteile zeigen – für den Hanseatischen Seerechtskreis sehr eigenständige abschließende Wertungen trifft[56]. Die Entscheidung des Gerichts hat zur Folge, daß Langenbeck in seinem Kommentar die an den holländischen Seerechten orientierte Meinung aus seinem Assecuranzordnungsentwurf 1721/22 aufgibt, dem Gericht zustimmt und ein neues juristisches und wirtschaftliches Regelungsmotiv aus der Ratio der Gerichtsentscheidung entwickelt. Die in Lemvig c. diverse Assecuradeure 1726 geäußerte Rechtsmeinung des Admiralitätsgerichts findet eine derartige Akzeptanz, daß sie die entgegenstehende Vereinbarung der Hamburger Assecuradeure im Vergleich 1697, Art. 1, die eine umfassende Bezeichnungspflicht für versicherte Güter enthält, für das Feld der Geldversicherungen derogiert, als „hiesige Praxis“ in Hamburg anerkannt wird und schließlich den Gesetzestext über Versicherungsobjekte in der Endfassung der Hamburgischen Assecuranz- und Havareiordnung 1731 (Tit. IV, Art. 9) bestimmt: „Gold und Silber, gemünzet oder ungemünzet, wie auch Edelgesteine und Perlen, werden unter der allgemeinen Benennung von Kaufmannschaften mit verstanden“.

Ein anderes Beispiel für die Personalunion zwischen Richtern des Admiralitätsgerichts und Rechtswissenschaftlern ist Martin Lucas Schele, der von 1721 bis 1733 dem Gericht als Ratsherr angehörte und von 1740 bis 1743 als Gerichtspräses fungierte. M. L. Schele verfaßt 1707 in Helmstedt eine aufsehenerregende und vielzitierte Dissertation „de instrumento assecurationis vulgo polizza“, die sein Doktorvater Johann Werlhof in einer von Schele überarbeiteten Fassung mit zwei beigefügten Abhandlungen von Prof. Hermann v. d. Hardt und Prof. Michael Richey 1736 erneut veröffentlicht. M. L. Schele gilt seinerzeit auf grund dieser Arbeit und seines Richteramtes als „erfahrenster Rechts=Lehrer in See- und Assecuranz=Sachen“[57]. In der Dissertation löst sich Schele vollkommen vom römischen Recht, definiert den Versicherungsvertrag ohne dogmatische Anleihen beim Bodmereivertrag oder beim Bürgschaftsverhältnis prägnant als „contractus nomina-

---

[54] Vgl. M. Pöhls, Darstellung des gemeinen Deutschen und des Hamburgischen Handelsrechts für Juristen und Kaufleute, Assecuranzrecht, 1832, S. 181 m.w.N.; Benecke, Bd. II, S. 74 m.w.N.

[55] So später Emérigon, v. I, ch. 10, sect. 2, § 3, unter Berufung auf Casaregis, Santerna, Rocco und Marquard.

[56] Vgl. hierzu *Frentz*, S. 139f., 147, 160f., 162ff., 176f., 196ff.

[57] Klefeker, Bd. I, S. 29.

tus nudo consensu constans de periculi rerum et personarum, sive mari, sive terra transvehendarum aversione pro certo ac definito pretio“[58]. Schele's Darstellungssystematik ist erheblich weiter entwickelt als z.B. die in den Abschnitten über die Seeassecuranz in Johann Loccenius' Abhandlung „de iure maritimo et navali“ (lib. II, cap. V) und in Franz Stypmann's „Tractatus de iure maritimo“ (part. IV, cap. VII); sie nimmt stellenweise – in den Kapiteln über den Policeninhalt, über die zusätzlichen Klauseln und Bedingungen der Assecuranz, über den Umfang des versicherten Risikos – die Systematik der Hamburgischen Assecuranz- und Havareiordnung 1731 vorweg, an deren Ausarbeitung Schele beratend mitwirkte. Materiellrechtlich setzt sich Schele umfassend und manchmal kritisch mit der zeitgenössischen internationalen Seerechtsliteratur und -gesetzgebung auseinander und zieht hierbei auch Entscheidungen der Rota Genuensis heran. Den rechtsvergleichenden Ansatz, der die ganze Arbeit prägt, betont er vor allem im Bereich der Auslegung des Versicherungsvertrages: „Putem quoque interdum ad aliarum linguarum parallelismum, et similia juris vocabula recurrendum esse“[59].

In den Vordergrund seiner Überlegungen zur Rechtsnatur der Police als instrumentum liquidum oder guarentigiatum im Assecuranzprozeß stellt Schele die Rechtsprechung des Admiralitätsgerichts, das bis etwa 1740 die „Polizzen nach denen See-Rechten und nach unserer Gerichts-Ordnung de 1645 cap. 2 § 13 denen Instrumentis liquidis gleichschätzet“[60]. Das Gericht hält die Policen für „unläugbare Handschriften“, deren inhaltliche Richtigkeit durch ergänzende Beweisdokumente oder förmliche öffentliche Beurkundung soweit glaubhaft gemacht ist, daß sie alle dilatorischen und bestimmte peremtorische Einreden des Assecuradeurs mit Ausnahme der exceptiones in specie sic dicti ausschließen. Die so definierte eingeschränkte Exekutivkraft der Policen, die auch Schele befürwortet, bewirkt in der Rechtsprechungspraxis, daß der beklagte Assecuradeur die ihm verbliebenen Einreden erst nach gerichtlicher Hinterlegung der Schadenssumme im Reconventionsprozeß erheben darf. Ein vergleichbares Verfahren kennzeichnet im geltenden deutschen Handelsrecht die Klagen aus Bürgschaftsurkunden mit der Klausel „auf erste Anforderung zu zahlen“, bei denen der Bürge nicht nur auf die Einrede der Vorausklage verzichtet, sondern mit seinen gesamten sonstigen Einreden und Einwendungen erst im Rückforderungsverfahren gehört wird[61]. Mit der Anerkennung einer mittelbaren

[58] Schele, p. 9.

[59] Ebd., p. 50.

[60] Beispiel: Burmester c. Höckel, Rationes decidendi vom 12. 12. 1731, prod. Wetzlar 13. 4. 1733, Staatsarchiv Hamburg, Reichskammergericht, B 116; zur Bedeutung der instrumenta liquida im Hamburgischen Admiralitätsprozeß vgl. auch *Frentz*, S. 89ff. m.w.N.

[61] Bundesgerichtshof, Urteil vom 31. 1. 1985 – IX ZR 66/84 –, NJW 1985, 1694; vgl. ferner BGHZ 74, 244.

„execution parée“ bei Klagen aus Policen liegt das Admiralitätsgericht auf einer ähnlichen Linie wie z.B. die Florentinischen Assecuranzartikel vom 28.1.1523 und vom 15.6.1526[62], die Amsterdamer Assecuranzordnung 1598/1603, Art. 33, und die Ordonnance de la marine 1681, liv. III, tit. 6, art. 61[63], die noch weitergehend die provisorische Bezahlung der Versicherungssumme an den Versicherten vorsehen.

Andererseits wendet sich Langenbeck schon in seinem Assecuranzordnungsentwurf 1721/22 und später in seinem Kommentar[64] gegen die Privilegierung des klagenden Policeninhabers und kritisiert das Admiralitätsgericht, das „mit der Condemnation gegen die Assecuradeurs gar zu fertig gewesen“ sei. Daraufhin verzichtet das Admiralitätsgericht etwa ab 1740 zunehmend auf die Verweisung des Assecuradeurs ins Reconventionsverfahren und entfernt sich im Bereich der Seeassecuranz[65] von den Regeln des Exekutivprozesses. Hier läßt sich die wechselseitige Beeinflussung der Rechtswissenschaft in der Person Scheles durch die Rechtsprechung des Admiralitätsgerichts und umgekehrt der Rechtsprechung durch Langenbecks literarische Kritik besonders deutlich nachvollziehen.

Im übrigen bewirkt die versicherungsrechtliche Rechtsprechung des Admiralitätsgerichts bei Schele, daß er die ausschließliche örtliche und sachliche Zuständigkeit des Gerichts in kontradiktorischen Assecuranzsachen unterstreicht[66] – mit Absicht, denn in den bis zum Erlaß der Assecuranz- und Havareiordnung in Hamburg verwendeten holländischen Policenformularen ist immer noch die Klausel enthalten, sich in Streitfällen dem Antwerpener Börsenrecht und inzident der Entscheidung der dortigen Assecuranzkammer zu unterwerfen[67]. Schele verwirft diese seines Erachtens veraltete Gerichtsstandsvereinbarung und bereitet damit die Regelung in der Assecuranz- und Havareiordnung 1731, Tit. I, Art. 2, vor, die untersagt, sich in der Police „den Coustumen der Beurse von Antwerpen zu submittiren“.

Scheles Arbeit ist ein Beispiel dafür, daß die Rechtsprechung des Admiralitätsgerichts auch in der seerechtlichen Dissertationsliteratur sehr aufmerksam verfolgt wird. Die Dissertation „de bodmeria“ von Henricus Rademin (Halle 1697), die bis Mitte des 19. Jahrhunderts in der bodmereirechtlichen Diskussion beachtet wird[68], setzt sich mit zahlreichen Urteilen des

---

[62] Magens, p. 380, 386.

[63] Vgl. ferner Emérigon, v. II, ch. 20, sect. 4, §§ 2, 3 m.w.N.; Valin, p. 563, 564.

[64] Assecuranzordnungsentwurf, Anhang, Art. 1 und 2 ; Langenbeck, Anmerkungen . . ., p. 325.

[65] Nicht bei Klagen aus Bodmereibriefen und Konnossementen, die weiter als instrumenta liquida gewertet werden, vgl. *Frentz*, S. 90f.

[66] Schele, p. 46, 36.

[67] Vgl. dazu im einzelnen *Frentz*, S. 285ff.

[68] z.B. bei Klefeker, Bd. VII, S. 267; v. Kaltenborn, Bd. II, S. 240, Fußnote.

Admiralitätsgerichts zum notwendigen Inhalt des Bodmereibriefes, zum Beweis der Verwendung der Bodmereigelder „zu des Schiffes Besten", zur Sicherung des Bodmereigläubigers und zur Rangfolge mehrerer konkurrierender Bodmereigläubiger, zur Haftungsbegrenzung im Vermögen des Bodmereischuldners und zum Regreß des Bodmereischuldners an seine Reeder und Befrachter auseinander[69]. Entscheidungen des Admiralitätsgerichts zum Seeassecuranzrecht und zur Mascopey sowie zum Frachtvertragsrecht kommentieren und verarbeiten Henricus Kellinghusen in der Untersuchung „de discrimine tempestatis marinae, von Seeschaden" (Halle 1709) und Johann Julius Surland in der Dissertation „de literis maritimis, vulgo von Zee-Briefen" (Groningen 1715). Johann Julius Surland war der Vater des späteren Professors in Frankfurt/Oder Johann Jacob Surland, dem er umfangreiches Material für dessen bekannte „Grundzüge des Europäischen See-Rechts" (1750)[70] zur Verfügung stellte[71].

Die bisher genannten Seerechtsabhandlungen sind dadurch gekennzeichnet, daß sie die Admiralitätsjudikatur mit Einzelnachweisen zur Bestätigung der eigenen Auffassung oder zur Bildung von Lehrsätzen heranziehen, ohne den Sachverhalt der Streitfälle ausführlich mitzuteilen oder sogar die Entscheidungen des Admiralitätsgerichts zu einem bestimmten Seerechtsinstitut systematisch zu sammeln.

Eine Rechtsprechungssammlung im Sinne eines reinen Entscheidungsregisters[72] oder einer nur auf Relationen und Voten konzentrierten Spruchsammlung[73] hat es – soweit ersichtlich – für das Hamburgische Admiralitätsgericht nicht gegeben. Andererseits bestand ganz offensichtlich ein Bedürfnis für die Seerechtswissenschaft wie für die kaufmännische Praxis, die Erkenntnisse des Admiralitätsgerichts, bei denen nur der Entscheidungstenor, nicht aber die Entscheidungsgründe schriftlich abgefaßt wurden[74], in der Form der Relationen und Voten der Referenten kennenzulernen[75].

Dieses Bedürfnis befriedigt der von Johann Klefeker innerhalb seiner zwölfbändigen „Sammlung der Hamburgischen Gesetze und Verfassungen" 1769 herausgegebene Band VII über „die Handels=Rechte", in dem Klefeker das Hamburgische Seehandels- und das Seeassecuranzrecht behandelt. Die Kommentierung des Seehandelsrechts folgt der Systematik des Hamburgi-

69 Rademin, p. 23, 36, 38, 43 - 48.

70 Zur Bedeutung dieses Werks *K. O. Scherner,* Die Wissenschaft des Handelsrechts, in: Handbuch der Quellen und Literatur der neueren europäischen Privatrechtsgeschichte, hg. von H. Coing, Bd. II, 1, München 1977, S. 797ff., 953f.

71 Klefeker, Bd. I, S. 74f.

72 *Gehrke,* S. 1352f.

73 Ebd., S. 1354f.

74 *Frentz,* S. 108 m.w.N., 120.

75 So auch Klefeker, Bd. VII, S. 594, 293.

schen Seerechts 1603/05; für jedes Rechtsinstitut fügt Klefeker paradigmatische Admiralitätsverfahren in Gestalt der ihm von den Referenten des Admiralitätsgerichts zugänglich gemachten vollständigen Sachberichte, Relationen und Voten ein und entwickelt auf dieser Grundlage eigene Auslegungsregeln und Lehrsätze. Diese Methode kennzeichnet auch den Abschnitt über „Assecuranzen“ und die „Ausübung des Assecuranz-Rechts“, mit einer Besonderheit: Ausgangspunkt dieses Abschnitts ist die 1752 in Göttingen von Franciscus Michael Poppe verfaßte Dissertation „de litium assecurationis causa orientium decisione“, die Klefeker als Handbuch des Seeversicherungsrechts bezeichnet und an dieser Stelle ins Deutsche überträgt. Im Seeversicherungsrecht ist Poppe's Arbeit nach den Dissertationen von M. L. Schele und Kellinghusen für den deutschen Sprachraum die erste umfassende „systematische Abhandlung, worinn zugleich anderer Staaten Assecuranz-Rechte durch einander und mit der hiesigen (Hamburgischen Assecuranz- und Havareiordnung 1731) verglichen sind“[76]. Poppe hatte nach dem ersten Kapitel „Praemonita quaedam generalia de contractu assecurationis exhibens“ und dem zweiten Kapitel „quod explicat unde petendae sint litium de assecuratione ortarum decisiones“ einen dritten Abschnitt konzipiert, der nicht vollendet wurde: „de controversiis assecurationis causa orientibus earumque decisione“. In der gedruckt vorliegenden Fassung der Dissertation besteht dieses letzte Kapitel aus 45 Leitsätzen, die Poppe aus seiner privaten Sammlung von Relationen und Voten des Hamburgischen Admiralitätsgerichts herausgearbeitet hatte und denen er diese Relationen und Voten als „exemplum notabilis controversiae cum rationibus in utramque partem a litigantibus allatis, illustrationis causa“[77] beifügen wollte. Klefeker übernimmt diese Sammlung und veröffentlicht sie – neben neueren Seeversicherungsrelationen und -voten seit 1752 – vollständig mit Poppes Leitsätzen sowie mit eigenen ergänzenden Anmerkungen.

Einige Beispiele sollen zeigen, wie Poppe die Admiralitätsjudikatur in Leitsätze komprimiert:

1731 hat das Admiralitätsgericht in der Sache Burmester c. Höckel[78] die Frage zu klären, ob zum in der Police genannten Ladungsort Hamburg auch der elbeabwärts gelegene Hafen Glückstadt (für eine sukzessive Einladung) gehört. Da die gerade verabschiedete Hamburgische Assecuranz- und Havareiordnung den „Ort der Ladung“ und seine Erstreckung in Tit. V, Art. 11 und 12 sowie in Tit. I, Art. 4, Nr. 4 nicht präzise genug definiert, greift das Gericht auf eine Entscheidung der Amsterdamer Assecuranzkammer vom 23. 1. 1699 zurück, derzufolge zum Ladungsort, der den Beginn des

76 Ebd., S. 292, 293.

77 Poppe, p. 46, 47.

78 Staatsarchiv Hamburg, Reichskammergericht, B 116.

Risikos der Assecuradeure markiert, nicht nur der in der Police genannte Hafen im engeren Sinne gehört, sondern alle „circumjacentien desselben Ohrtes bis die gemeldte Seemündung inclusive". Die niederländische Ordonnantie Philipps II. von 1563 bezeichnete in Tit. VII, Art. 2, als Ausgangspunkt der Gefahrtragung etwas enger „poort, haven oft reede" des Ladungsortes der Police. Das Urteil des Admiralitätsgerichts faßt Poppe zusammen: Nomen loci in instrumento nominati non solum denotat ipsum nominatae urbis portum, sed alia quoque loca circumiacentia, ubi naves onerandae atque levandae sunt.

1765 weist das Gericht in J. S. c. Scheel[79] die Klage eines Reeders ab, dessen versichertes Schiff nicht den in der Police genannten Abgangshafen Ahus/Dänemark erreicht, sondern den entfernter liegenden Ort Landöhafen, der nachweislich nicht zum Seerevier von Ahus gehört. Die Entscheidung des Gerichts ist ersichtlich durch den Rechtsgedanken in Ordonnance de la marine 1681, liv. III, tit. 6, art. 36 beeinflußt. Poppe formuliert: Iter non mutatum videtur, saltem non dissolvitur assecuratio, si navis portum nominato propiorem intravit, ibique merces expositae sunt. Explicatur et limitatur recepta regula, quod iter salva conventione abbreviari, non prolongari possit.

1767 macht das Gericht in Brouker c. Jenisch[80] deutlich, daß eine Güterversicherung auf eine „Kiste Leinen" die Versicherung einer Warengattung darstellt, die sich sowohl auf die Materialien Cattun und Leinen als auch auf verschiedene Verarbeitungsformen des Leinen (gestickte Manschetten, Leinentücher) erstrecken kann. Damit folgt das Gericht dem holländischen Regelungsvorbild[81] und weist konsequent Klagen eines versicherten Befrachters ab, wenn statt der versicherten Warengattung Güter einer anderen Gattung eingeladen werden und verunglücken[82]. Poppes Leitsatz: Fieri potest, ut ob mutationem mercium irrita sit assecuratio, etiamsi periculum sub generali vocabulo mercium, Waren, Güter, Kaufmannschaften translatum sit. Certo mercium genere definito, toties coruit assecuratio, quoties loco mercium in instrumento nominatarum, alius generis merces, invito assecuratore, navi impositae sunt.

Die Publikation der Sammlung exemplarischer Relationen und Voten des Admiralitätsgerichts und ihre Kommentierung durch Poppe bzw. Klefeker findet weite Verbreitung; bis ins 20. Jahrhundert werden Urteile des Admiralitätsgerichts nach Klefekers Wiedergabe zitiert[83].

---

[79] Klefeker, Bd. VII, S. 476.

[80] Ebd., S. 327.

[81] Vgl. hierzu *Frentz,* S. 147f. m.w.N.

[82] Beispiel: Wybrandt c. Schlüter, Klefeker, Bd. VII, S. 360.

[83] So z.B. in den nachfolgend genannten Werken von Pöhls und Benecke sowie bei Ladehoff („de havaria discrimine in primis ex legibus Germaniae septentrionalis", Kiel 1773), bei Soltau („de eo, quod iustum est circa havariam particularem", Lippe

Zwei Autoren, deren Werke in die Bemühungen um die Kodifikation eines Deutschen Handelsgesetzbuches im 19. Jahrhundert hineinwirken und die ihrerseits durch Entscheidungen des Admiralitätsgerichts erheblich beeinflußt werden, sind Wilhelm Benecke und Meno Pöhls.

Benecke legt zwischen 1805 und 1810 sein vierbändiges[84] „System des Assecuranz- und Bodmereiwesens" vor, das in einer spezifischen Wechselwirkung vom Admiralitätsgericht als rechtswissenschaftliche Rechtsquelle bei der Entscheidungsfindung verwertet wird[85] und gleichzeitig zahlreiche Erkenntnisse des Gerichts dokumentiert und der Seerechtsentwicklung dienstbar macht[86]. Denn Benecke übernimmt die Admiralitätsjudikatur mit teilweise ausführlichem Sachbericht einerseits direkt von den Referenten des Admiralitätsgerichts, andererseits aus der Klefeker'schen Sammlung, integriert sie in ein einheitliches, aus europäischer Seerechtsliteratur und -gesetzgebung abgeleitetes System von versicherungsrechtlichen Rechtsgrundsätzen und vollzieht an Hand der Urteile nicht nur eine Rechts-, sondern in einigen Fällen auch eine Rechtsprechungsvergleichung. Dieser vergleichende Ansatz erstreckt sich vor allem auf die englische Praxis, weil Benecke mehrere Jahre bei Lloyds in London arbeitete. So vergleicht Benecke z.B. den Admiralitätsprozeß Jencquel c. von Vinnen, in dem das Gericht 1728 die Anzeigepflichten des Versicherten und den Umfang des versicherten Risikos nach Informations- und Gefahrenkreisen der Vertragsparteien abgrenzt[87], mit den in England gerichtlich entschiedenen cases Mayne v. Walter und Carter v. Bochm. Burr[88]. Weitere Beispiele für den Rechtsprechungsvergleich mit der englischen Gerichtspraxis sind das Urteil des Admiralitätsgerichts in Wybrandt c. Schlüter, in dem es um die Differenzierung verschiedener versicherbarer Warengattungen geht[89], die Entscheidungen in dem bereits erwähnten Verfahren Burmester c. Höckel[90], in Matthießen und Sillem c. J. M. Schmidt et al.[91], in Hockmeyer c. 2. Assecuranzcompagnie[92]. Benecke's „System" – und damit auch die von ihm kommentierte Rechtsprechung des Hamburgischen Admiralitätsgerichts und der englischen Gerichte – findet internationale Verbreitung. Es erscheint

---

1774), bei *W. Hammacher* (Die Grundzüge des allgemeinen Seeversicherungsrechts in der deutschen Gesetzgebung des 18. Jahrhunderts vor dem Hintergrund der älteren europäischen Seeversicherungsgesetzgebung, Diss. iur. Bonn 1982) und bei *G. Lau* (Das Hamburgische Seehandelsrecht im 18. Jahrhundert, Diss. iur. Hamburg 1975).

[84] 1821 erscheint ein fünfter Ergänzungsband.

[85] *Frentz,* S. 131.

[86] Vgl. nur Benecke, Bd. I, S. 383f.; Bd. II, S. 40ff., 76ff., 216ff., 234ff.; Bd. III, S. 34f., 131f., 177ff., 202ff., 242f., 200ff.

[87] Klefeker, Bd. VII, S. 424.

[88] Benecke, Bd. III, S. 130ff.

[89] Benecke, Bd. II, S. 76f., 70f.

[90] Ebd., S. 216ff.

[91] Ebd., S. 40ff., 46f.

[92] Ebd., S. 234ff., 240f.

1828 in Triest in einer italienischen Übersetzung von Rossetti, bereits 1824 in London in einer eigenen Übertragung Benecke's unter dem Titel „A treatise on the principles of Indemnity in Marine Insurance, Bottomry and Respondentia“ und 1825 in der französischen Übersetzung von Dubernad. Vincent Nolte veröffentlicht Benecke's „System“ in einer Neuausgabe 1851/52 in Hamburg.

Benecke's „System“ beruht – wie Scherner für das allgemeine Handelsrecht bereits nachgewiesen hat[93] – auf dem Gedanken der Einheit des europäischen Seerechts, das sowohl in der Rechtsprechung des Admiralitätsgerichts[94] als auch in Benecke's Vorstellung als europäisches Seehandels- und Seeversicherungsrecht den Charakter einer subsidiären Rechtsnorm aufweist. Benecke erklärt in der Vorrede zu seinem „System“, es sei notwendig, „auf die Gesetze und Gebräuche fremder Länder beständig Rücksicht zu nehmen ..., weil sich einheimische Einrichtungen oft nach fremden verbessern lassen, und man, ohne mit dem Geiste der fremden Gesetze bekannt zu sein, oft Gefahr läuft, einzelne Meinungen auswärtiger Schriftsteller zu mißdeuten“. Um sein Ziel zu erreichen, „die wahren Grundsätze des Assekuranz- und Bodmereiwesens auf eine allgemeine, dem Versicherer, Kaufmanne und Rechtsgelehrten aller Nationen gleich brauchbare Art ... aus der Natur der Sache und mit beständiger Rücksicht auf die Gesetze und Gebräuche aller wichtigen handelnden Staaten zu entwickeln“, stellt er das europäische Assecuranz- und Bodmereirecht als Ergebnis des Zusammenwirkens „gerichtlicher Verhandlungen wichtiger Assekuranzstreitigkeiten, der vorzüglichsten Schriftsteller aller Nationen ... und der Gebräuche der größten Handelsstädte Europens“ vor.

Diese drei Faktoren der Rechtsentwicklung erkennt auch Meno Pöhls an; er nutzt sie aber, anders als Benecke, als Quellen für eine neue wissenschaftliche Zielsetzung, die der Obertitel seiner zwischen 1830 und 1834 erschienenen Abhandlungen zum Seerecht und Assecuranzrecht indiziert: „Darstellung des gemeinen Deutschen und des Hamburgischen Handelsrechts für Juristen und Kaufleute“. Pöhls bereitet den Weg zu einem allgemeinen Deutschen Handelsrecht mit Einschluß des Seerechts unter Verwertung der partikulären in- und ausländischen Seegesetze und der internationalen Seerechtswissenschaft. Die Rechtsprechung des Hamburgischen Admiralitätsgerichts, die auch Pöhls ganz überwiegend nach der Klefeker'schen Sammlung zitiert, erlangt bei ihm seerechtliche Normwirkung: Das Urteil des Admiralitätsgerichts tritt an die Stelle eines kodifizierten Rechtssatzes. Einige Beispiele:

Die Entscheidung des Gerichts in Burmester c. Höckel, die die Benennung des Ladungsortes/-hafens in der Police auch auf dessen Seerevier und Ree-

---

[93] *Scherner,* in: Ius Commune, Band VII (1978), S. 129ff.

[94] Vgl. hierzu *Frentz,* S. 126ff., 132ff.

den erstreckt, stellt Pöhls in Parallele zu den kongruenten gesetzlichen Regelungen in Holland und Spanien[95]. Entsprechendes gilt für das Urteil in Jencquel c. von Vinnen[96], in dem das Admiralitätsgericht in Fortentwicklung des Rechtsgedankens der Genuesischen Statuten 1610 lib. IV, cap. 17 („notitia ... per famam legitime probatam ...") ein bestimmtes berufsbezogenes Sonderwissen des Assecuradeurs abgrenzt von den Tatsachen, die in der Informationssphäre des Versicherten liegen, und für börsenkundige Tatsachen eine spezielle Offenbarungs- und Anzeigepflicht des Versicherten ablehnt. Auch die oben erwähnten Urteile des Admiralitätsgerichts in Brouker c. Jenisch (1767) und in Wybrandt c. Schlüter (1747) über die Zulässigkeit der Versicherung von Warengattungen unter dem Begriff der „allgemeinen Kaufmannschaften" und die Folgen unrichtiger Bezeichnung des Versicherungsobjekts zitiert Pöhls wie kodifizierte Regelungen, die die insoweit gegebenen Gesetzeslücken in der Hamburgischen Assecuranz- und Havareiordnung 1731 ausfüllen und als generelle Normen im gemeinen Seerecht gelten sollen[97]. Andere Präjudikate des Admiralitätsgerichts würdigt Pöhls im Vergleich mit der europäischen Seerechtswissenschaft oder mit allgemeinen Rechtsgrundsätzen[98].

Die Rechtsprechung des Admiralitätsgerichts entwickelt spätestens bei Pöhls eine gewisse Eigengesetzlichkeit, die erheblich über die ursprünglich vom Gericht geleistete Einzelfallentscheidung hinausgeht und die es rechtfertigt, das Gericht in seiner Wirkung auf die Seerechtswissenschaft in eine Linie mit der Rota Genuensis und den seegerichtlichen Spruchkörpern in England zu stellen.

IV.

Die Auswirkungen der Rechtsprechung des Hamburgischen Admiralitätsgerichts auf die seerechtliche Gesetzgebung sind unmittelbarer und mittelbarer Natur.

Ein unmittelbarer Einfluß ist bei den Vorarbeiten und der Kodifikation der 1731 verabschiedeten und am 1. 1. 1732 in Kraft getretenen Hamburgischen Assecuranz- und Havareiordnung festzustellen.

Das „Project zu einer Assecurantz-Ordnung"[99], das Hermann Langenbeck 1721/22 nach vorangegangenen ergebnislosen Kodifikationsversuchen 1603/05, 1656 und 1674[100] formuliert, weist gesonderte Randbemerkungen

[95] Pöhls, Assecuranzrecht, S. 383, Fußnote 3.

[96] Ebd., S. 592, Fußnote 24, S. 560.

[97] Ebd., S. 186, Fußnote 3, 4, S. 169f.

[98] Vgl. z.B. ebd., S. 591, Fußnote 16, S. 593.

[99] Staatsarchiv Hamburg, Senat Cl. VII, Lit. Lb, No. 2, Vol. 3.

[100] Vgl. hierzu *Frentz,* S. 121f.

auf, aus denen sich die für den Gesetzentwurf herangezogenen Rechtsquellen rekonstruieren lassen. Neben der Bezugnahme auf Johann Marquard, holländische Policenformulare und die Gerichtspraxis der Amsterdamer Assecuranzkammer dominieren die kodifizierten Rechtsquellen – vor allem die französische Ordonnance de la marine 1681, die „Ordonnantie van de Zeevart" Philipps II. von 1563 und die Amsterdamer Assecuranzordnung 1598/1603, gefolgt vom Consolato del mare, vom Hamburgischen Seerecht 1603/05 und vom Wisbyschen Seerecht sowie von dem Hamburgischen Reglement des Dispacheurs von 1705 und den als „pacta inter privatos" geltenden Vergleichen der Hamburgischen Assecuradeure von 1687, 1693, 1697 und 1704[101]. Dieser erste Befund legt es nahe, den Gedanken von Coing, Rechtsvergleichung – im Sinne einer Gesetzesvergleichung – könne Grundlage von handels- und wirtschaftsrechtlicher Gesetzgebung sein[102], auf die Kodifikation des Seerechts in der Hamburgischen Assecuranz- und Havareiordnung zu übertragen. Andererseits ist zu berücksichtigen, daß die Assecuranz- und Havareiordnung in ihrer endgültigen Gestalt nach weiteren Entwurfsbeiträgen Langenbecks bis zu dessen Tod 1728 sowie aufgrund der Mitwirkung von M. L. Schele und Johann Julius Surland und nach Beratung mit Vertretern der Hamburgischen Kaufmannschaft in mehreren nicht unwesentlichen Punkten von dem Entwurf 1721/22 abweicht; das impliziert insoweit ein Abweichen von den in diesem Entwurf verarbeiteten ausländischen Rechtsquellen. Als eine Ursache dieser Abweichungen muß man die noch stärkere Verwertung der Rechtsprechung des Admiralitätsgerichts, und zwar besonders der Rechtsprechung in den Jahren zwischen 1721 und 1731, in der Endfassung der Assecuranz- und Havareiordnung ansehen.

Das Beispiel des Prozesses Rendtorff c. Brandt soll diese Schlußfolgerung bestätigen[103]. Das Admiralitätsgericht hat 1725 über die Frage zu entscheiden, ob die nachträgliche Versicherung eines bereits verunglückten Schiffes zulässig ist und ob dem versicherten Reeder die Versicherungssumme zusteht. Das Gericht verurteilt den Versicherten zur Vorlage sämtlicher an seinen Kommissionär gerichteten Ordrebriefe zum Beweis dafür, daß er bei Vertragsschluß über den inzwischen eingetretenen Schiffsuntergang nicht informiert war. Die den Assecuranzordnungsentwurf 1721/22 mitprägende Ordonnantie van de Zeevart 1563 (Tit. VII, Art. 4) verbietet die Versicherung auf bekannten Untergang uneingeschränkt: „gheen asseurantien .. op schepen, goeden .., niet uitghesondert, die ten tyde van der asseurantie sullen wesen ghepericliteert". Auch die ältere Seerechtsliteratur und die Rota Genuensis sehen das objektive „periculum futurum" als Wesensmerkmal der Assecuranz an: „Re deperdita aut salva non adest Subjectum, super

[101] Ebd., S. 123.

[102] *H. Coing*, Rechtsvergleichung als Grundlage von Gesetzgebung im 19. Jahrhundert, in: Ius Commune, Band VII (1978), S. 160ff., 162.

[103] Staatsarchiv Hamburg, Reichskammergericht, R 18.

quod assecuratio fieri potest. Suscipiunt (assecuratores) in se periculum futurum non praeteritum, quandoquidem Contractus assecurationis est contractus conditionis, at natura conditionis est inspicere futurum casum non praeteritum“[104]. Von dieser apodiktischen Auffassung, die für die Wirksamkeit der Assecuranz auch nicht den subjektiven Mangel der Kenntnis der Vertragsparteien vom Eintritt des Versicherungsfalles genügen läßt, nehmen die meisten Assecuranzgesetze des 17. und 18. Jahrhunderts Abschied und gestatten die Versicherung eines bereits in See verunglückten Gegenstandes unter der Voraussetzung beiderseitiger Gutgläubigkeit, aber mit zwei Besonderheiten, die das Admiralitätsgericht in Rendtorff c. Brandt in sehr eigenständiger Wertung nicht akzeptiert:

Sowohl nach den Assecuranzordnungen von Middelburg (1689), Rotterdam (1721) und Amsterdam (1598/1603) als auch nach den Genuesischen Statuten 1610, lib. IV, cap. 17 („post casum sinistrum secutum tali tempore“), nach der spanischen Recopilation de leyes de los reynos de las Indias 1681 (tom. IV, Lib. IX, tit. 39, ley 7) und nach der Ordonnance de la marine 1681, liv. III, tit. 6, § 39, obliegt der Nachweis, daß der Versicherte den Eintritt des Schadensfalles kannte oder hätte kennen können, nicht dem Assecuradeur, sondern wird durch die unwiderlegliche gesetzliche Vermutung ersetzt, daß die Nachricht mit einer Geschwindigkeit von 3 Meilen auf 2 Stunden bzw. 1½ Meilen auf 1 Stunde oder von 1 - 2 Meilen auf 1 Stunde vom Unglücksort zum Ort des Versicherungsabschlusses gelangt. Nach der Rechtsprechung französischer Seegerichte ist die Vermutung auch nicht durch den Nachweis des klagenden Versicherten, daß das Eintreffen der Unglücksnachricht zur Zeit des Vertragsschlusses objektiv unmöglich war, zu widerlegen, sondern es bleibt bei dem Grundsatz: „Les présomptions juris et de jure ne peuvent être détruites, et la partie contre qui elles militent, n'est pas admise à prouver le contraire“[105].

Diese praesumtio iuris lehnt das Admiralitätsgericht ab und differenziert stattdessen danach, ob die Wahrscheinlichkeit nach dem Parteivortrag eher gegen oder eher für den Mangel der Kenntnis des Versicherten bzw. Versicherungskommissionärs spricht und erlegt dementsprechend den Parteien Beweis oder Gegenbeweis der behaupteten Kenntnis auf. Diese Auffassung vertritt das Gericht in gefestigter Rechtsprechung auch in anderen Verfahren 1726 und 1727[106] und sehr konsequent in Fällen, in denen die Kenntnis des Versicherten nach dem Sachverhalt praktisch ausgeschlossen ist – Strandung des zu versichernden Schiffes vor der holländischen Küste am Nachmittag vor dem Tag, an dem morgens in Hamburg die Police gezeichnet

---

104 Rota Genuensis, decis. 36, n. 9, zitiert nach Emérigon, v. II, ch. 15, sect. 2; Loccenius, lib. 2, cap. 5, § 8.

105 Emérigon, v. II, ch. 15, sect. 4, § 2 m. w. N.

106 Z. B. Jantzen c. Watkinson, Klefeker, Bd. VII, S. 405f.

wird[107] –; hier verzichtet das Gericht gänzlich auf weitere Beweiserhebung und verurteilt die Assecuradeure uneingeschränkt zur Zahlung der Versicherungssummen.

Die zweite Besonderheit der genannten zeitgenössischen Assecuranzgesetze liegt darin, daß die praesumtio iuris (nur dann) entfällt, wenn die Police „op goede ende quade tyding" / „lost or not lost" / „auf gute oder schlechte Nachrichten" gezeichnet ist; diese Klausel verlagert bei behaupteter Kenntnis vom Schadenseintritt die Beweislast in vollem Umfang auf den Assecuradeur. Dieser zwingenden Konnexität und der nicht einzelfallbezogenen Beweislastverteilung widerspricht das Admiralitätsgericht in seinen Entscheidungen in Rendtorff c. Brandt (1725), in Jantzen c. Watkinson (1726) und in Peinhorst c. Meckenhauser (1721). Der unmittelbare Einfluß dieser Rechtsprechung auf die Kodifikation der Hamburgischen Assecuranz- und Havareiordnung läßt sich an Hand folgender Gegenüberstellung zeigen: In Art. 11 des Assecuranzordnungsentwurfs 1721/22 heißt es für die Versicherung auf ein verunglücktes Schiff noch: „Wer aber in solchen zweifelhaften fall assecurantz thun lassen will, der soll in der Police die Conditio setzen: Auf gute oder böse Zeitung, welche Condition zwar in allen assecurancien allgemein ist, aber in diesem fall soll sie expresse wiederholet, und ausgedrücket werden". Unter Verzicht auf die „lost or not lost"-Klausel bestimmt die Assecuranz- und Havareiordnung dagegen in der Endfassung des Tit. V, Art. 9 in einer Formulierung, die im Obersatz wörtlich den einschlägigen Entscheidungen des Admiralitätsgerichts entspricht: „Ist ein Schiff, zur Zeit, da die Assecuranz geschiehet, bereits vergangen oder verloren, und kann der Assecurirte allenfalls eydlich erhärten, daß er von dem Schaden und Verlust des Schiffes, zu der Zeit, da er die Versicherung thun lassen, oder solche zu thun befohlen, nichtes gewußt; so hat die Assecuranz, wann sie eher geschlossen worden, als der Assecurirte Nachricht von dem Schaden erhalten, oder, falls derselbe ausserhalb Landes sich befindet, ehe solche Nachricht von ihm hieher geschrieben und allhier kund werden können, an beyden Seiten ihre Richtigkeit, und müssen die Assecuradeurs den Schaden, ihrer Verpflichtung gemäß, bezahlen".

Der Einfluß der Rechtsprechung des Admiralitätsgerichts ist auch erkennbar in der Entwicklung des versicherungsrechtlich essentiellen Begriffs des „Interesse", der in der Hamburgischen Assecuranz- und Havareiordnung für den Hanseatischen Seerechtskreis erstmals dogmatisch gesicherte Konturen erhält.

Das Admiralitätsgericht hat 1656 in Hübner c. von der Krentze[108] über eine Klage auf Zahlung der Versicherungssumme aus einer Police zu ent-

---

[107] Beispiel: Clamer c. Schnittler, Protocollum Admiralitatis 15. 2. 1748/28. 3. 1748, in: Staatsarchiv Hamburg, Senat Cl. VII, Lit. Ma, No. 6, Vol. 1 b.

[108] Staatsarchiv Hamburg, Admiralitätskollegium A 13.

scheiden, in der ein bereits in See gegangenes Schiff „mit oder ohne Interesse“ gegen eine Prämie von 75% versichert war. Das Gericht verzichtet auf eine Klagabweisung a limine, verlangt vielmehr den Nachweis der bestrittenen Prämienzahlung und dokumentiert dadurch, daß es eine Versicherung auf Noninteresse bzw. eine Wettassecuranz – die dem Fall zugrundelag – nicht a priori für unzulässig hält. Diese Auffassung ist zum Teil damit zu erklären, daß im Zeitpunkt der Entscheidung in Hamburg noch kein Gesetz den Mangel eines legalen versicherten Interesses kritisiert; erst im 18. Jahrhundert normiert der Hamburgische Senat durch Mandate die Unverbindlichkeit von Wetten und die Unzulässigkeit von Klagen aus Spiel- und Wettforderungen[109]. Die zeitgenössischen ausländischen Assecuranzordnungen, die wie z.B. die Ordonnantie van de Zeevart 1563 (Tit. VII, Art. 4), die Assecuranzordnungen von Middelburg 1689 (Art. 2) und von Rotterdam 1721 (Art. 28) die Wettassecuranz verbieten, verknüpfen das Verbot weniger mit dem fehlenden versicherten Interesse als vielmehr mit der Unzulässigkeit von „weddingschappen“ oder „Weddinge van Rysen“ in einem Vertrag, der der Sicherung gegen Seegefahren und -verluste dient. Vor allem wird der Begriff „Interesse“ noch nicht dogmatisch erfaßt und kodifiziert.

In diesem Sinne bieten einen Ansatz für die Abgrenzung zur Wettassecuranz die Genuesischen Statuten 1610, lib. IV, cap. 17: „Securitates non possint fieri pro se, neque pro aliis, *nisi extet risicum,* vel in mercibus, vel in navigiis, vel rebus quibusvis assecuratis mediaté, vel immediaté, principaliter, vel indirecté“. Der terminus technicus „Interesse“ wird hier zwar noch mit dem Begriff des Risikos umschrieben; erkennbar ist jedoch, daß der Versicherungsvertrag ein bereits bestehendes direktes oder indirektes Sicherungsinteresse voraussetzt, während ein erst durch den Vertrag begründetes Interesse – mit der bloßen Absicht der Gewinnerzielung bei Eintritt der Seegefahr – dem Zweck der Assecuranz zuwiderläuft.

Um die Wende zum 18. Jahrhundert ist eine immer noch kasuistisch geprägte Konkretisierung des Begriffs des notwendigen Interesses in Abgrenzung zur Wettassecuranz in der Admiralitätsjudikatur zu beobachten, die sich in Langenbeck's Assecuranzordnungsentwurf 1721/22, Art. 9, so niederschlägt: „Es kan niemand assecurantz thun lassen, es sey den daß Er würcklich *effecten, Interesse oder Risigo,* entweder selbst, oder auf ordre von andere, bey dem Schiff habe, sonst ist die assecurantz an sich null und nichtig“. In Entscheidungen zwischen der Vorlage des Entwurfs und dem Inkrafttreten der Assecuranz- und Havareiordnung, z.B. in Peinhorst c. Meckenhauser[110] und in Schrack c. Halsey[111], verdichtet sich dagegen die Rechtsprechung des Admiralitätsgerichts allein auf den Begriff des

[109] *Frentz,* S. 146 m.w.N.

[110] Staatsarchiv Hamburg, Reichskammergericht, P 11.

[111] Klefeker, Bd. VII, S. 553ff.

bestimmten, in Geld schätzbaren Interesses, und in dieser gegenüber dem Entwurf konzentrierten Terminologie findet er in Gestalt des „würcklichen Interesse" Eingang in die Endfassung der Assecuranz- und Havareiordnung (Tit. XIII, Art. 2 und Tit. II, Art. 3).

An dieser Stelle ist auch noch einmal das Verfahren Lemvig c. diverse Assecuradeure zu nennen, in dem das Admiralitätsgericht in seiner Entscheidung 1726 gegen Langenbeck's Assecuranzordnungsentwurf (Art. 12) votiert und unmittelbar der Bestimmung in Tit. IV, Art. 9 der Assecuranz- und Havareiordnung 1731 den Weg bereitet.

Die gezeigten Beispiele sollen verdeutlichen, daß die Endfassung der Assecuranz- und Havareiordnung nicht auf schrankenloser Übernahme überwiegend ausländischer Seegesetze beruht, sondern diese Gesetze in der Form verarbeitet, die sie – abgesehen von dem Beitrag der Seerechtswissenschaft – in der richterrechtlich differenzierten Rezeption durch das Admiralitätsgericht gefunden haben.

Über die Hamburgische Assecuranz- und Havareiordnung 1731 hat die Rechtsprechung des Admiralitätsgerichts mittelbar auch auf andere Seerechtskodifikationen des 18. Jahrhunderts gewirkt.

Schon in der Praefatio der Assecuranz- und Havareiordnung mißt der Hamburgische Senat dem neuen Gesetz nicht nur Geltung für Hamburg zu, sondern begründet das hinausgeschobene Inkrafttreten (am 1. Januar 1732) damit, daß das Gesetz „nothwendiger Weise in fremden Orten vorhero bekannt gemacht werden muß". Zeitgenössische Quellen bezeichnen die Hamburgische Assecuranz- und Havareiordnung als „Muster ihrer Art", die als unmittelbares Vorbild bei den Kodifikationsarbeiten für die Assecuranz- und Havareiordnung für sämtliche Königl. Preußischen Staaten 1766, für die Amsterdamer Ordnung „Van Assurantie en Avarye" von 1744, für die Dänischen Assecuranzbedingungen von 1746 und für die Schwedische Ordnung „Försäkrings- och Haweri-Stadga, Art. ‚Om Försäkring'" von 1750 herangezogen wird[112]. Gesetzgeberische Parallelentscheidungen sind beispielsweise festzustellen in der Schwedischen Assecuranzordnung 1750, Tit. Von Assecuranzen, Art. 9, 10, 11 und in der Hamburgischen Assecuranz- und Havareiordnung 1731, Tit. X, XVIII, XI – das Schwedische Recht übernimmt auch den Gedanken der nach versicherbaren Interessen differenzierten Musterpolicen aus der Hamburgischen Ordnung –, in der Preußischen Assecuranz- und Havareiordnung 1766, §§ 40, 46 und in der Hamburgischen Assecuranz- und Havareiordnung Tit. II, Art. 4 und Tit. V, Art. 7, 8, sowie in der Amsterdamer Assecuranzordnung 1744, Art. 7, 14 - 16, 17, 58 - 61 und in

---

112 Staatsarchiv Hamburg, Senat Cl. VII, Lit. Lb, No. 2, Vol. 7a; Hammacher, S. 60f., 66f.; Klefeker, Bd. I, S. 8, Bd. VII, S. 505; Pöhls, Assecuranzrecht, S. 18; *Scherner,* in: Ius Commune, Band VII (1978), S. 121f.

der Hamburgischen Assecuranz- und Havareiordnung Tit. III, Art. 3, Tit. III, Art. 1 und Tit. X, Tit. III, Art. 2, Tit. I, Art. 1 und Tit. I, Art. 3.

Vielleicht hat sogar ein Urteil des Admiralitätsgerichts direkt auf die inhaltliche Formulierung einer Vorschrift der Amsterdamer Assecuranzordnung 1744 Einfluß genommen. In deren Art. 4 ist der Begriff des Ladungsortes in der Police nicht nur als „circumjacentien" des Abgangshafens, sondern präziser – auch präziser als in den eigenen niederländischen Vorbildregelungen – definiert als „niet alleen de Plaats der Ladinge, maar ook de Zeegaten en Zeehavens, en voorts alle de Tonnen, Bakens, of diegelyke Teekenen, zoo daar eenighe moghen zyn, tot dat de Scheepen dezelve sullen zyn gepasseert". Von dieser Ratio war das Admiralitätsgericht auch in Burmester c. Höckel ausgegegangen, einem der meistzitierten Urteile des Gerichts überhaupt[113]. Da zwischen dem Hamburgischen Admiralitätsgericht und den verschiedenen holländischen Admiralitäten und Seegerichten ein Briefkontakt bestand[114], da ferner die Richter der holländischen Assecuranzkammern und Admiralitäten beratend an der Ausarbeitung der Amsterdamer Assecuranzordnung 1744 mitwirkten[115], kann eine Wechselwirkung zwischen der neueren Admiralitätsentscheidung im Verfahren Burmester c. Höckel 1731, dem älteren Urteil der Amsterdamer Assecuranzkammer vom 23. 1. 1699, die ähnlich wie das Admiralitätsgericht tenoriert, und der Endfassung der Amsterdamer Assecuranzordnung 1744, Art. 4, nicht ausgeschlossen werden.

V.

Im Blick auf die zahlreichen Beispiele für Wirkungen der Hamburgischen Admiralitätsjudikatur auf das zeitgenössische Rechts-Umfeld soll abschließend die Eingangsfrage noch einmal gestellt werden. „Non sibi sed orbi" – Programm, Anspruch, Wirklichkeit?

Offensichtlich haben seit Gründung des Admiralitätsgerichts 1623 seine Mitglieder nach einer Leitvorstellung gehandelt, die man dahin zusammenfassen kann, daß seerechtliche Rechtsprechung der oft grenzüberschreitenden Förderung der Rechtssicherheit und Streitschlichtung nur dann wirksam dient, wenn sie die Beschränkungen der lex fori überwindet. Die Brücke zwischen den lokalen Seegesetzen und den analogiefähigen ausländischen

[113] Vgl. nur Klefeker, Bd. VII, S. 456ff., 548ff., 590f.; Benecke, Bd. II, S. 216f.; Pöhls, Assecuranzrecht, S. 383, Fußnote 3; *F. Plaß,* Geschichte der Assecuranz und der Hanseatischen Seeversicherungsbörsen Hamburg, Bremen und Lübeck, Hamburg 1902, S. 63ff.

[114] Staatsarchiv Hamburg, Senat Cl. VII, Lit. Ca, No. 2, Vol. 1b (Nr. 91).

[115] *S. Lammel,* Die Gesetzgebung des Handelsrechts, in: Handbuch der Quellen und Literatur der neueren europäischen Privatrechtsgeschichte, hg. von H. Coing, Band II, 2, München 1976, S. 571ff., 774.

Regelungsmodellen bildet dabei nicht nur das kaufmännische Gewohnheitsrecht in Gestalt der internationalen Usancen oder Coutumen der See; die Richter des Hamburgischen Admiralitätsgerichts setzen sich auch ohne Vermittlung des Gewohnheitsrechts im Wege der Rechtsvergleichung direkt mit den Konfliktlösungsideen fremder Seerechte auseinander.

Damit korrespondiert die Beobachtung, daß auch nicht rechtsgelehrte – kaufmännische – Mitglieder des Gerichts sich auswärtiges Seerecht erschließen, indem sie private Gesetzessammlungen anlegen (z.B. mit den Amsterdamer Assecuranzordnungen, der Ordonnantie van de Zeevart Philipps II. von 1563 und in der Fassung von 1570/1571, der Instruktion für den ersten niederländischen Dispacheur Diego Gonzales Gante vom 11. Oktober 1570)[116].

Während in der Aufbauphase des Gerichts diese bewußte Rechtsvergleichung noch die Erschließung ergänzender Rechtsquellen – neben den Hanseatischen Seerechten – zum Ziel und damit den Einfluß fremder Seerechte auf Hamburgische Rechtsfindung zur Folge hat, verursacht die Rechtsprechung des Admiralitätsgerichts im Laufe einer gefestigten Gerichtspraxis wegen der differenzierten Behandlung der rezipierten Rechtsquellen wiederum eine Rückwirkung auf die Rechtsprechung anderer Seegerichte, auf die Seerechtswissenschaft bis ins 19. Jahrhundert und auf die seerechtliche Gesetzgebung des 18. Jahrhunderts. Im Jahr 1690 muß der Satz „non sibi sed orbi" mindestens als Programmsatz und Leitidee des Hamburgischen Admiralitätsgerichts verstanden werden; die tatsächliche Wirkung seiner Rechtsprechung ist zweifellos schon damals wesentlich umfassender gewesen, als es einer ins Bescheidene abgewandelten Inschrift „non sibi sed urbi" auf dem Portugaleser entsprochen hätte.

[116] Vgl. beispielsweise die privaten Gesetzessammlungen der Admiralitätsmitglieder Johann v. Spreckelsen 1624 (Commerzbibliothek Hamburg S/468) und Paul Jenisch 1720 (Staatsarchiv Hamburg, Senat Cl. VII, Lit. Ca, No. 2, Vol. 1b, Nr. 90).

CHRISTOPHER P. RODGERS

Continental Literature and the Development of the Common Law by the King's Bench: c. 1750 - 1800

Lord Mansfield (Chief Justice of King's Bench 1756 - 1788) has traditionally been regarded as the "creator" of English commercial law[1]. To talk of Mansfield, however, as the "founder" or "creator" of English commercial law probably overstates his achievement. While he undoubtedly contributed greatly to the foundation, for the first time, of a systematic body of mercantile jurisprudence in the common law, he was nonetheless not an original thinker. Many of the principles absorbed into the common law during this period were derived from continental learning on the law merchant and *jus gentium*. This influence was particularly marked in mercantile cases, but was also evident in cases with a "public" international law element, and in the development of the private law of obligations.

Law and Fact in Commercial Cases

As a preliminary to any study of the commercial law of this period, and of the role played by continental literature, it is necessary to look at the function of the jury, and the relationship between questions of law and fact in commercial cases.

In the mediaeval period the law merchant had been administered in its own special courts, e.g. the piepowder courts, and Admiralty. During the sixteenth and seventeenth centuries, the developing action of *assumpsit* provided a mechanism by which mercantile custom could be recognised by the common law. The courts began to accept that custom could be proved, as a question of fact, to found a legal duty in an action on the case. The use of juries in commercial cases, to adjudicate on questions of fact, was not new in Mansfield's time. They had been used sporadically since at least the beginning of the seventeenth century, and by an Act of 1730 each party was entitled to a special jury for the trial of any issue, provided he paid the

[1] A reputation which goes back to the well-known discourse of his contemporary, J. Buller in *Lickbarrow* v. *Mason* (1787) 2 T. R. 63 at 73.

expenses incurred[2]. Lord Mansfield institutionalised the system, and used special juries of merchants in most commercial cases. If an important principle was at issue, his practice was to direct the jury to state a case for the opinion of the court, which could then translate the mercantile custom applied at trial into a rule of law for future cases. According to the traditional theory, mercantile custom was in this way incorporated into the common law, without at the same time losing its flexibility to adapt to changing commercial practice[3]. Under Mansfield's guidance, the courts ceased to treat mercantile custom as a matter of fact and evidence, and began to treat it as a source of legal obligation. For this reason, Mansfield is normally recognised as having engineered the absorption of the law merchant into the common law.

Recent scholarship was suggested that the process of incorporation was in fact more complex. *J. H. Baker* has shown[4] that the common law courts *did* take cognizance of mercantile custom before 1700, and provided remedies in commercial cases through the existing forms of action at common law. The action of *onerabilis assumpsit* provided a remedy based on the law merchant, custom in this instance being expressly pleaded to found an obligation to pay. Custom could also be invoked at trial in a general assumpsit declaration, to support the implication of an undertaking to pay on the facts of the case, although there might be no mention of custom on the face of the pleadings. Customs "incorporated" in this way were not regarded by contemporary lawyers as importations from a coherent body of international law – the "law merchant". For this reason, foreign treatises on maritime and commercial law seem to have been rarely quoted before English courts before the eighteenth century. The incorporation of the law merchant had begun in the sixteenth and seventeenth centuries; it was simply that before Mansfield's time it had not manifested itself in the development of a body of *rules* within the common law itself. The use of special juries and the case stated procedure was the mechanism by which this change could occur.

It is now possible, using the evidence provided by Mansfield's own Judge's Notebooks, to analyse more closely the way in which the transformation of many issues from the realm of fact to that of law took place[5]. It is evident from the Notebooks that the use of special juries became a regular

---

[2] 3 Geo. II c. 25.

[3] See, inter alia: *Fifoot*, Lord Mansfield, p. 104 ff.; *Holden*, History of Negotiable Instruments in English Law, p. 114 ff.; *Holdsworth*, History of English Law I, p. 572; *Scrutton*, 3 Select Essays in Anglo-American Legal History, p. 13.

[4] Law Merchant and the Common Law before 1700 (1979) C. L. J. 295.

[5] Mansfield's Notebooks were discovered at Scone Palace, Perth, in 1967. They contain mostly notes of evidence in cases heard before Mansfield in King's Bench, made in his own hand. For a general description, see *E. Heward*, Lord Mansfield's Notebooks (1976) 92 L. Q. R. 438 - 455. Some of the Notebooks are missing, but they otherwise provide a record of cases heard before Mansfield between 1756 and 1786.

Table 1

Commercial cases heard before Lord Mansfield 1757 - 1786 (excluding those heard on circuit)

	Subject Matter							
	Insurance	Bills of Exchange	Charter-party	Bill of Lading	Ransom contracts	Seamens Wages	Salvage	Maritime Collision
1757		2						
1758	2	1						
1759	8		1					
1760		1						
1761	9		1	2	1		1	
1762	7	1	1					
1763	7	1	1	2		4		
1764	12	3				1		
1765	3	3						
1766	3	1				1		
1767			(Notebooks covering 1767 missing)					
1768	1	6			1	1		
1769	6	3	4			1		1
1770	5	12						1
1771	1	3						
1772	12	4	1					
1773	3	2						
1774			(Notebooks covering 1774 and 1775 missing)					
1775								
1776	8	10						
1777	9	3						
1778	18	11						
1779		1						
1780	3	3						
1781	38	21	1		1			
1782	25	20	1					
1783	10	17			2			
1784	11	12	3		1	1		
1785			(Notebooks covering 1785 missing)					
1786		3						

Source: Lord Mansfield's Judges Notebooks, Scone Palace, Perth.

feature of King's Bench procedure soon after Mansfield's appointment in 1756. The first recorded account of his relationship with the jurors was given in *Lewis* v. *Rucker* (1761)[6], but special juries had clearly become a

[6] (1761) 2 Burr. 1167.

common feature before this. The first case in which Mansfield noted the presence of a jury in his Notebook was *Green* v. *Rucker* (8th December 1759)[7]. He noted on this occasion that "but five of the special jury appeared", indicating perhaps that their use was not at this stage well established. The presence of a jury is evidenced by the Notebooks in one other case in 1759 (*Gardiner* v. *Croasdale*[8]), and in one case in 1762 (*Green* v. *Butler*[9]). From July 1766 onwards, the presence of a special jury in virtually every commercial case in the King's Bench is indicated by a standard entry to this effect in the headnote of each commercial case noted in the Notebooks[10]. The use of juries had become standard practice by 1766, and remained so for the next twenty years.

The process by which the juries' findings of fact became law involved more than their simple incorporation, wholesale, into the common law. To have done so would have sacrificed the flexibility of customary rules, for once incorporated into the law they would, naturally, be subject to the rule of *stare decisis*. On the other hand, Lord Mansfield recognised that a primary policy of the law must be to promote certainty in commercial transactions. He reconciled the conflicting interests of flexibility and certainty by incorporating into the common law the general principles of the law merchant, while at the same time leaving a large number of subsidiary matters as questions of fact for the jury. This policy in commercial cases was outlined by Buller J. in *Lickbarrow* v. *Mason*, who tells us that before Mansfield's time, "... in courts of law all the evidence in mercantile cases was thrown together; they were left to a jury and they produced no established principle. From that time we all know the great study has been to find some *certain general principles* which shall be known to all mankind, not only to rule the particular case under consideration, but to serve as a guide for the future. The primary objective was to bring certainty into mercantile transactions – something which could not be achieved where the issue was left entirely to the jury, from whose general verdict it would be impossible to elicit any principle to govern future cases"[11]. Certainty was so important that Mansfield frequently directed a case to be stated for the opinion of the court, even where the issue was not in doubt[12]. The desire for certainty came

---

7 Notebook, Vol. 455, 8 Dec. 1759 – 19 Feb. 1760.

8 Notebook, Vol. 455 ibid. p. 66.

9 Notebook, Vol. 458, 22 Feb. 1762 – 9 June 1762, p. 51.

10 A standard entry, "S. Jury", is made in the heading of each case entry in the Notebooks, starting with *Webster* v. *Edie* (2 July, 1766) (Vol. 456, 17 May 1766 - 2 Dec. 1766).

11 (1787) 2 T. R. 63 at 73.

12 See *Hankey* v. *Jones* (1778) 2 Cowp. 745 at 750. Also Mansfield's comments in *Vallejo* v. *Wheeler* (1774) 1 Cowp. 145: "It is not easy to collect with certainty from the general verdict, or from notes taken at Nisis Prius, what was the true ground of decision. Therefore in this case, as in all doubtful cases, I wished a case to be made for the opinion of the court" (at p. 153).

also from the merchants themselves. In a number of cases, Mansfield noted in his Notebook that he had given leave for a case to be stated at the request of jurors and witnesses, often where the issue was not in doubt[13]. Once a rule of law was settled, however, the role of the jury was at an end[14].

The nature, and generality, of many of the rules incorporated from the law merchant meant that the jury retained an important role in their application to individual cases. Many of these rules were 'open textured', in that their future application could change in accordance with changing mercantile morality and practice. It was established, for instance, that the indorsee of a negotiable instrument which was dishonoured must give notice to the drawer within a reasonable period. What constituted a "reasonable" period of notice was a question of law for the court. The mode of giving notice and its adequacy according to mercantile usage remained, however, a question of fact for the jury[15]. Similarly, in the law of marine insurance, the rules as to when a loss must be proved to have occurred, and the principle that a venture must be frustrated if the loss was to be 'total' (and not simply 'average'), were matters of law. What measure of loss would suffice to frustrate the venture, however, remained a question of fact for the jury[16]. In this way an element of flexibility in the application of the law was maintained, notwithstanding the translation into rules of law of many of the principles of the law merchant. In many other instances, mercantile usage was considered unsuitable for incorporation into the law, either because of its subsidiary nature or because the usage itself was not settled. In such cases its application remained a question of fact for the jury, leaving scope for development and change. Moreover if issues of fact were uncertain, Mansfield would seek the advice of expert witnesses, a practice which is evidenced throughout his Notebooks, e.g. in insurance cases he frequently sought the advice of the directors of the leading insurance companies[17].

---

[13] For instance, *Stevenson* v. *Snow* (1761) Notebook, Vol. 456, p. 168 ("There seems no doubt at all in this case. I reserved it only because asked"); *Green* v. *Butler* (1759) Notebook, Vol. 458, p. 51 ("I gave them [the jury] leave to move the court by a new action").

[14] *Edie* v. *East India Coy.* (1761) 1 W.Bl. 295 ("The point of law is here well settled; and, once solemnly settled, no particular usage shall be admitted to weigh against it; this would send everything to sea again"); *Buller* v. *Harrison* (1777) 2 Cowp. 565.

[15] *Tindal* v. *Brown* (1786) 1 T.R. 167.

[16] *Goss* v. *Withers* (1758) 2 Burr. 683; *Hamilton* v. *Mendes* (1761) 2 Burr. 1200.

[17] For instance in *Grant* v. *James* (15 May 1759), Notebook, Vol. 453. Mansfield noted the evidence of Mr. Barker, a Director of the London Assurance Co., as to the insurability of freight. In other insurance cases evidence was sought from underwriters (e.g. *Green* v. *Butler,* 1762, Notebook, Vol. 458, p. 51) and brokers (e.g. *Green* v. *Rucker,* 8 Dec. 1758, Notebook, Vol. 455, p. 1).

The Role of Continental Literature

Continental literature on the *jus gentium* and law merchant played an important role in the translation of usage from fact into law. The leading continental works provided the sources from which many of the general principles of the law merchant incorporated into law were taken. The transformation of custom into law, via the special jury system, meant that from the mid-eighteenth century onwards English lawyers began to treat the literature of the law merchant as a potential source of legal obligation, and not simply as evidence of issues of fact. English lawyers' perception of the law merchant itself had also changed. Before Mansfield's time, views as to its nature had differed. Some, such as Malynes[18], regarded it simply as the custom of merchants, while others saw it as part of the universal *jus gentium,* akin to international law. Blackstone asserted that "the affairs of commerce are regulated by a law of their own, called the Law Merchant or *Lex Mercatoria,* which all nations agree in and take notice of; and in particular it is held to be part of the law of England, which decides the causes of merchants by the general rules which obtain in all commercial countries, and that often even in matters relating to domestic trade, as for instance in the drawing, accepting and transfer of inland bills of exchange"[19]. Lord Mansfield belonged emphatically to the latter school, holding the law merchant to be part of the universal *jus gentium,* as evidenced by the practice of merchants, and as such part of the law of England. "The law of nations is in its full extent part of the law of England, and ... [is] to be collected from the practice of different nations and the authority of writers." (*Triquet* v. *Bath,* 1764)[20].

This view had been popular with some English writers, notably Zouche and Sir John Davies, during the seventeenth century[21]. During the eighteenth century, it became the accepted view of the status of the law merchant. This was undoubtedly due to the influence of the natural law theorists, and particularly to the works of Grotius and Pufendorf. Mansfield's views reflect Grotius's theory that the *existence* of natural law can be proved by the universal practice of states, and by the opinions of jurists[22].

---

[18] Lex Mercatoria (1622) pp. 2 - 3.

[19] Commentaries, i, 273.

[20] (1764) 3 Burr. 1478. See also dicta in *Heathfield* v. *Chiltern* (1764) 4 Burr. 2051; "the privileges of ministers and their retinue depend upon the law of nations, which is part of the common law of England".

[21] R. Zouche, Jurisdiction of the Admiralty in England Asserted (1686) p. 89; J. Davies, The Question concerning Impositions (1656) pp. 10 and 27 – both cited by *Scrutton,* "Roman Law Influence", 1 Select Essays in Anglo-American Legal History at pp. 238 - 9.

[22] De Jure Belli ac Pacis 1.1.12. and Prolegomena. *P. Stein* has drawn attention to the contrast between Grotius's *a posteriori* method of proof, and the *a priori* method adopted by Pufendorf in De Jure Naturae et Gentium (Legal Evolution, 1980, p. 4).

The apparent acceptance of Grotius's views by Mansfield facilitated reference to the continental works, which provided evidence of the practice of states and merchants, and therefore of the *jus gentium* itself. The continental literature played an important part in two ways. In the first place, many of the leading principles of the law merchant were to be found in the continental compilations widely used by practitioners. Mansfield frequently relied, for instance, upon the *Guidon de la mer* and Colbert's *Ordonnance de la Marine* of 1681. Secondly, in cases where there was no settled principle or uniform commercial practice, reference could be had to the more theoretical works on the *jus gentium,* and particularly to the leading works of the natural lawyers such as Grotius's *De Jure Belli ac Pacis,* Pufendorf's *De Jure Naturae et Gentium,* and Bynkershoek's *Questiones Juris Publici.* In cases where there was no settled practice, or the opinions of the writers differed, Mansfield was able to synthesize the views of the authorities to arrive a satisfactory principle of law. To this limited extent, he can truly be described as the "creator" of English commercial law.

The literature relied upon by Mansfield in his judgements can, for the purposes of analysis, be divided into four broad categories. It may be useful to make some general observations as to the use made of each type of literature before giving a detailed analysis of the citation of foreign works in different areas of English law. The continental codes and other models of commercial law, the technical treatises on the law merchant, the theoretical works of the natural lawyers, and the leading works of the continental civilians, all played differing roles in the development of the common law.

Where the law merchant was settled, reliance was commonly placed on the continental commercial codes and compilations of mercantile custom as evidence of the *jus gentium.* The model most often cited by Mansfield was Colbert's *Ordonnance de la Marine* of 1681, which was admitted by counsel in one of the leading marine insurance cases to be "in some measure a digest of the general law of merchants relative to maritime causes"[23]. Valin's influential *Commentaire sur l'Ordonnance de la Marine* (1760) was also frequently cited before Lord Mansfield[24]. The Ordinance of 1681 and Valin's commentary were the source of many of the principles incorporated into the common law. Other continental models relied upon included the *Guidon de la Mer*[25], the Rules of Oleron and the Laws of Wisby. The Guidon was itself one of the earliest treatises on marine insurance and set out many of the principles of insurance law adopted into English law by Mansfield. The

---

[23] *Bermon* v. *Woodbridge* (1781) 2 Doug. 781.

[24] R. J. Valin, Nouveau Commentaire sur l'Ordonnance de la Marine du Mois Août 1681 etc. (1760).

[25] A treatise on insurance, bottomry and average, by an unknown author. It was drawn up for the use of merchants at Rouen in 1561.

Guidon, the Rules of Oleron and the Laws of Wisby were included in an annotated compilation by Cleirac[26]. This edition became the most authoritative of the compilations in England and was the source from which Mansfield drew many of the principles of English maritime law. An English translation of Cleirac's work was included in Justice's *General Treatise of the Dominion of the Sea,* of which three editions appeared between 1705 and 1724[27]. The latter also included the Rhodian laws and much Roman law material, and was relied upon by Mansfield in a number of cases.

Where more complex issues of law were involved, reliance was often placed on the more technical treatises on the law merchant. Of such works, Roccus's *De Navibus et Naulo, item de Assecurationibus Notabilia* (1655) was particularly influential, and was cited on numerous occasions by Mansfield[28]. Reliance was also placed on a number of other treatises including Loccenius' *De Jure Maritimo et Navali* (1650)[29], and Marquard's *De Jure Mercatorom et Commerciorum* (1662)[30].

It has been noted that Mansfield's attitude to the law merchant was itself founded in natural law philosophy. The writings of the leading natural law theorists – particularly Grotius, Pufendorf, Barbeyrac, Burlamaqui and Bynkershoek – also contributed to the development of the substantive commercial law. They were frequently cited in cases where the extant works on the law merchant provided no guidance, or where the opinions of the writers conflicted. Grotius's *De Jure Belli ac Pacis* (1625) and Pufendorf's *De Jure Naturae et Gentium* (1672) were regularly cited as authorities for the basic principles of the law of contract, and on insurance. Both works were well suited for this purpose. Book II of Grotius's *De Jure Belli ac Pacis* had little to do with international law, being a systematic treatment of the various branches of private law according to the dictates of the law of nature. Similarly, of the eight books of Pufendorf's *De Jure Naturae et Gentium,* only Book Eight deals specifically with the law of Nations. Books Three and Five

---

[26] E. Cleirac, Us et coustumes de la mer, contenant les Jugemens d'Oleron, Ordonnances de Wisburg, de la Hanse-Teutonique et autre pieces, 4 Vols. (1647, 1661 and 1671, Bordeaux and Rouen). An English translation of the rules of Oleron was also published under Cleirac's name in London in 1686. It seems curious that Mansfield should have used Cleirac's compilation, as he must have been aware of the Guidon's inclusion in the Black Book of Admiralty.

[27] A. Justice, General Treatise of the Dominion of the Sea, and a compleat body of the Sea Laws, containing what is most valuable of that subject in Antient and Modern Authors, and particularly the antient laws of the Rhodians and Romans, those of Oleron, Wisbuy and other countries, as also the sea laws lately published in France ... with adjudged cases in several courts, opinions on important maritime cases. etc. 4 Vols. (3rd ed. 1724).

[28] Published at Naples 1655. There were two Dutch editions extant, published at Amsterdam in 1708 and 1737. An English translation was not available until 1809.

[29] J. Loccenius, De Jure Maritimo et Navali libri tres. 8 Vols. (Stockholm 1650).

[30] J. Marquard. De Jure Mercatorum et Commerciorum singulari, libri IV. (Frankfurt 1662).

deal with the law of obligations from the point of view of natural law, and were the source of many of the innovations introduced by Mansfield in this area. The most frequently used edition of Pufendorf was that by Barbeyrac, whose own commentary on the text was itself cited with approval in a number of cases[31]. Of the other standard natural law texts, Burlamaqui's *Principles of Natural Law* (1748)[32] was frequently referred to. Bynkershoek's *Questiones Juris Publici* (1737)[33] was also influential (particularly in cases involving issues of private and public international law).

The influence of works by continental civilians was more limited. The Roman law itself knew nothing of many of the transactions with which the English courts now had to deal. Civilian learning was thus of little use in developing areas of commercial law such as insurance and bills of exchange. Like the natural law works, civilian learning was of some use in formulating general principles, particularly in the law of contract and restitution. Huber's *Praelectiones Juris Romani et Hodierni* (1689) had a strong influence on the development of principles of conflict of laws in contract cases. Vinnius's Commentary on the Institutes of Justinian (1642)[34] was also cited with approval in a number of cases, principally those involved with contract law. The works of Johanne Voet were also relied upon in this context.

Lord Mansfield must himself have possessed many of the leading continental works on the civil and maritime laws. He is known to have kept an extensive library at his home in Bloomsbury Square, but this was destroyed when the property was burned in the Gordon Riots of 1780[35]. He must have re-acquired, or at least had access to, many of the standard works for use in his remaining years in office, for he is reported on a number of subsequent occasions as drawing counsel's attention to relevant foreign treatises[36]. The Mansfield family papers contain an anonymous inventory, described simply as a "Catalogue of Lord Mansfield's Books in Lincoln's Inn Fields, June 1793". Mansfield maintained a town house at No. 57/8 Lincoln's Inn Fields

---

[31] Le Droit de la Nature et des Gens de S. Pufendorf ... traduit par J. Barbeyrac. Avec des notes du traducteur (Amsterdam, 1706). I have used the 1749 English edition.

[32] J. J. Burlamaqui, On Natural Law, translated into English by Nugent, 8 Vols, 1748. Burlamaqui's Principles of Political Law was translated and published in 1752. The two were published together in translation as Burlamaqui's Principles of Natural and Political Law (2 Vols.) in 1752. Several editions appeared subsequently.

[33] C. van Bynkershoek, Questiones Juris Publici (1737) 2 Vols.

[34] In quatuor libros Institutionum imperialium Commentarius academicus et forensis (Leyden 1642).

[35] Campbell's Lives of the Justices II, p. 524. The destruction of his law library was evidenced by the fact that, when speaking on the legal issues raised by the use of the militia to quell the Gordon riots of 1780, Mansfield informed the House of Lords that he had to speak from memory because "he had no books to consult" – Campbell op. cit. p. 527.

[36] Thus in *Anton* v. *Fisher* (1781) 2 Doug. 649 he specifically drew counsel's attention to Valin's Commentary on the Marine Ordinance.

until his death in March 1793, and his will refers to household effects stored in the basement there[37]. Further biographical research will be necessary to establish the provenance of the catalogue, but it seems possible that it was made following Mansfield's death, and possibly for probate purposes. Its chief interest lies in that it lists over sixty works of continental origin, providing circumstantial evidence that Mansfield must have possessed many of the leading continental works. An abstract of those continental treatises listed in the Catalogue is printed at Table 2. As might be expected, Mansfield may well have possessed copies of the standard works on natural law, notably Grotius's *De Jure Belli ac Pacis* and both Pufendorf's *De Jure Naturae et Gentium* and his *De Officio Hominis*[38]. He also seems to have possessed many of the leading French works of this period, including not only Valin's commentary, but also Denisart's *Collections de Decisions*[39], Delacombe's *Recueil de la Jurisprudence Civile*[40], and the Institutions of both Gabriel Argou[41] and of Loisel[42]. He also possessed copies of the French Ordinances. The leading maritime treatises are also in evidence, including editions of Loccenius and Justice's *Treatise of the Dominion of the Sea*[43]. Mansfield also appears to have possessed a large collection of the works of the leading civilians. These include Voet's Commentary on the Digest[44], and his *Elementa Juris*[45], and the works of Vinnius, Böckelmann, Corvinus, Oldendorp and Van Leeuwen.

Tracing the precise influence of these works on the development of English commercial law presents a number of problems. In some cases, the use of foreign treatises is explicit, as when the writer and original source are directly quoted. In many other cases, however, evidence of their use is more indirect. A doctrine known to have originated in certain of the continental literature is discussed and relied upon, but without directly attributing its source. An examination of Mansfield's judgements reveals both types of influence. In the absence of direct attribution, it is only possible to speculate as to the source of some of the rules discussed[46]. The knowledge that Mans-

---

[37] *E. Heward,* Lord Mansfield (1979) p. 25.

[38] De Officio Hominis et Civis Juxta Legem Naturalem Libri Duo (1673). The catalogue also includes Pufendorf's Introduction à l'Histoire Universelle.

[39] J. B. Denisart, Collections de decisions nouvelles et de notions relatives à la Jurisprudence Actuelle.

[40] Delacombe, Recueil de la Jurisprudence Civile.

[41] G. Argou, Institution au droit françois (1692).

[42] A. Loysel, Institution au droit françois.

[43] As to which, see notes 27 and 29 supra.

[44] J. Voet, Commentarius ad Pandectas (1698 - 1704).

[45] J. Voet, Elementa juris secundum ordinem Institutionum Justiniani in usum domesticae exercitationis digesta (1700). This was an elementary student textbook, designed to enable students to follow his lectures without making notes – as to which, see *Feenstra* and *Waal,* Seventeenth Century Leyden Law Professors (1975), p. 40.

[46] Mansfield's Notebooks contain only notes of evidence, and do not throw any light on the sources on which he relied in many leading cases.

Table 2

Catalogue of Lord Mansfield's Books in Lincoln's Inn Fields, June 1793

Page in	*Folio Volumes*
catalogue. 6	Bronchorst. de Verborum Significatione.
fo. 8	Fachinus. de Controversiis Iuris. [Fachinaeus, A; Controversiarum iuris libri tredecim].
	Marquardus. de Jure Mercatorum. [Marquard, J. De Jure Mercatorum et Commerciorum Singulari. 4 Vols. 1662].
	De Mercatura Decisiones, et Tractatus Varii (anon.).
fo. 10	Jo. Voet. Comment. ad Pandectas. 2 Vols.
	Quarto Volumes
fo. 11	Police of France. [anon. but probably the work of this name by Sir Wm. Mildmay].
	Treatise of the Dominion of the Sea. (anon.) [Justice, A. General Treatise of the Dominion of the Sea etc.].
	J. B. Denisart, Collections de decisions [nouvelles et de notions relatives à la jurisprudence actuelle] 3 Vols.
	Delacombe, Recueil de la jurisprudence Civile.
	Valin, Commentaire sur l'Ordonnance de la Marine.
	Salle, Esprit des Ordonnances & c. de Louis XV. 2 Vols.
	Pacquet, Traité des Fiefs.
fo. 13	Mysinger, de Institutionibus Justiniani.
	Fritschi, Sylloge variorum Tractatum Juris Publici et privati.
	M. Berlichius, de Novercarum Jure.
	U. Huber, Praelectiones [Juris Romani et Hodierni] 2 Vols.
	Hottingem, de Legibus Hebraeorum.
	"Extracts from Marine Treaties" (anon.).
	Coustumes de la Mer (anon.).
	A. Corvinus, Summarium Jurisprudentiae Romanae.
	"Code de Henry IV" (anon.).
	Françon, Coutume de Paris.
	Peregrinus, de Jure et Privilegiis Fisci.
fo. 14	Mertertius, de Justitia Romanorum Legum.
	Bachovius, Tractatus de Pignoribus & Hypothecis. [Frankfurt, 1627].
fo. 15	Russian Code of Laws (anon.).
	Magens on Insurance, Vol. 2.
fo. 16	Bynkershoek, Opera, Vols. 2, 3, 4, 5, 6.
	Bynkershoek, Questions Juris Publici, 2 Vols.
	Octavo & c.
fo. 17	Commentaire Sur l'Ordonnance Criminelle. (anon.).
	Pufendorf, de Officio Hominis.
	Corpus Juris Civilis (edition unidentified).
fo. 18	Park on Marine Insurance (2 copies).
fo. 19	Traité des Prises, 2 Vols in 1 (anon.).

Table 2 (continued)

fo. 20	Grotius, de Jure Belli ac Pacis, 2 Vols.
fo. 21	Lengnich, Jus Publicum Regni Poloni, 2 Vols.
fo. 23	Collection of Treaties, 4 Vols. (anon.). Warville, Bibliotheque du Legislateur, 4 Vols. Warville, Theorie des Loix Criminelles, 2 Vols.
fo. 24	Principes de la Jurisprudence François, 2 Vols. G. Argou, Institution au Droit François, 2 Vols. Recueil des Ordonnances du Roi de Portugal, Vols 1 - 4 (anon.). Justinian's Institutes (edition unidentified).
fo. 26	Vinnius, de Jurisdictione. Böckelmann, Compendium Institutionum Justiniani. [Lugduni Batav 1679]. A. Duck, de usu Juris Civilis. Vinnius, Questiones Juris.
fo. 27	A. Corvinus, Elementa Juris Civilis. [Amsterdam 1664]. Grotius, Florum Sparsio ad Jus Justinianeum.
fo. 28	Refuge, Traité de la cour. Oldendorp, Miscellanea.
fo. 30	Grotius, de Jure Belli ac Pacis. J. Voet, Elementa Juris. [Lugduni, Batav. 1700].
fo. 31	Loccenius, de Jure Maritimo [et Navali libri tres (1650)]. Leewius, de origine Iuris Civilis Romani [presumably S. van Leeuwen, De origine et progressu juris civilis & c. (1671)]. Ordonnances de Louis XIV. (anon.).
fo. 33	Loisel, Institutes Coutumieres, Vol. 1. [A. Loysel, Institution au droit françois].
fo. 34	Pufendorf, Introduction à l'Histoire Universelle, Vol. 4.
fo. 35	Commentaire sur l'Ordonnance Civile, Vol. 1. (anon.). Commentaire sur l'Edit de 1695. (anon.).

Note:

The Catalogue contains legal works of both English and continental origin, and works of a non legal nature. Only those works identifiable as of foreign origin, and works on commercial law, are abstracted here.

The Catalogue is written in a rough hand. Entries are reproduced above as they appear in the Catalogue itself.

field may well have possessed many of the treatises suspected as source material does, however, make such speculation more fruitful than would otherwise be the case. The following discussion concentrates on the use of continental literature in the areas of commercial law, private international law, and the law of contract. Foreign influences on the development of these branches of the common law are known to have been strong, although further research may reveal the extent of this influence in other areas of the common law.

Maritime Law

The international character of maritime law, and the fact that Mansfield saw English law as part of the universal *jus gentium,* meant that continental literature was bound to exert a strong influence on the development of this branch of the common law. Mansfield was particularly concerned that the law applied in England should be the same as that applied elsewhere, and his work in the field of maritime law was accordingly an early attempt at legal harmonisation. Continental literature played a leading role in two areas of English maritime law: the law of marine insurance, and the development or rules as to the enforceability of ransom bills.

So confused was common law thinking on the law of marine insurance that it was unclear until 1746 whether an insurable interest was necessary for a valid contract of insurance or not, viz. whether wagering policies were valid, or void on grounds of public policy. This pre-existing uncertainty was noted by Blackstone in the *Commentaries,* where he observed,

> "The learning relating to marine insurance hath of late years been greatly improved by a series of judical decisions, which have now established the law in such a variety of cases, that (if well and judiciously collected) they would form a very complete title in a code of commercial jurisprudence. But being founded on equitable principles, which chiefly result from the special circumstances of the case, it is not easy to reduce them to any general heads in mere elementary institutes[47]."

Blackstone's discussion of bottomry and marine insurance was itself inserted into a description of contracts of hire and borrowing, and is very perfunctory. He discusses bottomry and wagering contracts, but says virtually nothing about contracts of marine insurance as such, except that they are contracts of utmost good faith. By 1788 the position had been transformed. The King's Bench had laid down most of the leading principles of the modern law of insurance in a clear and intelligible form, and treatises devoted to the new jurisprudence had appeared. Notable among the latter was Park's treatise on *Marine Insurance* (1787)[48], a book which is commonly regarded as a digest of the law developed in the previous thirty years by Lord Mansfield.

Two considerations influenced Mansfield's work on the law of marine insurance. The first was that the basic principles of the law should be contained in clear and certain general principles, and that with difficult cases recourse should always be had to basic principles so as not to cloud the issues with legal technicalities. Secondly, when interpreting policies he was concerned to ensure that they should be interpreted in the same way and

---

[47] Commentaries, ii, 461.

[48] Sir J. A. Park, System of the Law of Marine Insurance, with three chapters on Bottomry, Insurance on Lives and on Insurance against Fire (1787).

have the same legal effect in England as they would abroad. Whether formulating general principles to be applied to future cases, or interpreting technical language in policies, Mansfield encouraged the citation of continental authorities.

Given the uncertainty of the law, the first task was to settle a clear definition of the nature of the contract of insurance itself. In *Goss* v. *Withers* (1758)[49], counsel cited Bynkershoek's definition of insurance (*Questiones Juris Publici,* 1.21) viz. "insurance is nothing else than an engagement for the security of another's property by which the owner is liberated from the risk, which is assumed by the insurer in consideration of a certain fixed premium." This was not challenged, and formed a basis for the detailed rules later laid down by Mansfield. The reporter noted that "Lord Mansfield spoke extremely well of Bynkershoek's writings ... and recommended especially as well worth reading his book on Prizes" *(Questiones Juris Publici)*[50]. Bynkershoek's *Questiones* was also an important source for the general principles of other areas of maritime law. Blackstone cites *Questiones Juris Publici,* 3.16, as authority for his description of contracts of bottomry[51]. Grotius (*De Jure Belli ac Pacis,* II, 12, 3.5) defined insurance, further, as "the act of guaranteeing indemnity against chance losses" and a "guarding against risk". The nature of the contract as one of indemnity was recognised by Lord Mansfield, and incorporated as one of the basic principles of English insurance law. "The insurer runs the risk of the insured and undertakes to indemnify: he must therefore bear the loss actually sustained and can be liable for no more[52]."

One of the most important problems in practice was to distinguish between average and total losses. Under the common form of marine insurance, the rights of the insured varied according to whether the loss sustained was 'total' or merely 'average'. If the ship and cargo survived some calamity in transit, but the commercial purpose of the voyage was completely frustrated, the insured was entitled to claim a total loss, surrender his interest to the insurers and claim upon the policy. If the venture was not frustrated, the loss might be partial (or 'average'), in which case the insured could recover only the damage actually sustained. In the leading cases of *Goss* v. *Withers* (1758) and *Hamilton* v. *Mendes* (1761), Mansfield laid down the basic principles of the English law on total and average losses. Continental learning was very influential in their development.

In *Goss* v. *Withers,* an English merchantman was captured by a French privateer, but, after eight days, was recaptured and taken to Milford Haven.

---

[49] (1758) 2 Burr. 683.
[50] (1758) 2 Burr. 683 at 692.
[51] Commentaries, ii, 459.
[52] *Goss* v. *Withers* (1758) 2 Burr. 683, supra.

A quarter of the cargo had been lost in a storm at sea, and the rest perished while she was lying off Milford. Argument turned on whether detention for eight days was sufficient to transfer title in the vessel to the French, thereby rendering the loss total in law. The plaintiffs relied upon Grotius's *De Jure Belli ac Pacis,* 3.6.3.2[53] for the proposition that property passes after twenty-four hours' detention in enemy hands. The defendants relied on Bynkershoek, *Questiones Juris Publici,* 1.4, for the contrary view that length of time alone cannot divest an owner of property, and that the *spes recuperandi* must be entirely gone before property can pass – the captor has a possessory title, which only becomes absolute when resonable hope of recovery has gone. Burlamaqui's *Principles of Natural Law,* 1.6 and 2.7, was relied on to the effect that fresh pursuit prevents possessory title becoming absolute. Mansfield's knowledge of the continental authorites was shown by the fact that he corrected counsel's version of Bynkershoek's views. Faced with the contradictory views of the authorities, a separate ground for decision was required. Whether the property had been transferred to the enemy was held to be irrelevant as between the insurerer and insured. Lord Mansfield therefore started from the principle that nothing should be taken to have changed until all pursuit had ceased – a proposition he drew from Voet's Commentary on the Pandects, 49.15.2.1155. The insurer runs the risk of the insured, and undertakes to indemnify – he must therefore bear the loss actually sustained. That loss must be judged at the date when it actually happened. Here the loss was total when the ship was captured, for half the remaining cargo would have to be paid for salvage even if it was recaptured, and the cargo was perishable. Being in the nature of an indemnity, however, the contract should be liberally construed, so that an average loss might occur where the entire cargo was recaptured after a short time. The definition of the right to abandon a claim on a total loss was adopted by Mansfield from the *Guidon de la Mer,* 7.1, viz. where there had been a capture "or such other disturbance as defeats the voyage, or makes it not worthwhile, or worth the freight, to pursue it". Mansfield's source was the translation of the *Guidon* included in Cleirac's *Us et Coustumes de la Mer*[54].

It was common for owners to attempt to cut their losses where there was a falling market by claiming a total loss, and surrendering their goods to the insurers. The decision in *Gross* v. *Withers* encouraged this practice and the court was faced in *Hamilton* v *Mendes* (1761) with a more questionable claim for a total loss where a whole cargo had been delivered in London after recapture. Counsel for the plaintiffs argued for a total loss on the basis

[53] The citation in Burrow's report of the case, which refers to De Jure Belli, 3.6, pa 814, appears to be inaccurate.

[54] (1758) 2 Burr. 683 at 698. Mansfield quotes the Guidon which, he says, is contained "in the second part of the Usage and Customs of the Sea (a French book translated into English)".

of the length of time (17 days) that the vessel had been in enemy hands, relying on Grotius, Bynkershoek and Roccus[55]. The defendants, like their counterparts in *Goss,* argued that the hope of recovery could only be considered gone when the vessel was taken *infra praesidia hostium.* Article 45 of the *Ordonnance de la Marine* of 1681 and the *Consolato del Mare* were adduced to support this, and the correct views of Bynkershoek and Roccus debated[56]. Lord Mansfield reiterated that the basic principle of English law was stated in the *Guidon,* 7.1. The most important thing was to adopt a certain principle of law. If the result "is to depend upon speculative refinements, from the law of nations or the Roman *jus postliminii* concerning the changing or revesting of property, no wonder the merchants are in the dark, when doctors have differed upon the subject from the beginning and are not yet agreed"[57]. Insurance being in the nature of an indemnity, the insured must establish some injury at the time his action is brought. This conclusion was itself based on the general principles recognised by the continental authorities who, Mansfield asserted, all agreed "that if the thing is recovered before the money paid, the insured can only be entitled according to the final event." As authority for this view, Mansfield relied on Roccus, not. 50, which "collects the opinions of all the authors before his time." The nature of the plaintiffs' injury here was merely a delay and obstruction in delivery, and the loss was therefore average. These two decisions laid down the basic principles of the law of average and total losses, and were followed in subsequent cases[58].

Another important principle recognised by the law merchant, and incorporated into English law by Lord Mansfield, was that insurance contracts are contracts *uberrimae fidei,* viz. the parties are under a duty of utmost good faith. A failure to disclose material facts will avoid the contract, whether the failure is deliberate or not. Mansfield's treatment of the subject in his reported decisions owes much to civilian learning, although no direct citation is apparent.

The requirement of good faith derives from the nature of insurance as an indemnity against chance occurrences. Pufendorf (*De Jure Naturae et Gentium,* 5.9) discusses insurance in conjunction with wagers, lotteries and raffles, i.e. what modern civilians would term aleatory contracts. "This contract is null, if either the insurer knows for certain that the goods be already safe, or the merchant that they be lost. For the matter of this contract is sup-

---

[55] De Navibus et Naulo, respons. 34.

[56] Bynkershoek, Questiones Juris Publici, 1.5., holds that ships and other moveables become the absolute property of the captor only when brought within the praesidia. Roccus, op. cit., Not. 50 was also cited for the proposition that "a ship cannot be abandoned as long as it can swim".

[57] (1761) 2 Burr. 1200 at 1214.

[58] See for instance *Milles* v. *Fletcher* (1779) 1 Doug. 231.

posed to be a loss considered as uncertain. Whereas, if the insurer is certain that the goods are arrived safe, he runs no risk; and if the owner knows that they are lost, he cannot demand another to run the risk of them; for what is not in being cannot be liable to risk."[59] These principles were worked into English law in *Stevenson* v. *Snow*[60] (1761) and *Carter* v. *Boehm* (1766)[61].

In the former it was held that premiums must be repaid where a vessel does not undertake its voyage, for no risk is run. Magens's *Essay on Insurances*[62] provided proof that return of premiums was the rule in other jurisdictions, and the Ordinances of Konigsbergh and Stockholm were cited as examples. Under the continental codes, a small percentage (half a per cent) was usually retained to cover the cost of effecting the policy, with the remainder of the premium being repaid. Mansfield was prepared to rely on the more general ground that insurance, being a contract of the *jus gentium,* should be construed liberally and not *stricti iuris.* Equity implies a condition "that the insurer shall not receive the price of running a risk, if he runs none." Wilmot J. was more explicit, holding that, "these kinds of contracts are by the writers ... called *contractus innominati;* and the rule which they lay down concerning them is that they are to be determined *secundum bonum et aequum*". The materiality or otherwise of disclosure was discussed in *Carter* v. *Boehm* (1766), in which Mansfield held that good faith forbids either party from drawing the other into a bargain by concealing what he privately knows. Each party may innocently be silent as to the grounds open to both, and the insured need not divulge to the underwriter what he ought to know. An innocent concealment of something outside the underwriter's sphere of knowledge would, however, vitiate the contract if it changed the risk insured against under the policy. Similarly, a policy would be void against an underwriter if he insured a ship on a voyage when he privately knew it had already arrived – the example given by Pufendorf. The influence of the works of Pufendorf and other natural law writers was hinted at in *Hodgson* v. *Richardson* (1764) by Yates J. who (concurring with Mansfield) observed that "the concealment of material circumstances vitiates all such contracts upon the principles of natural law"[63].

Mansfield's approach to the construction of insurance policies proceeded on the premise that mercantile documents should have the same meaning before English courts as abroad. "From the nature, object and utility of this kind of contract, consequences have been drawn, and a system of construc-

---

[59] De Jure Naturae et Gentium 5.9.8. Pufendorf himself cites Loccenius's De Jure Maritimo as authority for some of the propositions in his passage on Insurance.

[60] (1761) 3 Burr. 1237.

[61] (1766) 3 Burr. 1905.

[62] N. Magens, Essay on Insurances, illustrated by cases; a Collection of all the foreign Ordinances of insurance and forms of policies, etc. (1755).

[63] (1764) 1 W. Bl. 464.

tion established upon the ancient and inaccurate form of words in which the instrument is conceived. The mercantile law, in this respect, is the same all over the world. For from the same premises, the sound conclusions of reason and justice must universally be the same."[64] Moreover, being contracts *de jure gentium,* their interpretation depended upon equitable considerations, and not upon the strict legal import of the terms in the contract[65]. It was natural that the courts should rely heavily on the more technical foreign treatises to ascertain the meaning of phrases hitherto unfamiliar to English courts. Reference was also made to the continental mercantile codes for guidance. The inaccurate phraseology used by merchants meant that disputes as to interpretation were common.

In *Pelly* v. *Royal Exchange Assurance Co.* (1757) the true meaning of the phrase "in the *ordinary* course of a voyage" had to be decided. The works of Loccenius, Marquardus and Roccus[66], and other foreign writers, were cited to the effect that the insurer is liable for all loss occurring as a result of something usually done in the course of a voyage, including refitting. This was accepted as law by Lord Mansfield. Another concept unknown to English law was that of "barratry", viz. the misconduct of a ship's master, which was usually insured against. This usually manifested itself in cases where the master had deviated from his proper course in order to collect contraband or engage in smuggling on his own account. Could the owners claim on the policy when damage to the vessel occurred during the course of such a deviation? In *Vallejo* v. *Wheeler* (1774), a wide-ranging investigation of the history and continental usage of the phrase was conducted. The plaintiff argued for the wide interpretation that every peril is insured against, except such as happen with the consent or knowledge of the owner. Magens provided a source of examples of court usage taken from the Ordinances of Middleburgh (s. 14), Rotterdam (s. 52), Amsterdam (s. 6), Hamburg (4.6, 5.1 and 7.1) and Stockholm (Art. 5, s. 11, 16, and Art. 6, s. 14). Postlethwaite's *Universal Dictionary of Trade and Commerce,* a work itself modelled on Savary's *Dictionnaire de Commerce,* was also cited[67]. Mansfield accepted this definition, as it would be inappropriate for policies to be given a narrower interpretation in English courts than obtained on the continent. In doing so, he investigated the Italian origins of the phrase, indicating that he had also looked into the foreign materials for guidance. The contrary argument that the phrase only encompassed direct and intentional injury to the owners – itself argued from Savary's *Dictionnaire de Commerce* – was

---

[64] *Pelly* v. *Royal Exchange Assurance Co.* (1757) 1 Burr. at 347.

[65] *Stevenson* v. *Snow* (1761) 1 W. Bl. at 319.

[66] Loccenius, De Jure Maritimo 2.5.10. Marquardus, De Jure Mercatorum 2.15.148. Roccus, De Navibus et Naulo, Not. 138.

[67] (1778) 1 Cowp. 143. M. Postlethwayt, Universal Dictionary of Trade and Commerce, 2 vols., 1751 - 5.

rejected. The principle adopted in *Vallejo's* case represented a synthesis of the various views expressed in the continental literature and the codes. This was recognised in *Lockyer* v. *Offley* (1786)[68] where Willes J. observed that "many definitions of barratry are to be found *in the books,* but perhaps this one may comprehend almost all the cases. Barratry is every species of fraud or knavery in the master of a ship by which the freighters or owners are injured".

Continental authorities were invoked to aid the interpretation of other mercantile documents, notably charterparties. In *Luke* v. *Lyde* (1759)[69], Lord Mansfield had to decide the proportion of freight payable where a vessel carrying fish had been captured 17 days out of Newfoundland and 4 days from her destination. She had been subsequently recaptured, and half the value of her cargo paid as salvage. Some freight was clearly owing, but how much? In the absence of any guidance from English authorities, it was decided that a *pro rata itineris* rate should be payable in such cases. In this case freight was therefore payable on 17/21 of the value of half the cargo, the other half having been paid as salvage. Authority for this common sense solution was found in the continental models. Lord Mansfield referred to the Rhodian laws, the *Consolato del Mer,* the Laws of Wisby and the Rules of Oleron, using as his source for the latter Cleirac's *Us et Coustumes de la Mer.* Colbert's Ordinance of 1681 was also invoked as an example of the continental practice as to payment of freight in cases of shipwreck and ransom. Roccus's *De Navibus et Naulo,* not. 81, was relied upon and provided the express ground for the judgement.

Of the continental authorities referred to by the Enlish courts, the preeminent model was Colbert's *Ordonnance de la Marine* of 1681. This was only to be expected. It was highly influential in the rest of Europe and, given Mansfield's treatment of English commercial law as part of the *ius gentium,* it was inevitable that it would have a strong influence on the development of English Law. In addition to the instances already mentioned, it was cited as authority on the interpretation of "free from average" clauses[70] and the divisibility or otherwise of insurance contracts[71].

Mansfield also had an opportunity to bring English law into harmony with the *jus gentium* in a number of cases involving ransom contracts. It was common practice for a ship's master, following capture by privateers, to sign a written bill promising payment in return for the release of his vessel. The enforceability or otherwise of such contracts was a matter of public debate. The principle consistently adopted by Lord Mansfield was that, if the agree-

[68] (1786) 1. T. R. 252. See also *Nutt* v. *Bourdieu* (1786) 1. T. R. 323.

[69] (1759) 2 Burr. 382, 1 W. Bl. 190.

[70] *Wilson* v. *Smith* (1761) 3 Burr. 1237.

[71] *Bermon* v. *Woodbridge* (1781) 2 Doug. 781.

ment would be enforced by the courts of the captor's domicile, then it should be accepted as enforceable in English law. Continental authorities would inevitably have to be invoked to establish the position of such agreements in foreign domestic law.

The first case in which the problem arose was *Ricord* v. *Bettenham* (1765)[72]. The master of a French privateer sued on a ransom bill, in circumstances where the hostage had died naturally before payment had been made. Argument centred on whether the contract survived the death of the hostage. The plaintiff relied upon the Digest, 20.5.9., to argue that a hostage was merely collateral security, and that the obligation survived his death. Cleirac's *Us et Coustumes de la Mer,* the *Guidon,* Grotius 3.20.58 and 3.23.16, and the Ordinance of 1681, were adduced to prove that the contract was valid in international law. The defendant, not surprisingly, relied on the narrower gound that no action could arise on a contract made with an enemy alien. Counsel confessed that "it astonished him that all foreign writers (except Grotius and Pufendorf) are silent upon this subject; and they do not say much about it". The views of Grotius and Pufendorf were explored in argument, and found to favour the enforceability of such agreements. Grotius, *De Jure Belli ac Pacis* 3.23.16 holds that a hostage is merely "assessory to the principal act". Pufendorf's *De Jure Naturae et Gentium* 8.7.14 has little to say, and reference was therefore made to Barbeyrac's commentary, which (we are told) "has cleared Grotius from the imputation of inconsistency". Barbeyrac also supported the enforceability of such compacts, holding that "when an Officer has gone beyond his private instructions, the sovereign is no less obliged by such a compact; otherwise the execution of all sorts of treaties would or might be evaded"[73]. The enforceability of such pacts being recognised by all the authorities, it was decided that in principle judgement should be entered for the plaintiff, subject only to evidence being furnished that the agreement would be enforced abroad. Blackstone undertook to write to the Pensionary of Rotterdam, and to an Avocat of the Parlement de Paris, and on being advised that the contract would be upheld in

[72] (1765) 3 Burr. 1734. See also *Cornu* v. *Blackburn* (1781) 2 Doug. 648 and *Anton* v. *Fisher* (1781) 2 Doug. 649 (Note) (discussed below).

[73] Barbeyrac's note to Pufendorf 8.7.14. in fact deals with pacts made by military officers, but its reasoning was evidently applied here to those made by the masters of merchant vessels also. "The Sovereign is obliged to keep the compacts which are made by his Generals, Commanders and other Military Officers, when they contain nothing beyond the power of their posts, or the extent of private orders they were charged with, give them, whether they are executed openly in the view of the whole world or privately known to those with whom they treat. But if a compact be made without orders, and afterwards ratified by the Sovereign, by an express or tacit consent; it is plain that, in that case, it ought to be kept the very same as if it had at first been made by his authority. Nay, When an Officer has gone beyond his private instructions, the Sovereign is no less obliged by such a compact; otherwise the execution of all sorts of treaties would or might be evaded." (Note 1 to Puf. 8.7.14.). I have used the 1749 English edition of De Jure Naturae, with Barbeyrac's notes.

France and Holland, judgement was given for the plaintiff. The action was something of a test case, and a number of other ransoms were paid as a result.

Actions on ransom bills were not uncommon, and Mansfield's Notebooks disclose that there were at least half a dozen such actions during his tenure of office in addition to the leading cases reported in the printed reports. The validity of such contracts again arose in two leading cases in 1781. In *Cornu* v. *Blackburn,* a ransom bill had been given to a French privateer which had then been captured by British warships. The French captain had concealed the ransom bill itself from his captors in order to preserve the obligation to pay. It was argued that the ransom bill itself must be recaptured, for the rights of spoliation in war are "odious" and should not be extended to anything not absolutely seized and reduced to possession – a principle advocated by Grotius (*De Jure Belli ac Pacis* 3.21.28). Valin's Commentary on the Ordinance of 1681 was adduced as evidence that the contract would be enforceable in France. Mansfield accepted this line of reasoning and upheld the enforceability of the bill, commenting that "the authority from Grotius is very strong on this last ground". The plaintiffs also invoked Pufendorf (*De Jure Naturae* 8.6.23) to the effect that the existence of a right did not, in any event, depend upon the document which evidenced it.

A similar problem arose in *Anton* v. *Fisher,* with the difference that the French master in this instance had fraudulently concealed the ransom bill after being asked to hand over all his papers. Lord Mansfield directed the case to be argued by a civilian on each side. We are told that "a great variety of new authorities were cited, chiefly from foreign writers, and particularly many passages from Valin's Commentary on the French Ordinance of 1681, which had been pointed out by Lord Mansfield". Valin's opinion was that only the recapture of the bill itself could put an end to the obligation[74]. At this juncture the legislature intervened. By the Statute 22 Geo. 3, c. 25 it was made unlawful for any British subject to enter into a ransom contract, and all such contracts were declared void. When Anton's case came on for judgement in 1783, judgement was given *pro forma* for the plaintiff, but reversed on a writ of error in the Exchange Chamber on the ground that the statute of 1782 had removed the court's jurisdiction over ransom bills.

Lord Mansfield's success in incorporating the *ius gentium* into English law was on this occasion shortlived. The Act of 1782 did not, however, prevent further litigation relating to ransom bills. In *Yates* v. *Hall* (1785)[75], an action was brought by a seaman who had agreed to act as hostage, provided his wages continued to be paid. He was imprisoned for almost four years,

[74] Valin, Commentaire sur l'Ordonnance de la Marine, Vol. 2, 3.9. art. 19.

[75] (1785) 1 T.R. 74.

and later sued the owner to recover his wages. This was a unique action, and (as Lord Mansfield noted) "there is no case like this in the civil law or the law of England". He had clearly looked to the continental authorities for guidance without success. Roccus's *De Navibus et Naulo,* not. 32 was adduced in argument to support the view that the ship's master can validly bind his principal without financial limit. It was decided that, in the absence of direct authority, the correct principle was that the master can bind his principal up to the value of the ship and cargo, and the owners were therefore liable to account for the unpaid wages. Ransoms continued to be a matter of public concern. Lord Mansfield's Notebook discloses that, in addition to *Yates* v. *Hall,* there were in 1783 a further two actions on ransom bills, in both of which the plaintiff succeeded[76].

Private International Law

When, under Mansfield's guidance, the King's Bench began to incorporate the law merchant into the common law, the common law courts were presented for the first time with problems of the conflict of laws. To what extent should foreign laws be given extra-territorial effect in England? There was a paucity of English learning and the doctrines of the Dutch jurists – especially Ulrich Huber and the Voets – exercised a strong influence on the development of this branch of the common law. Lord Mansfield was directly responsible for introducing English lawyers to their writings. Continental authorities are known to have been cited in conflicts cases before the Court of Session in Scotland. After the Union in 1707, it seems probable that these authorities must also have been cited in Scottish appeals to the House of Lords, although the reports provide no overt evidence of this[77]. Mansfield had himself acted as counsel in a number of Scottish appeals before 1756, and his acquaintance with the Dutch jurists' works may therefore owe something to his Scottish connections.

A strong influence was exerted by Huber's title *De Conflictu Legum* in his *Praelectiones Juris Romani et Hodierni* (1689)[78]. Huber's theories were first discussed in *Robinson* v. *Bland* (1761)[79], in which an action was brought on a bill of exchange given in France to secure monies won by gaming. Evidence was given that the debt would be enforceable in France as a debt of honour in the court of the marshalls. It was unenforceable in English law.

---

[76] *Castagnier* v. *Selby* 25 July 1783, Vol. 498. p. 11. *Poreau* v. *Hartley* 1 Aug. 1783, Vol. 498, p. 87. The ground on which these claims were upheld is not apparent.

[77] On the Scottish origins of the continental influence, see *Anton,* The Introduction into English Practice of Continental Theories on the Conflict of Laws (1956) I.C.L.Q. 534.

[78] On Huber's influence generally, see *Llewelfryn Davies* (1937) B.Y.I.L. 49.

[79] (1760) 1 W. Bl. 234, 256; 2 Burr. 1077.

After the case had been argued once, Lord Mansfield directed that it be reheard and "threw out a few hints to be spoken to the next time", including the distinction between personal and real statutes. When the matter was reargued, counsel for the plaintiffs relied on the writings of Voet, Huber, Grotius (*De Jure Belli ac Pacis* 2.11.5), Vinnius and Duck for the proposition that all mixed and personal contracts should be governed by the *lex loci contractus*. The defendants relied upon Domat and Delamare's *Traité de la Police* (3.4.4) to the effect that the contract was not enforceable in France in any event, as it became due after the death of the defendant. Lord Mansfield relied upon the principles set out in Huber's *Praelectiones*, and ruled that as a general rule the *lex loci contractus* should govern. "The general rule established *ex comitate et jure gentium* is that the place where the contract is made, and not where the action is brought, is to be considered in expounding and enforcing the contract." Huber himself, however, admitted an exception where the parties themselves had a view to a different law. The general rule, therefore, was that the law of the place where the contract was to be executed should apply. As the bill of exchange was payable in England, English law applied to render the debt unenforceable. Mansfield is reported to have commended Huber's work as "clear and distinct", and pointed out that Voet's conclusions were to the same effect.

Huber's *Praelectiones Juris Romani et Hodierni* was also relied upon in *Holman* v. *Johnson* (1775)[80]. Action was brought to enforce payment for tea which had been sold at Dunkirk in the knowledge that it was to be smuggled into England. Mansfield relied upon Huber's general principle that the law where the cause of action arose should govern: "The doctrine Huber lays down is founded in good sense and upon general principles of justice. I entirely agree with him". The contract was enforceable as the vendor was not himself involved in the smuggling.

The principles enunciated in *Robinson* v. *Bland* and *Holman* v. *Johnson* were followed in subsequent cases, notably *Briggs* v. *Lawrence* (1789)[81] and *Waymell* v. *Reed* (1794)[82]. Huber's doctrine on the enforceability of contracts consequently became the accepted English rule. The opportunity did not arise for Mansfield to adopt the theories of the continental writers in other areas of private international law. Their influence was more strongly felt at the end of the eighteenth and the beginning of the nineteenth centuries. In *Bruce* v. *Bruce* (1790)[83], the House of Lords heard argument from the writings of Huber, Vattel, Vinnius, J. Voet, Van Leeuwen and Denisart and accepted that intestate succession to moveable property is governed by the

---

80 (1775) 1 Cowp. 341.
81 (1789) 3 T. R. 454.
82 (1794) 5 T. R. 599.
83 (1790) 2 Bos. & Pul. 226.

law of the intestate's domicile. The continental authorities were also invoked in *Potinger* v. *Wightman* (1817)[84], where it was established beyond question that an infant's domicile follows that of his surviving parent. Counsel on this occasion admitted that "of authority on this subject, in the English law none exists ... but it has been much discussed by foreign jurists, to whose opinions ... our courts are accustomed to resort, on questions which (like the present) must be decided rather by general principles of law than by the peculiar doctrines of any local code"[85]. Sir William Grant, M.R. based his decision on the views of J. Voet, Bynkershoek and Pothier, and commented that "on the subject of domicile, there is so little to be found in our own law that we are obliged to resort to the writings of foreign jurists for the decision of most of the questions that arise concerning it"[86]. The principles laid down in *Bruce* v. *Bruce* were amplified in a number of subsequent cases, by reference to the foreign authorities[87].

By way of introduction, Huber set out in his *Praelectiones* three maxims which (he claimed) represent the fundamental principles of the subject. Huber's third maxim set out the comity doctrine: "Those who exercise sovereign authority so act from comity that the laws of each nation having been applied within its own boundaries should retain their effect everywhere so far as they do not prejudice the power or rights of another state or its subjects"[88]. Conflicts rules, according to Huber, owe their existence to "the convenience and tacit consent of nations, for although the laws of one country cannot have any direct force in another, yet nothing could be more inconvenient to the commerce and general intercourse of nations than that which is valid by the law of one place should be invalid elsewhere owing to a difference in the law". Lord Mansfield wholeheartedly accepted this reasoning. One of the grounds for his decision in *Holman* v. *Johnson* (1775) was that "the law of England says that in a variety of circumstances, with regard to contracts legally made abroad, the law of the country where the cause of the action arose shall govern". This theory is often criticised by modern jurists on the ground that it leaves the enforcement of rights as a matter of mere courtesy. It can be argued, however, that Huber saw conflicts rules as part of the *jus gentium,* and as such resting on the consent of nations. This was certainly Mansfield's view. Whatever the theoretical objections to the comity doctrine (for instance that it gives no guidance as to how one is to decide *which* rules will be enforced) Lord Mansfield can

---

[84] (1817) 3 Mer. 67.

[85] (1817) 3 Mer. 67 at 73 per Sir. S. Romilly.

[86] (1817) 3 Mer. 67 at 79 - 80.

[87] On the influence of continental theories *post* Mansfield, see *Anton* (1956) I.C.L.Q. 534.

[88] De Conflictu Legum, s. 2.

share at least some of the credit for introducing English lawyers to the theoretical foundations of private international law.

Public International Law

Questions involving what we now call "public" international law rarely came before the common law courts during the eighteenth century. The natural law jurists, particularly Grotius and Pufendorf, were pioneers in the systematic study and exposition of the subject. It was only natural, therefore, that their writings would have a strong influence in those cases where questions of public international law arose. Indeed, Lord Mansfield's judgements in cases of sovereign immunity are still quoted today to support the "incorporation" theory of the relationship of municipal and international law, i.e. that international law, found in the opinions of the writers on the subject, is *automatically* part of the common law of England.

By the Statute 7 Anne, c. 10, sovereign immunity from suit extended to "ambassadors and other public ministers". Mansfield was counsel in *Barbuit's case* (1737) in Chancery[89], in which the relevant principles were first discussed at length. The case was "solemnly argued and decided by Lord Talbot on considering and well weighing Barbeyrac, Bynkershoek, Grotius, Wincquefort and all the foreign authorities; for there is little to be said by our own writers on this subject"[90]. It was decided that immunity only attaches to ambassadors entrusted to transact matters of state between two nations, and was not to attach to mere consuls with no such authority.

Lord Mansfield was clearly familiar, therefore, with the continental authorities on the subject at an early stage in his career. He had an opportunity to review the law in a judicial capacity in *Triquet* v. *Bath* (1764)[91]. The court had to decide the legal position of the servants of diplomats and those engaged in trade on their own account. The debtor was an English secretary employed by the Bavarian minister in London and claimed immunity from suit. Blackstone, for the plaintiffs, argued from the authority of Grotius's *De Jure Belli* and Bynkershoek's *De Foro Legatorum,* c. 15, that by the law of nations the servants of legitimate ministers have immunity, but that mere traders do not. Lord Mansfield accepted this, holding that "the law of nations is in its full extent part of the law of England". In the event, however, the defendant was able to produce evidence to establish his status as a

---

[89] (1737) Cases T. Talbot 281.

[90] Heathfield v. Chiltern (1767) 4 Burr. 2015 per Lord Mansfield. Some English writers, however, were clearly aware of the continental literature on the law of ambassadors. For instance, Sir Edward Littleton's unfinished treatise ("The Newe Littleton") makes extensive use of foreign authorities in it's discussion of the subject; see *J. H. Baker* (1974) C.L.J. at p. 151.

[91] (1764) 3 Burr. 1478.

bona fide servant, and so claim immunity. These principles were reiterated in *Heathfield* v. *Chiltern* (1767), where it was held that a servant must be an ambassador's employment at the actual date of his arrest in order to qualify for the privilege of immunity.

The law of prize was a matter for the Admiralty jurisdiction. Questions of the law of prize, however, sometimes arose incidentally in actions before the common law courts, as for instance where property the subject of a trespass action was claimed to be prize by a defendant. When questions of this nature arose, it was natural that the extensive continental literature would be referred to for guidance. An example is the decision in *Land* v. *Lord North and the Bank of England* (1785)[92]. Coins belonging to an enemy alien were found aboard a Prussian ship which had foundered on the Goodwin Sands. Lord North (as Warden of the Cinque Ports) seized them and declared his intention of having them condemned as prize in Admiralty. In an action of detinue to recover the coins, the captain of the Prussian vessel relied on Grotius, *De Jure Belli* 3.6.12, to argue that moveables taken outside the course of public service belong to their captor[93]. Lord Mansfield, however, overruled the previous rule which had reflected Grotius's view, and held that all enemy property coming within the realm belongs to the Crown.

The Law of Obligations

Lord Mansfield's attempts to reform the English law of contract are well known. It may be fruitful, however, to speculate as to the civilian origins of some of his attempts at reform. The development of the action of *assumpsit* meant that an ever-wider range of promises were becoming enforceable at common law. As a result, the courts were faced with the problem of establishing criteria to distinguish seriously intended promises which they should enforce from merely gratuitous promises, which they would not. This problem was familiar to civilians, of course, and most of the contemporary works on the civil law discussed the problems of *nudum pactum* at length. Both Grotius and Pufendorf classified promises into three types (*De Jure Belli* 2.11.3 - 4, *De Jure Naturae* 3.5.1 - 9):

(i) Bare assertions, i.e. an expression of a present opinion. Such promises were not binding either by the law of nature or the civil law.

(ii) An "imperfect" promise which obligates the promisor but confers no rights on another. An imperfect stipulation, which morally obligates

---

[92] (1785) 4 Burr. 266.

[93] "Subjects, by the law of nations, have a right to seize the goods of the enemy. But things moveable, whether with or without life, are either taken in public service or out of it; if they are not taken in public service they are the captors" (De Jure Belli ac Pacis, 3.6.12.).

the stipulator by the law of nature but does not create a civil obligation, would fall within this category, e.g. "I have made up my mind in all seriousness to do this or that for you and I hope you will take my word for it."[94]

(iii) A "perfect" promise which obligates the promisor by both civil and natural law. According to Grotius, the promisee acquires a legal right provided the promise is accompanied by "an outward sign of the intent to confer the due right upon the other party" (*De Jure Belli* 2.11.4.). Similarly, Pufendorf holds that "it is a perfect promise when a man not only declares his will for a future time to do something for another, but also shows that he gives him a right whereby the other is fully entitled to demand of him the thing promised" *(De Jure Naturae 3.5.7.)*.

How should the law assess the seriousness of the promise made? For the civilians this question resolved itself into a discussion of the content of the doctrine of *causa,* viz. the requirement of the civil law that, to be enforceable, a promise must have a sufficient "cause". This was a topic of some debate in the seventeenth and eighteenth centuries. Some, principally Francois Connan[95], argued that for an obligation to arise a promisee must derive a benefit from the promise, and the promisor a detriment, such that the promisee would suffer a detriment if the promise was not performed. Grotius and Pufendorf countered this, holding that any seriously intended promise, even if gratuitous, was enforceable. Both held that the loss of a prospective benefit, if a promise remained unperformed, amounted to a sufficient detriment to the promisee and that a gratuitous promise could not, therefore, he said to be without cause. Barbeyrac, in his note to *De Jure Naturae* 3.5.9., explained the prevalent view as follows: "if a promise, purely free, may confer a real right, the person who has received it certainly loses that right. To say nothing of the mischief which would ensue, from being always being deceived by a person, who seems to promise seriously and on whose word we depend. This damage may often be as sensible as the most real loss, which may otherwise attend it"[96]. The natural lawyers' position was that any seriously intended promise should be enforceable, provided it manifested a present intent – whether gratuitous or otherwise, and whether or not evidenced in writing.

The common law adopted a characteristically more pragmatic solution. To create an enforceable contract, there must be a present exchange of values, i.e. consideration must flow from the promisee to the promisor in return for the promise made. The only exception was where the contract was executed under seal. Forseeing some of the problems to which this requirement would

94 The example given by Pufendorf (De Jure Naturae 3.5.).

95 Comment. Juris Civilis, 5.1.

96 De Jure Naturae, 3.5.9. note 4, p. 271.

give rise, Mansfield attempted to influence the development of the doctrine of consideration in two ways. He tried to reduce it to the status of an evidentiary requirement, and in so doing to uphold the enforceability of written agreements unsupported by consideration. Secondly, he recognised "moral" consideration as sufficient in itself to support an unwritten promise. Much has been written about his attempted reforms by historians of the English law of contract. What interests us here, however, are the sources from which the principles introduced by Mansfield were derived. Both lines of development appear to draw heavily on contemporary civilian learning. Although citation of continental litrature is less common than in (for instance) maritime cases, there can be little doubt that continental treatises provided the source material from which many of Mansfield's innovations were derived. The lack of direct citation makes it difficult, however, to specify accurately the sources of this civilian influence.

The use of writing to evidence contracts, instead of the seal, had been encouraged by the Statute of Frauds 1677, Section 4 of which required writing for five categories of contract. These were all types of contract which had become enforceable through the action of *assumpsit,* e. g. promises by an executor to pay legacies out of his own estate, promises to pay another's debts, marriage agreements, and agreements for the sale of land. Writing was also required for any agreement which was to be performed within one year of being entered into.

One consequence of introducing writing as a formal requirement for the conclusion of a binding contract was to reduce the significance of consideration as a purely evidentiary requirement. The position of the doctrine of consideration was reviewed in *Pillans* v. *Van Mierop* (1765)[97], in which a written undertaking to meet a bill of exchange, unsupported by consideration, was sued upon. Mansfield took a broad view, citing no authority, and held that as consideration was a requirement of evidence only it was not necessary in agreements evidenced by writing. Justification for this view could be found in the Statute of Frauds "which proceedeth on the same principle". Wilmot J. was more specific. Having traced the theory of *nudum pactum* in Roman and English law, he relied on Vinnius's Commentary on the Institutes[98] for an explanation of its rationale and utility: "if by stipulation (and *a fortiori* by writing) it was good without consideration. It was made requisite in order to put people on attention and reflection, and to prevent obscurity and uncertainty; and in that view either writing or certain formalities were required". Consideration, in other words, was merely a guard against "rash inconsiderate promises". If, however, a promise was made "upon deliberation and reflection", as for instance where writing was

[97] (1765) 3 Burr. 1663.

[98] Book 3, De Obligationibus.

used, then it was binding. He relied upon Grotius (*De Jure Belli* 2.11. above) and Pufendorf (*De Jure Naturae* 3.5. above) for authority that such promises were obligatory by the law of nations. This innovation was, as is well known, short-lived. In *Rann* v. *Hughes* (1774)[99] the Exchequer Chamber re-established the traditional distinction between agreements by Specialty (under seal) for which consideration was not required, and parol agreements which must be supported by consideration to be enforceable. The existence of a third category of agreement, viz. written agreements without consideration, was expressly rejected. The civilian learning on *nudum pactum* therefore failed to gain a foothold in the common law. It is noteworthy, however, that Lord Chief Baron Skynner made a point of asserting in the Exchequer Chamber that Wilmot J. was "contradicted by Vinnius in his Commentary on Justinian". Vinnius's authority was such, even in England, that it was felt necessary to ascertain his views on the question in point – and these were clearly felt by the Exchequer Chamber to be at variance with the interpretation placed upon them in *Pillans* v. *Van Mierop*.

The second line of development pursued by Mansfield was to attempt to change the substance of the requirement of consideration itself, by holding that a moral obligation could constitute a valid consideration. This also reflected contemporary continental learning on the doctrine of "causa". In the classical civil law an element of reciprocity had been required to clothe an agreement with enforceability. In the medieval period the requirement that a promise must have a valid "cause" changed significantly as a result of canonist influences, until in the sixteenth and seventeenth centuries civilian writers generally held any agreement to be enforceable, provided it was seriously intended to create an obligation. Where the agreement was bilateral, the engagement of one party provided the foundation (or cause) for that of the other. In the case of gratuitous contracts, however, the gratuitous intent of the grantor was held to be a sufficient "cause" for his obligation to give. As Pothier put it, "Dans les contrats de bienfaisance, la liberalité que l'une des parties veut exercer envers l'autre, est une cause suffisante de l'engagement qu'elle contracte envers elle"[100]. This view was propounded also by Domat, with the result that the doctrine of cause was limited to the role of explaining the invalidity of illegal and illicit contracts, a role it retains in the modern civil law[101]. It had ceased to have any objective meaning as a requirement for the formation of contractual obligations, a development encouraged by the teaching of the natural lawyers. Grotius and Pufendorf both held that agreements should be enforceable *ipso facto,* provided evidence of the seriousness of the parties' intent was available. The only limita-

---

[99] (1774) 4 Brown P.C. 27, 7 T.R. 350n.

[100] Traité des Obligations, Art. 42, quoted by *Walton,* Cause and Consideration in Contracts (1925) 41 L.Q.R. at 316.

[101] See e.g., C.c. Arts 1131 and 1133.

tion they recognised was that a promise should not be enforceable if it conferred no benefit on the other party. So, Pufendorf explains "cause" thus: "I cannot compel someone to do something unless I am going to receive an advantage for myself – while for the promisor's part it is against all reason to undertake something from which no good and only evil will result" (*De Jure Naturae,* 3.5.9.). Virtually any agreement, seriously intended, would be enforceable.

Mansfield's doctrine of moral obligation, if accepted, would have brought the common law very nearly into conformity with the continental learning. Reflecting Mansfield's views, Blackstone asserted that "any degree of reciprocity will prevent [a] pact from being nude; nay, even if the thing be founded on a prior moral obligation (as a promise to pay a just debt, though barred by the Statute of Limitations) it will no longer be *nudum pactum*"[102]. In a number of early cases Lord Mansfield was able to mitigate the effects of the doctrine of consideration by relying on principles of estoppel by conduct[103]. The first opportunity to widen the scope of the doctrine itself arose in *Trueman* v. *Fenton* (1777)[104]. Action was brought on a promissory note given by an undischarged bankrupt, in return for which the plaintiff had agreed not to prove in the bankruptcy. Although the note was void, the promise to pay was held to be enforceable, for "the debts of a bankrupt are due in conscience ... although all legal remedy be gone the debts are clearly not extinguished in conscience". The moral obligation to pay, in accordance with the promise given, furnished a sufficient consideration. An opportunity to develop this theme arose in a number of cases brought by legatees against executors who had promised to pay legacies out of their assets. There was no legal obligation to pay legacies in this way, the only justification for enforcing payment being that an executor is under a moral obligation, once he has received the deceased's assets, to administer the estate according to his wishes. If an executor had sufficient personal assets to back his promise to pay, he was clearly under a moral obligation to pay, and his promise would be enforced as a binding contract. This was established beyond doubt in *Atkins* v. *Hill* (1775)[105] and *Hawkes* v. *Saunders* (1782)[106]. In the latter Lord Mansfield commented: "Where a man is under a moral obligation which no court of law or equity can enforce, and promises, the honesty and rectitude of the thing is a consideration ... though the promise gives a compulsory remedy where there was none before in law or equity, yet as the promise is to do what an honest man ought to do the ties of conscience upon an upright mind are a sufficient consideration."

---

[102] Commentaries, ii, 445.

[103] See for instance *Montefiori* v. *M.* (1762) 1 W. Bl. 363.

[104] (1777) 2 Cowp. 544.

[105] (1775) 1 Cowp. 284. (Reversed on its facts by *Rann* v. *Hughes,* supra).

[106] (1782) 1 Cowp. 289.

This development was reflected in other areas of the law of contract. It was held that, even where the pre-existing debt was wholly void, a subsequent promise to pay would be enforceable[107]. Likewise a subsequent promise to pay a debt barred by the Statute of Limitations. The doctrine of moral consideration was finally overruled in *Eastwood* v. *Kenyon* (1840)[108] in which the boundaries of the modern doctrine of consideration were laid down. Earlier authorities were returned to and it was clearly held that a moral obligation could never be a valid consideration, with the result that a precedent void debt could no longer found an enforceable subsequent promise to pay. Denman C. J., in rejecting Mansfield's views, observed that "the doctrine [of moral consideration] would annihilate the necessity for any consideration at all, inasmuch as the mere fact of giving a promise creates a moral obligation to perform it"[109]. In the earlier case of *Lee* v. *Muggeridge* (1813), a similar interpretation of Mansfield's views was put forward by counsel, who observed that "Lord Mansfield thought the rule of *nudum pactum* much too strict, and that it was competent for parties to make their own agreements on deliberation and ... they must be subject to them"[110]. Mansfield's cases never, in fact, went this far. They were based on the premise that there must be a pre-existing moral obligation to support a subsequent promise to pay. Had the additional step been taken of recognising that a promise to pay *in itself* imported a moral obligation recognised by law, then the identification of the doctrine of consideration with contemporary civilian learning on *causa* would have been complete. Mansfield's approach nevertheless went a long way towards adopting the principles enunciated by Grotius, Pufendorf and other of the continental authorities.

Civilian doctrine also seems to have exerted a strong influence on the development by Mansfield of the restitutionary action for money had and received. Much has been written about this innovation, but it may prove fruitful, once again, to speculate as to the origins of some of the rules introduced by Mansfield into English law. The principles of the modern law of quasi-contract derive from Mansfield's judgement in *Moses* v. *Macferlan* (1760)[111]. Despite a lack of direct citation, the views of Pufendorf and other continental authorities are clearly reflected in Mansfield's judgement. The problem with which the courts were faced was to classify the situations in which an action of *indebitatus assumpsit* could be brought to recover sums

---

107 *Barnes* v. *Hedley* (1809) 2 Taunt. 184.

108 (1840) 11 Ad. & E. 438.

109 (1840) 11 Ad. & E. at 450.

110 (1813) 5 Taunt. at 42.

111 (1760) 2 Burr. 1002; 1 W. Bl. 219. For an exhaustive discussion of the civilian influences evident in Mansfield's judgement, see: *P. B. H. Birks,* English and Roman Learning in Moses v. Macferlan, (1984) 37 Current Legal Problems 1. There is little that can fruitfully be added to Birks' survey, and the account given here concentrates on the possible literary sources of some of these influences.

paid to another's use, but in which no express contract could be pleaded. In *Moses* Mansfield laid down as a general principle that "if the defendant be under an obligation, from the ties of natural justice, to refund, the law implies a debt, and gives this action, founded in the equity of the plaintiff's case, as it were upon a contract ("quasi ex contractu" as the Roman law expresses it)"[112]. The action in quasi contract is therefore explained as deriving from an implied contract to repay. In adopting the implied contract theory, Mansfield was reflecting Pufendorf's interpretation of the Roman category of claim arising *quasi ex contractu:* "these actions are said to depend upon a kind of imaginary contract. For when we deliver the thing without intending it for a matter of pure bounty, it is supposed to be given by the one party, and received by the other on this condition, that it shall be delivered back, in case there appear no reason why it was given" (*De Jure Naturae* 4.13.5.). This was a controversial topic among contemporary civilians, many of whom dispensed with the fiction of implying an agreement into what was, in essence, an involuntary obligation. Barbeyrac, for instance, in his note to Pufendorf's *De Jure Naturae* disagreed with the author and dispensed with the implied contract theory[113]. Mansfield was probably aware of the dispute, and adopted Pufendorf's interpretation, which fitted more easily with the nature of the action as a species of *assumpsit.*

Civilian influence is also evidenced by the fact that the heads of recovery enumerated by Lord Mansfield in *Moses* reflect the categories of restitutionary *condictiones* of Roman law, and (again) approximate to the description in Pufendorf's *De Jure Naturae* (4.13.5.). The heads of recovery recognised in *Moses* v. *Macferlan* were:

(i) Where there had been a mistake of fact (cf. the *condictio indebiti* of Roman law).

(ii) Where there had been a failure of consideration (cf. the *condictio causa data causa non secuta*).

(iii) Where there had been extortion, imposition, oppression, or undue influence (cf. the *condictio ob turpem vel iniustam causam*).

The only significant limitation of the action was that it would not lie to recover monies which the defendant had a moral (if not a legal) right to retain, e.g. money paid by the defendant as a debt "in point of honour and

[112] (1760) 2 Burr. at 1008.

[113] De Jure Naturae 4.13.5. note 7; "there is no necessity for a consent, either express or tacit, the authority of the law, or the nature of the thing itself being sufficient to establish an obligation; and so there is no need of feigning the formal consent of a person wholly ignorant of what passes".

honesty". This doctrine was also prominent in the writings of contemporary civilians. Thus Pufendorf (*De Jure Naturae* 3.4.5.):

> "Grotius observes that the lawyers sometimes call a thing of natural obligation, the doing of which Nature shows to be good and honest, although it be not strictly a debt ... When any thing of this kind is voluntarily paid, a man cannot recover it again, on pretence that it was not due, although he might at first have refused to pay it."

Barbeyrac's note to this passage makes the point that in the Roman law, the *condictio indebiti* was "a Right requiring a thing in justice, which one has paid, but was not due"[114]. The same might equally be said of the action for money had and received, as outlined by Mansfield in *Moses* v. *Macferlan,* and developed by him in later cases.

Conclusion

Although Mansfield's reputation as the founder of English commercial law is well established, his frequent use of continental sources illustrates clearly that he was not an original thinker. Many of the leading principles of English commercial law were derived from continental sources, as this paper has endeavoured to show, and simply adopted by Mansfield into the common law. It is evident from recent research into the earlier history of the law merchant that the process of incorporation had begun before the eighteenth century. Mansfield's most important achievement was to develop the *means* by which the English courts could give expression, in the form of a coherent body of legal rules, to the developing body of continental jurisprudence on the law merchant and *jus gentium.* The introduction of special case procedures as a regular feature of court procedure, and the consequent transformation of mercantile usage from fact to law, provided the means by which this could be achieved.

This paper has concentrated on identifying the sources of some of the rules incorporated into English *commercial* law, an area where continental inluence is known to have been strong. Mansfield's attempts to introduce civilian concepts into the private law of obligations were less successful. Nevertheless, continental literature undoubtedly played a leading role in the development of the common law here also, albeit in a less direct manner. By 1781 Sir William Jones, in his *Essay on Bailments,* could comment that Pothier's *Traité des Obligations* was a book "... the greatest part of which is law at Westminster as well as at Orleans"[115]. In the absence of any systematic treatment of obligations by English writers, it was inevitable that the

---

114 De Jure Naturae, 3.4.5. note 5, page 263.

115 Essay on Bailments, p. 29.

extensive continental literature would exert a strong influence. Further research may throw light on specific areas of the common law of contract and tort where this influence manifested itself. It is also likely that continental learning coloured Mansfield and Blackstone's attitude to equity and his attempts to reform English property law[116]. Further research may well shed some light on the sources of some of his attempts at reform in these, and other, areas of the common law.

[116] See *Holdsworth* (1929) 43 H.L.R. 1. Blackstone's treatment of equity in his lectures draws on the Digest and Gravina's Origins Juris Civilis – see Holdsworth's Note at (1929) 43 H.L.R. 28 - 9.

KNUT WOLFGANG NÖRR

Procedure in Mercantile Matters: Some Comparative Aspects

The differentiation of a society can be traced in the growth of new sections of the legal order and sometimes in a shift within the elements that stamp the conception of law. Thus in the middle ages the law of interregional commerce and the law of ecclesiastical benefices bear witness to the rise of the two most significant social branches that joined the ancient and traditional rural and feudal categories. In both cases the *instrumental* element of law began to prevail, law devotes itself to external purposes, the promotion of commerce and the economical backing of the ecclesiastical service. In the case of commercial law the instrumental character was favoured by the need of evading the dogma of usury. It is no accident that both times the solemn forms of litigation were rejected; no more the individual in its entirety is at stake nor the law itself which covers man and his fate. The conflict, instead, turns to demarcated and depersonalized issues. The second reason for unceremonious proceedings was the *multitude* of transactions in the commercial as well as in the benefice spheres (and for this reason also matrimonial cases were assigned to summary procedure).

My task, however, is not to continue these parallels, but to turn to some judicial and procedural questions in the early history of mercantile law. There are, it seems to me, four major points in this respect[1].

1. Whatever mercantile law means, it contains special and often unwritten rules which the law-court had to be confronted with. This was no problem in case of mercantile courts with merchants as judges, as in the arti of medieval Italy, in the period of the consules mercantiae. Often the merchants were not alone, many statutes provided that a iurisperitus had to join as a judge or, at least, had to give the *consilium sapientis*. Hence the uses of the merchants and the Roman and canon law rules had to be conciliated one way or another. The principle was that the curia mercatorum is not bound

[1] Italy: *Benvenuto Straccha,* Tractatus de mercatura, ed. Lugduni 1610; *Alessandro Lattes,* Il diritto commerciale nella legislazione statutaria delle città italiane, 1884, p. 242ss. – England: *A. H. Thomas,* Calendar of Select Pleas and Memoranda of the City of London, a.d. 1381 - 1412, 1932, p. VIIss; *Theodore F. T. Plucknett,* A Concise History of the Common Law, 5th ed. 1956. – In general *Levin Goldschmidt,* Handbuch des Handelsrechts I, 2. Aufl. 1875; 3. Aufl. (Universalgeschichte des Handelsrechts, 1. Lieferung) 1891.

to the *apices iuris* but free to judge according to *negotii veritatem*[2] that is to the circumstances of the case in question. Through the *facti veritas* the usages of the merchants entered the court, but they were shaped in conformity with the technics of the *ius commune*. In ordinary courts with professional judges the mercantile customs like other customs had to be pleaded and proved. This was a widespread rule throughout Europe whereas the way of showing them, of course, varied. In the west, for instance, we find the device of the inquisition *par turbe;* it was used in the Netherlands until the 18th century[3].

In medieval England mercantile matters were handled by a variety of local courts; the merchants in the town or the port acted as suitors and gave the pertinent judgements. As soon as the jury prevailed, the fundamental dichotomy of law and fact plays a part. For example, the Mayor's Court in London was assisted by the Aldermen which in mercantile matters had to have knowledge of the law merchant. As to the jury the Statute of Merchants of Edward I 1285 established the so-called jury of the moiety: in cases between English and foreign merchants one half of the jury should consist of citizens, the other half of foreigners visiting the place. The latter were probably taken, if available, from the place or the nation of the foreign party[4]. The Statute of the Staple 1353 assigned two alien merchants ("lun devers le Suth et lautre devers le North") to the court of the Mayor and Constables[5]. But the merchants were not limited to litigation in the local courts, they appeared as parties in the central courts, too. In the view of the law as administered in Westminster the law merchant originally was no law, but a matter of fact, therefore to be proved[6]. But later, during the 17th century, the maxim turned up that the law merchant is part of the law of the land.

---

[2] Bartolus Dig. 17.1.29 § Quedam; Baldus Cod. 4.35.10.

[3] *J. W. Bosch,* La preuve dans l'ancien droit néerlandais, La preuve II (Recueil Jean Bodin XVII), 1965, p. 475s.

[4] Questions of Conflict of Laws sometimes were clothed in the composition of the jury, cf. Liber Albus of London, Rolls Series XII p. 216: Item, les Viscountz de Loundres ount usez de tout temps de tener plees devaunt eaux par entre qicouncqes marchauntz, la ou ambedeux parties sount marchauntz, des touz bargaynes et contractz personelx qe touchent marchaundys faitz outre le meer a ville marchaunt ou a lieu merchaundable, lou les bargaynes et contractz sount faitz par expresse parole sur paiementz ou liveree des marchaundises, ou de rendre accompt deinz la dite citee de Londres. Et en tiel cas, si les parties descendent en issue denquest, adouncqes serra lenquest prys des gentz demorantz deinz mesme la citee, cestassavoir des marchauntz passauntz, qi usent de passer outre meer, qi poent meiltz avoir conisaunce de les bargaynes et contractz suisditz. Et sascun estraunge merchaunt et alien soit partie al pley, et tiel enquest soit a prendre, adouncqes le marchaunt alien avera la moite de lenquest de sa lange.

[5] Also in Italy we find, at a later date, foreign merchants as judges, for instance Ancona 1593 and Nizza 1613, v. *S. Lammel,* Die Gesetzgebung des Handelsrechts, Handbuch, ed. Coing, II.2 p. 973, 974.

[6] For instance Select Cases in the Court of King's Bench Under Edward I, ed. *G. O. Sayles,* vol. II (S.S. 57), No. 34, p. 71s.

The crucial question arises how the fact became law, a question recently revived by Dr. *Baker*[7]. The result, anyway, as practised by Holt and Mansfield, was the distinction between the general and better known customs, of which the courts took judicial notice, and the special and particular customs, which had to be pleaded. In the latter case merchants were chosen in order to explain their uses and customs, either as members of the jury or as authorities within an informal inquiry. This was the way how the common law courts were shaping the commercial law. We find a striking parallel in the continental *ius commune*[8] and especially in the approach of the Rota Genuensis. Customs which were notorious and general, need not be alleged and proved, and the judge took notice *"etiam per solam famam"*[9], whereas other customs or stiles of the merchants had to be proved; they were usually attested by *parere* of merchants[10] or of *iurisconsulti, procuratores* and *practicantes,* as a decision of the Rota reads[11].

The concurrence of the general and the mercantile law could lead to tensions with practical results in a law suit. In Italy and Germany the legal literature developed certain rules for the relation between the common and the particular law, above all the statutes, but these rules, the *dottrina degli statuti,* were not distinctive of mercantile matters. In England the situation was different. There was no theory on the limits of operation, on the province of the common law, and so the lines had to be drawn as required. Thus the Statute of the Staple ordered the judges to apply the law merchant and not the common law, and in the well-known case of the carrier who broke bulk, the Chancellor in the Star Chamber in favour of an alien merchant advanced the law of nature, "que est appelle par ascunz ley marchaunt, que est ley universalle par tout le monde" against an inconvenient rule of the common law[12]. In this case the legitimation of the mercantile law in face of the common law was touched upon, a question which was to be discussed in a wider context since the 17th century[13].

2. A main obstacle to commerce is the formalism of litigation. Hence the merchants were exempted from the *vare* that is the vexatious procedural punctiliousness in the courts of northern Germany. The courts of the *foires*

---

7 Cambridge Law Journal 38 (1979), 295 ss.

8 Cf. *Wolfgang Wiegand,* Studien zur Rechtsanwendungslehre der Rezeptionszeit, 1977, p. 101 ss.

9 Ed. Venetiis 1582; dec. 16, nr. 12, 13; dec. 138 nr. 3, 4.

10 An example in Sigismondo Scaccia, Tractatus de commerciis et cambio, ed. Romae 1619, § 2, Glos. 5, nr. 61.

11 Dec. 206 nr. 2.

12 Select Cases in the Exchequer Chamber Before All the Justices of England, ed. *M. Hemmant* (S.S. 64), No. 12, p. 32; cf. Select Cases Concerning the Law Merchant, ed. *H. Hall,* vol. II (S.S. 46), p. LXXXV s.

13 *L. S. Sutherland,* The Law Merchant in England in the 17th and 18th c., Transactions of the Royal Historical Society, 4th series, vol. XVII, p. 149 ss.

in the Champagne and the piepowder courts in England applied procedural rules that were to cope with the mobility of the parties. English customs and statutes offered the merchants and mariners justice "from hour to hour, from tide to tide, from day to day", and the phrase *lex mercatoria* in the sources often sounded as a code word for the arrangements of speedy procedure. Or the ordinary courts granted special sessions such as the *gastrecht* in the Netherlands and in Germany. The romano-canonical procedure was just as inadequate, and so the courts proceeded *summarie* and *de plano* (not necessarily in the sense of the Clem. *Saepe*); and rejecting the *apices iuris* often aimed at the procedural subtleties. A good example of the mercantile procedure with romano-canonical background outside Italy is to be found in the Edict Charles IX's which created the court of the *juge et consuls des marchands* in Paris 1563[14]. The measures were similar all over Europe: Suits should be settled within a fixed period, summonses secured by efficient pressure, delays cut down in every stage of proceedings, exceptions and proof restricted, and the execution quickened and sharpened; in addition, sometimes the attorney or advocate is excluded, and the suspensive effect of appeal removed.

3. The law of evidence was frequently adjusted to the wants of the merchants. In many places they were exempted from the archaic judicial duel. A popular form of transaction was the tally; its value as evidence has been studied above all for the medieval English practice. If, in the common law courts, the plaintiff pleaded according to the law merchant, the defendant's offer to wage his law was not an apt answer, and the claimant normally was admitted to prove the tally by two or more witnesses[15]. Similarly, in London the sealed tally was of the same value as the written obligation and ruled out the compurgation as well. On the continent we may find comparable provisions, for instance in the Netherlands, where the tally equalled the merchant's book in the probative value[16].

But in the Dutch courts as throughout the continent these *libri mercatorum* were more in use than the tally. They held a prominent place in the system of proof[17]. Their value was emphasized by the statutes and the court practice against some reluctant voices of the *ius commune*. There are stat-

---

[14] Isambert XIV 153.

[15] Bandon's *alias* Comberton's Case (under Edward II), Select Cases Concerning the Law Merchant, ed. *H. Hall*, vol. II (S.S. 46), p. LXXXIss. Other cases listed in *Baker*, n. 23.

[16] *Bosch*, p. 479.

[17] Cf. *W. Endemann*, Zeitschrift für das gesamte Handelsrecht (ZHR) 2 (1859), p. 329ss.; *Lattes*, p. 283ss.; *Goldschmidt*, Universalgeschichte, p. 246ss.; *Paul Rehme*, Geschichte des Handelsrechts (Handbuch des gesamten Handelsrechts, hg. v. Victor Ehrenberg, I), 1913, p. 159, 215s.; *J. Kohler / F. Hecht*, Niederländisches Handelsrecht in der Blütezeit des Freistaates, ZHR 59 (1907), p. 262ss.; *Wilhelm Ebel*, Forschungen zur Geschichte des lübischen Rechts, I. Teil, 13 Stücke zum Prozeß- und Privatrecht, 1950, p. 122ss.; *Bosch*, p. 478s.; *Lammel*, p. 598s., and passim.

utes which ascribed full proof to the merchant's book even *pro scribente.* Other statutes confined this rule to a certain sum of money or required additional conclusive circumstances. But the predominant rule on the continent said that the merchant's book constitutes half proof and may be supplemented by oath[18]. The effect was indivisible that is a party who produces the book to his favour has to accept it also to his detriment, a controversial principle, however. The merchant's book had to meet certain requirements for its exterior arrangements as well as for the contents of the entries. The *libro maestro* was able to furnish proof, not the *giornale,* but the latter could destroy the credit of the former[19]. There were many more details of and discussions on this evidence, and statutes and legal literature were abundant through the centuries.

In England, however, the sources are scarce. A single custom, it seems[20], has survived from the late middle ages that tells about the judicial use of "books of entries"[21]. They are, once more, equated with obligations and debar the defendant from compurgation. We hear again of "shopbooks" in a statute of James I, where for reasons of abuse their probative force was limited to one year except between merchants or tradesmen[22]. Malynes (1622) inserted a chapter "Of merchants accompts kept by debtor and creditor" and mentioned the *liedger* (which corresponds to the *libro maestro*) and the journal; much credit had been given to them in law, if orderly kept, but Malynes does not specify the probative effect of the ledger or the journal in legal practice[23]. The higher courts rejected the book of the party himself as evidence *pro se* but accepted the book of his clerk or servant if the keeper was deceased or if he would take a suppletory oath[24]. Later the topic was discussed under the heading of a hearsay exception[25].

4. There was nothing more desirable for the merchants than a prompt execution when they had won their case. The regular course of the execution usually was insufficient; therefore exceptions from the normal course were granted. The Italian statutes, for instance, conceded that the execution begins with the attachment of the debtor, against the rule that first his prop-

---

[18] See for instance the practice of the *Reichskammergericht* according to Andreas Gaill, Pract. Observ. lib. II, ed. Venetiis 1613, obs. 20, nr. 2.

[19] Rotae Genuensis dec. 2, nr. 26, 27; dec. 173, nr. 11, 12.

[20] Statute 38 Edward III, stat. 1, c. 5 (Statutes of the Realm I, 384), speaks plainly of "papers" of London merchants and does not have in mind the formal merchant's books. But see *Plucknett,* p. 116.

[21] Lincoln 1481, c. 14, Borough Customs, ed. *M. Bateson,* vol. I (S. S. 18), p. 204.

[22] 7 James I, c. 12 (Statutes of the Realm IV.2, 1169).

[23] Gerard Malynes, Consuetudo vel Lex Mercatoria, Second Part, ch. 20, ed. 1685, I p. 250.

[24] *Price* v. *Lord Torrington,* 2 Ld. Raym. 873 = E.R. vol. 92, p. 84 (1703); *Lefebure* v. *Worden,* 2 Ves. sen. 55 = E.R. vol. 28, p. 36 (1750).

[25] See further *John Henry Wigmore,* A Treatise on the Anglo-American System of Evidence, § 1518, 3. ed. 1940, V p. 347 ss.

erty had to be levied (it was a good device also for the reason that merchants are wont to move fast). In case of appeal the execution shall not be stayed, a rule which we find in several continental laws and statutes[26].

But more significant than these and other measures were certain legal facilities which allowed an immediate access to the execution and which were, therefore, preferred by the merchants. One of the means was the instrument in which the debtor pledged his goods on the understanding that the creditor in case of non-performance may take possession of the goods without any intervention of the public authorities. This kind of a contractual and private right of execution is to be found in the registers of the notary Giovanni Scriba from Genova in the 12th century[27]. Another device was the instrumentum guarentigiatum or confessionatum[28]. This document enabled the creditor to demand the execution immediately, without undergoing the tiresome lawsuit; exceptions had to be advanced and proved without delay, and a swift execution was provided for. At the beginning these documents had to be drafted by notaries, too; but in the later middle ages the private writing of a merchant was sufficient[29]. Our modern civil procedure still ensures remedies which derive from these early notarial and mercantile models. Similar needs resulted in similar measures also outside Italy[30]. The merchants took advantage above all of the recognitions, a wide spread device of ensuring debts. They were an evidence and an executory instrument at the same time, and they represented indeed a common law throughout Europe though, of course, in different settings. Thus, to mention only one continental instance, the recognitions were the pivot of the transactions in the famous fairs of Champagne[31]. They were followed in case of the fugitive debtor by the *lettres de foire* which opened the spectacular process of international execution. In England[32] the Statute of Merchants (mentioned above) also provided an efficient kind of recognisances; they were taken before the mayor and a clerk of the town, who enrolled the debt; upon default the execution started immediately with the imprisonment of the debtor, and in the end the merchant, assisted by the Chancery, got hold even

---

[26] *Lammel*, p. 612 n. 3.

[27] A similar contractual expedient was in medieval Germany the *Pfändungsklausel* v. *Guido Kisch*, ZRG Germ. Abt. 35 (1914), p. 41 ss.

[28] *Hans Karl Briegleb*, Über executorische Urkunden und Executiv-Prozeß, 2. Aufl. 1845; *Lattes*, p. 294 ss.; *Giuseppe Salvioli*, Storia della procedura civile e criminale II, 1927, p. 658 ss.; *Adriana Campitelli*, Precetto di guarentigia e formule di esecuzione parata nei documenti italiani del sec. XIII, 1970.

[29] Executory force of merchant's books: *Lattes*, p. 297 n. 13; *Goldschmidt*, Universalgeschichte, p. 248 n. 42.

[30] Cf. *W. Mitchell*, Essay on the Early History of the Law Merchant, 1904, p. 110 ss.

[31] *H. Laurent*, Revue historique de droit fr. et étr. 1932, p. 660 ss.

[32] *K. Güterbock*, ZHR 4 (1861), p. 20 ss.; *H. Hall*, Introduction, Select Cases Concerning the Law Merchant, vol. III (S. S. 49); *Plucknett*, Legislation of Edward I, 1949, p. 136 ss.

of the land of his debtor until the debt was levied. Commerce makes an inroad into feudality, "the sacred freehold passes into the profane hands of the merchants" (Plucknett). For centuries the "statute merchant" was a popular means in order to enforce debts. A related system was set up in favour of the traders in the staple towns 1353 by the Statute of the Staple. Thus on the continent and in England the traditional legal forms were used, but to the same purpose, and the results were remarkably similar, tailored to the needs of the merchants, and directed by public interest in a swift and smooth traffic and trade.

Verzeichnis der Mitarbeiter

Asser, Daan, J. P. Sweelincklaan 6, NL-1401 CD Bussum

Frentz, Eva-Christine, Dr., Kaiserallee 3, D-2400 Travemünde

Nörr, Knut Wolfgang, Prof. Dr., Universität Tübingen, Forschungsstelle für internationale Privatrechtsgeschichte, Neue Aula, Wilhelmstraße 7, D-7400 Tübingen

Piergiovanni, Vito, Prof. Dr., Università di Genova, Istituto di storia del diritto, Via Balbi 30, I-16126 Genova

Rodgers, Christopher P., Lecturer in Law, University College of Wales, Department of Law, Hugh Owen Building, Penglais, Aberystwyth, Dyfed SY23 3DZ, Großbritannien

Savelli, Rodolfo, Prof. Dr., Università di Genova, Istituto di storia del diritto, Via Balbi 30, I-16126 Genova

MIX
Papier aus verantwortungsvollen Quellen
Paper from responsible sources
FSC® C105338

Printed by Libri Plureos GmbH
in Hamburg, Germany